# GAME AND GRAPHICS PROGRAMMII
# AND ANDROID® WITH OPENGL® ES 2.

# Game and Graphics Programming
## for iOS and Android®
## with OpenGL® ES 2.0

# Game and Graphics Programming
## for iOS and Android®
## with OpenGL® ES 2.0

Romain Marucchi-Foino

John Wiley & Sons, Inc.

## Game and Graphics Programming for iOS and Android® with OpenGL® ES 2.0

This edition first published 2012

Copyright ©2012 Romain Marucchi-Foino

*Registered office*

John Wiley & Sons Ltd, The Atrium, Southern Gate, Chichester, West Sussex, PO19 8SQ, United Kingdom

For details of our global editorial offices, for customer services and for information about how to apply for permission to reuse the copyright material in this book please see our web site at www.wiley.com.

978-1-119-97591-5
978-1-118-22400-7 (ebk)
978-1-118-23329-0 (ebk)
978-1-118-262221 (ebk)

A catalogue record for this book is available from the British Library.

# ABOUT THE AUTHOR

**ROMAIN MARUCCHI-FOINO** is the original author and founder of the popular mobile game engine SIO2 (`http://sio2interactive.com`). Formerly a game engine developer, Romain has dedicated his efforts to build a state-of-the-art game engine for mobile devices using OpenGL ES since the arrival of the iPhone. He is currently working as the lead 3D programmer for `sio2interactive.com`, the official developer of the SIO2 Engine, which powers thousands of games and 3D applications throughout the App Store and the Android market. His experience in the mobile game industry has led him to contribute his work to many online communities, publications, and blogs.

# ABOUT THE TECHNICAL EDITOR

**EFFIE C. LEE** is a self-employed game and graphics designer who has been working in the game industry for the last 4 years. With a bachelor's degree in Computer Science and a real passion for electronic games and computer graphics, she has been involved in multiple mobile game productions. With her wide range of knowledge in the game development process, she has been professionally working as a 2D and 3D graphics designer, game programmer (scripting), and web designer for game sites, as well as managing game quality assurance and localization. If you would like to reach her, send an email to `effiecl@gmail.com`.

# CREDITS

# CONTENTS

# INTRODUCTION

**WELCOME TO** *Game and Graphics Programming for iOS and Android with OpenGL ES 2.0.* This book is not your usual "OpenGL Hello Triangle" book — it's not meant to explain the "why" (Google is there for that), but rather, to show you the "how." This book will strictly teach you what works and what doesn't when it comes to game and graphics programming.

Using more than 50 unique tutorials (which also include some full game frameworks), this book adopts a straightforward practical approach (probably never seen before) that only focuses on what you need to learn to insure that you will be able to create a game.

You will learn all the necessary elements in order to create a full-fledged game with rich 3D graphics. If you are looking for an aggressive teaching method that enables you to quickly move forward to create your dream game, this book is for you!

## WHO THIS BOOK IS FOR

Be aware that this is not a beginner book. It is an intermediate-level book that assumes you are familiar with linear algebra (matrices, vectors, and quaternions), you have a strong C/C++ programming background, you have at least touched base with OpenGL or OpenGL ES, and you basically know how computer graphics work in general.

If you have this necessary knowledge, and want to make lightning-fast progress in game and graphics programming, then you have found the right publication. This book is written for people who want to learn the hardcore stuff fast in order to be able to create and push a full-fledged game on the App Store and the Android Market.

## WHAT THIS BOOK COVERS

Basically everything you need to know in order to create a full game is included in this book. You will learn about all aspects of creating a game, such as loading 3D geometries and textures; how to handle materials, shaders, sounds, cameras, clipping, physics, AI, pathfinding, skeletal animations; and a lot more.

By the end of this book you *will* be able to apply the knowledge you've learned and combine the different tutorials you've completed to create your own state-of-the-art game.

## HOW THIS BOOK IS STRUCTURED

This book is structured in such a way that pretty much all chapters depend on each other. Each chapter shows you progressively how to master the necessary techniques to be able to handle the next chapter.

Here is a list of all the chapters and what will be covered in each of them:

➤ **Chapter 1, "Getting Started"** — You will learn how to set up your development environment, download this book's SDK, import and re-compile the tutorials, and deal with the template project that you will be using throughout this publication.

➤ **Chapter 2, "Setting Up Your Graphic Projections"** — Since you have a running template, I will show you how to set up the necessary projection matrix to be able to handle 2D, 2.5D, or 3D. You will also learn how to draw simple geometry onscreen and handle a camera matrix.

➤ **Chapter 3, "Dealing with Complex Geometry"** — You will create a Wavefront OBJ viewer that will allow you to learn how to load complex geometry from disk. You will also learn how to load and create textures, deal with basic lighting, and respond to touch events.

➤ **Chapter 4, "Building a Scene"** — This chapter will extend the knowledge that you've learned in Chapter 3 and will explain how to handle a more complex scene. You will learn about drawing sequences and how to create reusable shaders.

➤ **Chapter 5, "Optimization"** — In this chapter, I will show you techniques that will allow you to optimize the performance of your drawing. You will touch base with texture compression and shader optimization, and learn how to convert triangles to triangle strips as well as other tips and tricks to get better FPS.

➤ **Chapter 6, "Real-Time Physics"** — Since you will know by now how to handle a scene properly, this chapter is about adding real-time physics behaviors to your scene using Bullet. I will show you how to create a physical world and add physical entities to it. You will then learn how to handle in code different techniques that will allow you to add logic upon collision callbacks or based on the contact points between two or more physical entities.

➤ **Chapter 7, "Camera"** — This chapter will focus entirely on cameras. You will learn to build frustum planes and will be able to determine the visibility of each object of your scene in the field of view of a camera. I will then show you how to implement multiple types of cameras, including a full-fledged first- and third-person camera with collision, ready to be used in your own apps.

➤ **Chapter 8, "Pathfinding"** — Artificial intelligence (AI) and pathfinding will play an important role inside your games, and that's what this chapter is all about. You will learn how to use the Recast and Detour libraries to build a navigation mesh and have entities moving automatically in the scene. In this chapter, I will also demonstrate how to use True Type Font to generate a font texture and draw dynamic text onscreen.

➤ **Chapter 9, "Audio and Other Cool Game Programming Stuff"** — This one is all about audio using OpenAL. In this chapter, you will learn how to load OGG Vorbis sound files and either stream them from memory in real time or statically store them in audio memory. I will also introduce how to create 3D positional and ambient sound sources and will touch base on how to use the accelerometer, along with how to animate textures and create other miscellaneous effects.

➤ **Chapter 10, "Advanced Lighting"** — This chapter will teach you how to apply dynamic lighting, probably one of the hardest things to master in game and graphics programming. You will create multiple types of lights from directional to spot lights and will learn how to handle them in real time.

➤ **Chapter 11, "Advanced FX"** — This chapter is all about special effects. You will learn how to create fullscreen post-processing effects, project textures, and real-time shadows, as well as how to handle particles.

➤ **Chapter 12, "Skeletal Animation"** — Last but not least, you will learn how to handle skeletal animation using the MD5 file format. I will teach you how to load and draw a mesh attached to a skeleton. You will then load action files and learn how to mix them using different types of blending methods.

You will find that this book will not simply show you the theory, but it will also show you how to apply the knowledge that you gain in each chapter to real game scenarios.

As you can see, this book is packed full of useful knowledge that you will need on a daily basis while programming games or 3D applications. There is plenty enough content in here to get you started with real game and graphics programming in no time!

## WHAT YOU NEED TO USE THIS BOOK

If you are planning to develop for iOS, all you need is a Mac that can support the latest version of the iOS SDK (for more information, visit http://developer.apple.com). An iDevice is optional since the iOS SDK provides out-of-the-box an iPhone/iPod Touch and iPad simulator, which you can use to develop and test your application. And it is fully compatible with everything contained in this book.

If you are planning to develop for Android, what you need is a Mac or a PC with an operating system that is supported by the Android SDK (for more information, visit http://developer.android.com). Also, you will need an Android device with OpenGL ES 2.0 support, because the simulator bundled with the Android SDK only supports OpenGL ES 1.0.

In addition, this book uses Blender as its 3D modeling software (because it is free and open source). So to be able to test, tweak, and re-export all the test scenes used in the book's SDK, go grab a copy at http://blender.org.

## CONVENTIONS

To help you get the most from the text and keep track of what's happening, the following conventions are used throughout this book:

➤ New terms and important words are in *italics*.

➤ File names, URLs, variables, and code within text are shown like this: templateApp.cpp.

➤ Code blocks are shown like this:

```
#include "templateApp.h"

TEMPLATEAPP templateApp = { templateAppInit,
                            templateAppDraw };
```

## SDK SOURCE CODE

The official SDK used in this book is available at www.wrox.com for download (packaged as a .zip file). The SDK contains the final end results of all the tutorials covered in this publication. It also includes the full source code of the SDK and all the original assets used in the tutorials, so you will have access to the 2D/3D scenes and can recompile them from scratch freely.

*Because many books have similar titles, you may find it easiest to search by ISBN; this book's ISBN is 978-1-119-97591-5.*

In addition, I also personally maintain the book's SDK (using GIT version control system) on the official website of the GFX 3D Engine (the free and open source mini 3D game and graphics engine that you'll be using in this book, featured in Figure 1), which is available at the following address: http://gfx.sio2interactive.com.

The latest SDK revisions of the book along with all quick bug fixes can be found at the GFX 3D Engine site instantly since it's easier for me to just update the source code using version control. It might take a bit more time for the official SDK at www.wrox.com to be updated since this official SDK version is carefully maintained by the publisher, but you could just be patient and wait for the official release. It's up to you.

MODELS AND TEXTURES GENEROUSLY PROVIDED BY KEN BEYER (http://www.katsbits.com) AND DAVID RADFORD (http://dmradford.com).

**FIGURE 1:** GFX 3D Engine

It is also worth mentioning that on the GFX 3D Engine site (http://gfx.sio2interactive.com), you can find support forums for this book's SDK as well as the latest version of the GFX 3D engine. This website also provides other 3D game and graphics-related demos, tutorials, and other materials that are fully compatible with this book's SDK.

## ERRATA

We make every effort to ensure that there are no errors in the text or in the code. However, no one is perfect, and mistakes do occur. If you find an error in one of our books, like a spelling mistake or faulty piece of code, we would be very grateful for your feedback. By sending in errata you may save another reader hours of frustration and at the same time you will be helping us provide even higher quality information.

To find the errata page for this book, go to www.wrox.com and locate the title using the Search box or one of the title lists. Then, on the book details page, click the Book Errata link. On this page you can view all errata that has been submitted for this book and posted by Wrox editors. A complete book list including links to each book's errata is also available at www.wrox.com/misc-pages/booklist.shtml.

If you don't spot "your" error on the Book Errata page, go to www.wrox.com/contact/techsupport.shtml and complete the form there to send us the error you have found. We'll check the information and, if appropriate, post a message to the book's errata page and fix the problem in subsequent editions of the book.

## P2P.WROX.COM

For author and peer discussion, join the P2P forums at p2p.wrox.com. The forums are a Web-based system for you to post messages relating to Wrox books and related technologies and interact with other readers and technology users. The forums offer a subscription feature to e-mail you topics of interest of your choosing when new posts are made to the forums. Wrox authors, editors, other industry experts, and your fellow readers are present on these forums.

At http://p2p.wrox.com you will find a number of different forums that will help you not only as you read this book, but also as you develop your own applications. To join the forums, just follow these steps:

1. Go to p2p.wrox.com and click the Register link.

2. Read the terms of use and click Agree.

3. Complete the required information to join as well as any optional information you wish to provide and click Submit.

4. You will receive an e-mail with information describing how to verify your account and complete the joining process.

 *You can read messages in the forums without joining P2P but in order to post your own messages, you must join.*

Once you join, you can post new messages and respond to messages other users post. You can read messages at any time on the Web. If you would like to have new messages from a particular forum e-mailed to you, click the Subscribe to this Forum icon by the forum name in the forum listing.

For more information about how to use the Wrox P2P, be sure to read the P2P FAQs for answers to questions about how the forum software works as well as many common questions specific to P2P and Wrox books. To read the FAQs, click the FAQ link on any P2P page.

# Getting Started

**WHAT'S IN THIS CHAPTER?**

➤ Learning about the software used in this book

➤ Downloading the book's SDK

➤ Understanding the SDK architecture

➤ Importing projects into your IDE

➤ Understanding this book's template application

➤ Learning how to work with the template code structure

In this chapter, you will first start by setting up your development environment to be able to work with this book's tutorials and examples.

You will then receive a quick introduction about this book's SDK and where to download it, and learn about the different directories it contains. Then you will learn how to import this book's existing SDK projects and templates into your favorite IDE, as you will do throughout this book when following the different tutorials.

Moving on to the last section of this chapter, you will learn about this book's cross-platform template project. And finally, this chapter concludes with a quick tutorial that will help you to get familiar with the events of the template, as well as with the tone that will be used for all the tutorials in this book.

# SOFTWARE REQUIREMENTS

This book's content is built to run on iOS 5.x+ as well as for Android 2.x+, the latest and most stable versions of these two mobile operating systems at the time this book was written.

## For iOS Developers

To use this book for iOS, all you have to do is to grab a copy of the latest iOS SDK available at http://developer.apple.com, and install it on your Mac.

Out-of-the-box the iOS SDK provides a simulator with full GLES v2 support, so even if you do not have an iOS device, or do not have an official iOS Developer Certification from Apple, you can still make full use of this book.

## For Android Developers

To set up your environment for Android, it is unfortunately not as easy as for iOS. First go to http://developer.android.com/sdk/installing.html and follow the instructions to install the Android SDK, Eclipse, and the ADT plug-in. Please note that the Android SDK version used for this book was v2.3.4, but later versions should also work as well.

All the code in this book uses C/C++, which means that you will have to install Android Native Code support. To finalize the installation of your development environment, follow these steps:

1. Grab a copy of the Android NDK at the following address: http://developer.android .com/sdk/ndk/index.html. The version used at the time of writing this book was r5c, but all examples and tutorials should work on later versions as well. Download the Android NDK zip package and decompress it on your machine where you have read and write access.

2. In order to compile and debug native code using Eclipse, you will need to install the Sequoyah plug-in. To do this, first enable the repository that is located (from the Eclipse main menu) in: Help ⇨ Install New Software ⇨ Available Software Sites ⇨ Sequoyah Metadata Repository. Then select the entry from the Work With combo box, and once the repository data is loaded, select and install the Sequoyah Android Native Code Support, as shown in Figure 1-1.

3. Once Sequoyah is installed, go to (from the main menu): Eclipse Preferences ⇨ Android ⇨ Native Development and specify the location where you extracted the Android NDK in step 1, as shown in Figure 1-2.

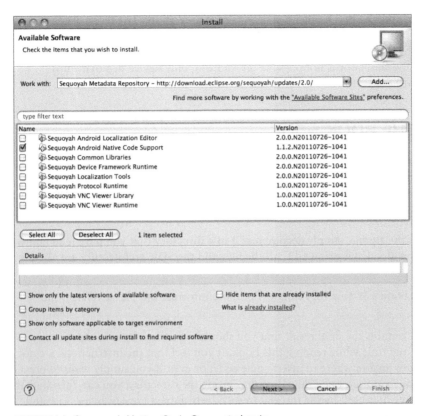

**FIGURE 1-1:** Sequoyah Native Code Support plug-in

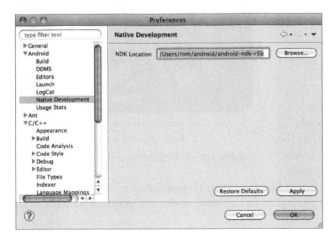

**FIGURE 1-2:** Specify the location of the Android NDK

Congratulations — your Android development environment is now all set! However, please note that in order to use this book with Android you will need an actual device with OpenGL ES 2.0 support. The emulator provided by the Android SDK supports only OpenGL ES 1.x, not OpenGL ES 2.0. So local deployment on the simulator is not possible on Android; only device deployment is supported when using GLES 2.

## DOWNLOADING THE BOOK'S SDK

Once your development environment is set up, you should now grab a copy of this book's SDK. The official SDK is available for download at http://www.wrox.com. Alternatively, if you wish to download it through GIT, go to the official GFX 3D engine website, http://gfx.sio2interactive.com, where you can find detailed instructions.

If you have downloaded the zip file, simply decompress it in a directory that you have read and write access to. If you have downloaded it using GIT, all the files and the SDK architecture are already available on your drive.

The architecture of this book's SDK is very simple. For more information, please refer to the following directory list:

➤ _chapter#-#: Contains the final result that you should reproduce by reading the tutorials in the book. At any time while reading this book, if you feel that the instructions are not clear, or if you are unsure where to insert some code, or even if you simply want to preview the final result of a tutorial, open this directory. Inside the directory, you can then find at the root the source files used by the tutorial (respectively named templateApp.cpp and templateApp.h) and two directories
that contain the project files for iOS and Android. You can then load the project into your IDE and rebuild it from scratch.

➤ common: Contains the free and open source GFX 3D engine (the mini game and graphics engine that you will be using in this book) source code of the version that was used to create the templates and tutorials for this book, along with the source of the libraries the engine depends on. The GFX 3D engine is a very small and lightweight graphic engine that is built with bits and pieces of my own professional engine. It is very small, fast, flexible, and scalable; and will allow you to render state-of-the-art graphics on your mobile device, as shown in Figure 1-3.

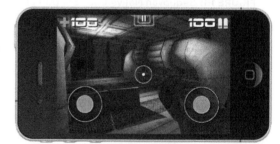

MODELS AND TEXTURES ARE GENEROUSLY PROVIDED BY DAVID RADFORD (http://dmradford.com).

**FIGURE 1-3:** An FPS demo using the GFX 3D engine

➤ data: In this directory, you can find all the original assets that were used in each tutorial. These assets are either linked dynamically to the projects (in the case of iOS) or simply duplicated inside the assets directory of each Android tutorial. Please note that all the original project 3D scenes are available as `.blend` (the default file extension of Blender). It is not mandatory, but highly suggested that you download a copy of Blender for your platform, which is available at `http://blender.org`. This will enable you to study the way the scenes are built and how the assets are linked and exported to the Wavefront OBJ (the official 3D model exchange format used in the book).

➤ `EULA`: In here, you can find all the End User License Agreements for the different libraries that this book's SDK relies on. If you plan to release a commercial application using this book's SDK, make sure that your application complies with all of these licenses.

➤ `glsloptimizerCL`: Contains the source to a simple yet powerful command line program that you can use to optimize your GLSL code (as demonstrated in Chapter 5, "Optimization").

➤ `md5_exporter`: A python script for Blender (v2.6x) that allows you to export bone animation sequences created in Blender to the MD5 version 10 file format (script generously provided by Paul Zirkle).

➤ `template`: The original template project that you will be using when creating a new project from scratch.

➤ `template_chapter#-#`: In order to speed up and avoid redundancies, you will duplicate these directories by following the tutorials throughout the book. This will give you a head start and save you from having to rebuild everything from scratch using the default template project.

## IMPORTING PROJECTS

This book has over 50 tutorials, varying from the demonstration of a single technique to full-fledged games. To be able load and rebuild the projects from this book into your IDE, you will have to import them. To do this, just follow the instructions in the subsection that corresponds to the type of developer you are.

## For iOS Developers

As usual for iOS developers, importing files is very easy. All you have to do to import a project into XCode is simply double-click the `.xcodeproj` file. To compile, simply click the `Build & Run` button.

## For Android Developers

Things are a little bit more tedious if you're using Eclipse. You need to import this book's projects as instructed in the following procedure. Of course, this procedure assumes that you have properly installed and configured Android SDK, Android NDK, Eclipse Classic, the ADT plug-in, and the Sequoyah Android Native Development plug-in (as described at the beginning of this chapter).

Once you have configured all the necessary prerequisite files, follow these steps to import this book's project files:

1. From the Eclipse main menu, select File ⇨ New ⇨ Android Project. The New Android Project dialog should appear.

2. In the Project name text box, enter the project name. Example: **chapter2-1**.

3. Select the Create Project From Existing Source option.

4. Click the Browse button, and then select the existing Android directory inside the chapter or template project. Example: *<path_to_sdk>*/SDK/_chapter2-1/Android.

5. Click the Finish button at the bottom of the dialog box.

Figure 1-4 illustrates each of these steps.

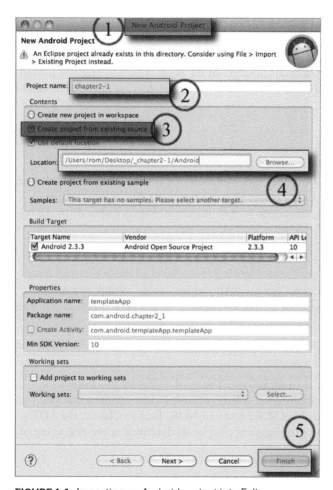

**FIGURE 1-4:** Importing an Android project into Eclipse

Every time you want to open an existing Android project using Eclipse, you will have to go through this importing procedure.

## THE TEMPLATE

As briefly mentioned earlier in this chapter, you will work mostly with the template project that is provided inside this book's SDK. This template is a C/C++ cross-platform project that initializes internally for you a vanilla, ready-to-use OpenGLES 2 context. In addition, the template provides an init and exit function callback, which you can just plug your creation and destruction code into.

The template also provides you with an easy-to-use callback mechanism that acts as a universal HUB to handle all the platform-specific events for you.

Using this mechanism, all you have to do is to link a function callback for the specific event you want to intercept, and you'll receive updates for this event in real time. This mechanism covers all of the touche events such as ToucheBegan, ToucheMoved, ToucheEnded, as well as the accelerometer data. In other words, everything is already set up for you. You can just go ahead and create the code as instructed in this book's tutorials without having to worry about platform-specific issues.

As the title of this chapter says, it's time to get started! In order to get familiar with both the template and the type of tutorials you will be studying throughout this book, follow these instructions:

1. Duplicate the template project directory at the root of the SDK and rename it **template_test**.

2. Load the template_test project (following the appropriate importing method for your platform as described previously) into your IDE, and then open the templateApp.cpp (for iOS developers, it is located under the templateApp directory inside the Project Navigator; for Android developers, you can find it under the jni directory inside the Project Explorer panel).

3. Read the code comments that explain what each function is doing.

4. Uncomment the following callbacks from the initialization (TEMPLATEAPP templateApp = {): templateAppToucheBegan, templateAppToucheMoved, and templateAppToucheEnded.

5. Move to the templateAppInit function and add the following code on the line before the end bracket of the function:

```
    /* Use the built-in GFX cross-platform API to print on the
console (XCode) or LogCat (Eclipse) that the execution pointer
passes the templateAppInit function. */
    console_print(
    "templateAppInit, screen size: %dx%d\n", width, height );
```

6. On the line before the end bracket of the templateAppDraw function callback, add the following code block:

```
    /* Specify that you want to use a chili red color to clear the
screen and spice up your app. */
    glClearColor( 1.0f, 0.0f, 0.0f, 1.0f );
    /* Report that the execution pointer was here. */
    console_print( "templateAppDraw\n" );
```

7. Add the following line before the end bracket of the `templateAppToucheBegan` function:

```
/* Print that the execution pointer enters the touche began
function and print the touche XY value as well as the number of
taps. */
    console_print( "templateAppToucheBegan,"
                   "touche: %f,%f"
                   "tap: %d\n", x, y, tap_count );
```

8. Repeat the same procedure as in step 7 for `templateAppToucheMoved` and `templateAppToucheEnded`, updating the `console_print` text with the appropriate callback function you are dealing with.

9. Move on to the `templateAppExit` function that has already been linked to the `atexit` built-in C function, and add the following line before the end bracket of the function:

```
    console_print( "templateAppExit...\n" );
```

10. Build and run the application. While the application is running, observe the console or LogCat (depending on which platform you are developing for). Touch the screen, move your finger around, and monitor in real time on the console how and in which sequence events are triggered internally.

## SUMMARY

By stepping through this chapter, you now have your development environment set up. You have this book's SDK resident on your drive and have learned how to find your way around its architecture.

You now know how to import new or existing projects into XCode or Eclipse, and have a good overview of what the default template project can do for you.

You are now ready to embark on a very challenging journey in game and graphics programming. Before moving on to the next chapter, make sure that you fully understand what has been covered inside the different sections of this chapter.

# Setting Up Your Graphic Projections

**WHAT'S IN THIS CHAPTER?**

➤ Understanding how the different types of projection matrices work, how to use them, and when

➤ Getting familiar with the template application that comes with the SDK and learning how to customize it for your specific needs

➤ Building your first practical application — learning how to set it up and use the different types of projections

Before you can draw any graphics onscreen, you first need to create a projection matrix. The type of graphics you plan to use will have a direct impact on the creation of this matrix. Whether it is 2D, 2.5D, or 3D, each type of projection matrix will require a different initialization, allowing you to create the necessary perspective for your specific needs.

In this chapter, you will learn about the three primary types of projections used in modern mobile games and how to use them.

In addition, this chapter will teach you how to work with this book's template project and walk you through three progressive exercises. In these exercises, you will learn how to manipulate the most common types of graphic projections and draw simple geometry onscreen; handle vertex and fragment shaders and link them to a shader program; manipulate vertex attributes and uniform variables; translate, rotate, and scale basic geometry; and create a simple camera *look-at matrix*.

# THE THREE BASIC TYPES OF PROJECTIONS

When drawing using OpenGL ES, you always have to keep in mind the sequence of your drawings and in which perspective space you want to draw. Needless to say, this sequence will directly affect the type of projection and the sequence of creation of your projection's matrix.

For example, if you want to draw a heads-up display (HUD) that contains your character data on top of your scene, you first need to set up a 2D, 2.5D, or 3D perspective (depending on the type of game you are working on), and then draw your game scene. After your scene is rendered in the color buffer, you need to render your character life bar, ammo, etc. on top of it. Simply scaling your HUD graphics onscreen to fit the current drawing perspective would deteriorate their overall aspect ratio, eventually making them distorted. Knowing this, the right way to draw the HUD of your game would be to create a projection matrix that has a ratio of 1 unit to 1 pixel. Since your HUD consists of multiple 2D graphics, and it is important to respect their ratio onscreen, a 1:1 2D projection will allow you to draw them consistently onscreen.

There are three distinct types of projections that can be used in any game genre:

➤ **Orthographic 2D Projection:** This type of projection is used to draw any HUD, as in the example described previously. This type of projection was also used in the "old school" side-scroller genre and other types of games, such as the classic Tetris and older grid-based role-playing games. As mentioned, this type of projection will have a 1:1 ratio onscreen, which means that the size of your drawing is directly affected by the size in pixels of the squares (quads) that you are sending to the GPU (graphical processing unit). In a more modern usage, this types of projection is mostly used only to draw menus, text, HUD, or other types of static (or semi-dynamic) 2D information onscreen. Since a third level of dimension is not available, and because the depth range is limited from -1 to 1 (with -1 being the nearest point onscreen and 1 the farthest), the use of the depth buffer is basically obsolete and should be turned off. In addition, the rendering sequence should be done from back to front to avoid overwriting pixels.

➤ **Orthographic (Ortho) Projection:** This type of projection allows you to draw in a semi-2D environment while still considering a third level of dimension, where the perspective is strictly based on the current screen ratio. This type of projection is the one used by every modern 2D/2.5D shoot 'em up-type game and real-time strategy games. When using this type of projection, you can still have access to a third level of dimension and make full use of the depth buffer. Figure 2-1 shows an example of a game that uses a 2D orthographic projection in conjunction with the depth buffer.

**FIGURE 2-1:** Ragdoll Launcher by SIO2 Interactive

➤ **Perspective Projection:** This type of projection matrix is the one that you see at work inside all fancy 3D games that render in real-time dynamic and realistic 3D worlds onscreen. With this kind of projection, you can simulate what a 3D world would look like from a real human-eye perspective. In addition to the screen aspect ratio, this sort of projection takes into consideration the field of view of the camera looking at the scene, as in the futuristic car game for iOS shown in Figure 2-2.

**FIGURE 2-2:** Sky Racer by SIO2 Interactive

# ORTHOGRAPHIC 2D PROJECTION

Now it's time to get your hands dirty and start looking at the necessary code to set up a 2D orthographic projection matrix.

In this section, you will create from scratch a simple program using the `template` project from this book's SDK. Your first app will use a screen projection to draw a scaled colored quad onscreen in absolute pixel coordinates.

**Available for download on Wrox.com**

Before diving into the code, first duplicate the `template` project directory located at the root of the SDK. In order to do this, simply right-click on it and create a local copy of the folder, and then rename it **chapter2-1**. Once the project is loaded into your favorite IDE, locate the `templateApp.cpp` source file and open it in the code editor.

The first step for you to get started with the tutorials of this chapter is to adjust your newly created `template` project by removing the callback functions that you will not need for the exercises in this chapter.

You will concentrate your efforts on the `templateAppInit` and the `templateAppDraw` function callbacks, so you can remove the rest of the callbacks and code comments and have a clean template to start working on. Modify the code so you get the following result:

```
#include "templateApp.h"

TEMPLATEAPP templateApp = { templateAppInit,
                            templateAppDraw };

void templateAppInit( int width, int height ) {
    atexit( templateAppExit );
    GFX_start();
    glViewport( 0, 0, width, height );
}

void templateAppDraw( void ) {
    glClear( GL_COLOR_BUFFER_BIT );
}

void templateAppExit( void ) {
}
```

# Program and Project Initialization

The following steps will guide you through the necessary procedure in order to set up global variables used by your first program. In addition, you will learn about the different types of structures provided in this book's SDK that will help you manipulate different aspects of your programs, such as shaders and loading assets from disk. You will also learn how to create your first 2D screen projection matrix, using the API provided in the SDK.

**1.** At the top of the `templateApp.cpp` source file (on the line just before the `templateAppInit` function declaration), define your vertex and fragment shader filenames as follows:

```
#define VERTEX_SHADER ( char * )"vertex.glsl"
#define FRAGMENT_SHADER ( char * )"fragment.glsl"
```

**2.** Declare a flag to toggle ON (1) or OFF (0) the shader debugging functionalities. No debugging usually means faster shader compilation, but no errors will be reported, and the result is undefined if an error does occur. Therefore, you should keep this flag toggle ON while you are developing your program.

```
#define DEBUG_SHADERS 1
```

**3.** Create an empty `PROGRAM` structure for managing all your shader programs, as follows:

```
PROGRAM *program = NULL;
```

The `PROGRAM` structure is the one that you are going to use throughout this book to handle shader programs. The full source code of the implementation is available inside the `SDK/common/program.cpp` and `program.h` source files. The code of the `SHADER` structures linked to the `PROGRAM` can be found inside the `shader.cpp` and `shader.h` source files, which are also located inside the `SDK/common` directory of the book's source code package. Basically, this pre-made structure handles all interactions between the vertex and fragment shaders and the main shader program. This allows you to compile your shaders and link them to a shader program automatically. In addition, this structure provides you with an easy-to-use way to gain access to uniform variable(s) and vertex attributes that are automatically assigned by the GPU. It also provides an easy-to-use callback mechanism that allows you to access, set, and modify these uniform variables in real time.

**4.** Declare a `MEMORY` structure pointer as follows:

```
MEMORY *m = NULL;
```

This object is also part of the SDK and basically behaves like `FILE` in C, with the exception that all the work is done in memory. On mobile devices, the system memory is the fastest way to deal with data. In this exercise, you are going to use this structure to read your shader files from disk. As a general rule, you should avoid disk access if possible. By using this structure instead, you will get a better loading speed and more flexibility when loading your assets.

**5.** In this step, you'll modify the content of `templateAppInit` to suit your needs. Since it's the first time you're working with this function, I'll explain a few things, starting with the first function call. This call uses the standard `atexit` function, which will allow you to get a feedback when the application exits. You can then program the necessary code to flush whatever is still alive in memory. For every tutorial and exercise in this book, make sure that the `templateAppExit` is always linked to `atexit`, as in the following line:

```
void templateAppInit( int width, int height ) {
    atexit( templateAppExit );
```

**6.** Start the GLES initialization using the GFX helper function, which is also part of this book's SDK:

```
GFX_start();
```

This line initializes all the OpenGL ES standard machine states to make sure that everything is set up properly, regardless of the current driver of the device you are using. For more information concerning the `GFX_start` function, do not hesitate to consult its source code located in `SDK/common/gfx.cpp`.

Quick side note on the GFX implementation: It also provides matrix manipulation functionalities that are not available in GLES2, and mimics the matrix mechanism found in GLES1 and GL desktop implementations.

By using the GFX helpers, you can easily push, pop, load, and multiply matrices and gain direct access to the model view, projection, normal, and texture matrix in a similar fashion as you would normally do with the older version of OpenGL ES and OpenGL.

**7.** Use the standard `glViewport` command to set the GL viewport with the current screen dimensions:

```
glViewport( 0, 0, width, height );
```

**8.** Now use the `GFX_set_matrix` mode function to tell the GFX implementation to focus the projection matrix in order for you to setup your 2D projection:

```
GFX_set_matrix_mode( PROJECTION_MATRIX ); {
```

**9.** Declare two temporary `float` variables to hold half of the screen width and height, as follows:

```
float half_width  = ( float )width * 0.5f,
      half_height = ( float )height * 0.5f;
```

**10.** Next you need to make sure that the current projection matrix is clean. To clean it up, simply load the identity matrix using the following function call.

```
GFX_load_identity();
```

**11.** Now you are ready to set up your 2D screen projection using the `GFX_set_orthographic_2d` function by passing in parameters half of the screen dimensions on both the positive and negative side of the origin of the viewport matrix (left, width, right, height). This operation will position the point of origin, or pivot point if you prefer, of the projection matrix right in the middle of the screen using a 1:1 ratio between GL units and screen pixels.

```
GFX_set_orthographic_2d( -half_width,
                          half_width,
                         -half_height,
                          half_height );
```

**12.** Next, in order to be consistent with OGL, translate the matrix to the bottom left of the screen as follows:

```
GFX_translate( -half_width, -half_height, 0.0f );
```

As you might already know, OpenGL uses the bottom-left corner of the color buffer as the 0,0 coordinate. The GFX_translate function call you've just inserted will translate the default location of the matrix to be aligned with the GL color buffer coordinate. This will ensure that all your drawings will be relative to the bottom-left corner of the screen.

**13.** As mentioned earlier in this chapter, you don't really need to use the depth buffer when using this type of projection because most of the time when using this mode, you simply want to overwrite the color buffer. So turn off the depth buffer as follows:

```
glDisable( GL_DEPTH_TEST );
```

**14.** Since the depth buffer is OFF, you can also turn OFF the depth mask.

```
glDepthMask( GL_FALSE );
}
```

## Vertex and Fragment Shader

Because the purpose of this book is to present you with a straightforward approach to implementing the different elements of a game and graphic engine, I will not go into detail about the specifics of the GLSL ES language. For more information about GLSL ES, feel free to visit http://www .khronos.org/registry/gles/specs/2.0/GLSL_ES_Specification_1.0.17.pdf.

Before moving on with core code to load the necessary vertex and fragment shaders for this exercise inside the templateAppInit function, you first need to create a vertex and fragment shader.

Since shaders are all text based, you can use any text editor that you want to write them. For this example, create two empty shader files. Name them **vertex.glsl** and **fragment.glsl**, and save them at the root of the current exercise directory (SDK/chapter2-1/).

To package these two shaders and make them accessible within your app bundle, you need to link them to your project.

If you are an XCode user, simply select the two .glsl files using Finder, then drag and drop them directly inside the Resources directory of your project tree, and confirm the operation.

If you are an Eclipse user, simply select the two .glsl, files and then copy and paste them inside the assets directory of your project.

For both iOS and Android, the shader files will be bundled within your application and will be accessible at runtime. In addition, please take note that from now on, I will refer to this procedure every time you will be required to link an asset to your project (since it will be the same for models, textures, sounds, physics files, etc.).

## vertex.glsl

For this example, you are simply going to draw a colored square onscreen. First, you need to write the necessary code to transform the vertices, and then you need to get the color for each vertex and send it over to the fragment shader for pixel processing. To do this, open the vertex.glsl file and execute the following steps:

**1.** On the first line of the vertex shader, you will have to define a uniform variable (meaning that the value of this variable can be manipulated within your C/C++ code). This variable is going to hold the result of the current projection matrix multiplied by the current model view matrix in order to transform each and every vertex that will be sent down to the shader to be displayed onscreen.

```
uniform mediump mat4 MODELVIEWPROJECTIONMATRIX;
```

**2.** Then you need to have a variable to contain the vertex position that the vertex shader is currently handling. In order to handle this type of variable, you need to declare it using the attribute specifier, and because it's handling the vertex position, call it POSITION, as shown here:

```
attribute mediump vec4 POSITION;
```

**3.** The quad will also receive a color associated with each vertex position. So declare another variable using the attribute keyword to define the color per vertex, and name it COLOR:

```
attribute lowp vec4 COLOR;
```

**4.** As mentioned previously, vertex shaders strictly deal with vertices, so in order to be able to pass the COLOR variable to the fragment shader for pixel processing, you have to use a middleman variable that will send this color over to the fragment shader. The specifier used for this type of task is varying, and since you have declared COLOR in uppercase as the attribute, you can call this one color (lowercase).

```
varying lowp vec4 color;
```

**5.** Next, you need to insert the main function of the shader. Just like in C/C++, every shader is required to have a main function in order to determine the default entry point of the execution pointer.

```
void main( void ) {
```

**6.** Every time you have to process a vertex and make it visible onscreen, you will have to use the built-in gl_Position variable. In order to be able to see this vertex onscreen, you will have to assign it the result of the vertex position multiplied by the projection matrix and the model view matrix, just like this:

```
gl_Position = MODELVIEWPROJECTIONMATRIX * POSITION;
```

7.  Only one crucial operation remains to set up your vertex shader: sending the vertex color to the fragment shader. In order to do this, simply assign the value COLOR to the varying variable color so the value can be associated with the similar variable inside the fragment shader that you will create in a minute.

```
color = COLOR;
} /* Close the main function */
```

8.  Save the file.

## A Few Words about Precision Qualifiers

Before moving on with the fragment shader code, you might already notice that before declaring any variables in GLSL ES, you have the opportunity to use a precision qualifier.

Especially implemented for GLSL ES, precision qualifiers can control the level of floating-point precision (including vectors and matrices) as well as integer variables. When used wisely, these qualifiers can drastically increase the performance of your shader programs and improve their execution time.

The less time it takes the GPU to execute your shader programs, the more GL instructions can be added, giving you the opportunity to render more complex drawing onscreen while keeping an acceptable frame rate.

Table 2.1 lists the precision keywords and their ranges for floats and integers.

**TABLE 2-1:** Precision Qualifiers Table

| PRECISION | FLOATING POINT RANGE | INTEGER RANGE |
|-----------|----------------------|---------------|
| highp | $-2^{62}$ to $2^{62}$ | $-2^{16}$ to $2^{16}$ |
| mediump | $-2^{14}$ to $2^{14}$ | $-2^{10}$ to $2^{10}$ |
| lowp | $-2.0$ to $2.0$ | $-2^{8}$ to $2^{8}$ |

## fragment.glsl

It's time to write the fragment shader for this exercise. As you might have guessed, the fragment shaders strictly deal with pixel-based operations. In this first example, there won't be too much code inside your fragment shader; however, as you are going forward in this book, the level of complexity will drastically increase.

Use the text editor of your choice to open fragment.glsl, and then follow these steps to create your first fragment shader:

1. Declare a `varying` variable named `color` using the same syntax as the one you declared in the `vertex.glsl` file. Since they are exactly the same, and since both of them are declared using the `varying` specifier, the shader compiler will automatically associate them and will send you the value that you have set in the vertex shader to your fragment shader for processing.

   ```
   varying lowp vec4 color;
   ```

2. Now create the main entry point of your fragment shader by inserting the `main` function:

   ```
   void main( void ) {
   ```

3. To assign the color that you specify in your vertex shader, simply assign the `varying` variable color to the built-in `gl_FragColor`:

   ```
   gl_FragColor = color;
   }
   ```

4. Save the file.

## Linking a Shader Program

It's now time to attack the necessary code to actually link your vertex and fragment shader to the `PROGRAM` structure.

Since this is the first example in this book, and since you are going to work with the `PROGRAM` structure and its functionalities in subsequent chapters, I'm going to walk you through the full initialization process.

Now let's go back to `templateApp.cpp`, or more precisely, back to the `templateAppInit` function.

1. First, you have to initialize your `program` variable pointer, so add the following line:

   ```
   program = PROGRAM_init( ( char * )"default" );
   ```

   This function will automatically assign the required memory and set the whole structure to be blank and ready to receive other commands in order to successfully link a shader program. The last parameter of this function, the name, is strictly there for your convenience. In this exercise, you are basically only going to deal with one `PROGRAM`. But you will have to deal with multiple `PROGRAM` structures as you are progressing throughout this book, so this function will enable you to associate a name with them for identification purposes.

2. Next, you need to create a new vertex and fragment `SHADER` pointer by calling their associated `_init` function as follows:

   ```
   program->vertex_shader = SHADER_init( VERTEX_SHADER,
                                         GL_VERTEX_SHADER );
   program->fragment_shader = SHADER_init( FRAGMENT_SHADER,
                                           GL_FRAGMENT_SHADER );
   ```

The first parameter of the SHADER_init function represents the internal name to use for the shader, and the second one represents the type so GLES can associate them accordingly.

As you can see, you have now initialized the two SHADER pointers of the PROGRAM structure. Alternatively, you could initialize them as independent SHADER pointers and attach them manually to your PROGRAMs before the linking phase, making them reusable.

**3.** In order to be able to load the shaders you've created from disk, you now need to load their content in memory. To do this, simply use the MEMORY structure like this:

```
m = mopen( VERTEX_SHADER, 1 );
```

The first parameter is the file name, and the next parameter lets you specify whether the path is relative to the application or not (either 1 for yes or 0 or no).

**4.** For safety purposes, and in order to see how the loading mechanism behind mopen works, effectuate a pointer check on the m variable as follows:

```
if( m ) {
```

Please take note that if the file fails to load, the pointer will be NULL. A non-empty pointer will confirm that the file has been loaded and currently resides in memory.

**5.** Now you need to compile your vertex shader code that is currently contained inside the MEMORY buffer pointer (m->buffer) by passing it to the SHADER_compile function as follows:

```
if( !SHADER_compile( program->vertex_shader,
                     ( char * )m->buffer,
                     DEBUG_SHADERS ) ) exit( 1 );
```

The first parameter of this function is, of course, a valid SHADER structure pointer that represents the shader you want to compile the code for. The next parameter is the shader source, which in this case is accessible from memory. The last parameter allows you to toggle debugging functionalities ON or OFF.

As you can see from the preceding code, if the SHADER_compile function fails to compile the code, the function will return 0. In this case, this will trigger an early exit and call the templateAppExit function.

**6.** Enter the following code to free the MEMORY structure pointer m, because you are going to reuse it for loading the fragment shader in the next step.

```
}
m = mclose( m );
```

**7.** It's time to load the fragment shader and compile it. To do this, simply reuse the same loading code structure that you used for the vertex shader, except this time, you have to specify the FRAGMENT_SHADER file as shown here:

```
m = mopen( FRAGMENT_SHADER, 1 );
if( m ) {
```

```
if( !SHADER_compile( program->fragment_shader,
                     ( char * )m->buffer,
                     DEBUG_SHADERS ) ) exit( 2 );
}
m = mclose( m );
```

You now have your vertex and fragment shader properly compiled and ready to be linked to your shader PROGRAM. Please note that it takes at least one valid and compiled vertex shader and one valid and compiled fragment shader to be able to successfully link a shader program; otherwise, the shader compiler will fail and report an error on the system console.

**8.** Call the PROGRAM_link function in order to execute the final linking phase of your vertex and fragment shader:

```
if( !PROGRAM_link( program, DEBUG_SHADERS ) ) exit( 3 );
```

Take note that similar to the previous SHADER_compile function, the last parameter of PROGRAM_link determines if the debug functionality should be used. And as previously mentioned, if an error occurs, the function will return 0 and the error message(s) will be reported on the system console.

## The Drawing Code

The next step in order to get your app up and running is to deal with the templateAppDraw function. In this function, you will plug in the necessary code to be able to actually render something onscreen. In addition, you will also set up the different vertex attributes and control the uniform variable within your application.

### Preparing the Frame

Before being able to actually start drawing something, you first have to prepare the data that you need in order render a single frame. At this point, one important piece is missing before any frame can be displayed onscreen. You need to actually declare all the vertices and the vertex color as well as the visual transformation that your quad will use to be displayed onscreen. To do this, just follow these steps:

**1.** Start by declaring some 2D positions (the vertices) that will then be linked together in order to draw a quad onscreen. To declare the vertices, insert the following declaration right after the start bracket of templateAppDraw:

```
static const float POSITION[ 8 ] = {
0.0f, 0.0f, // Down left (pivot point)
1.0f, 0.0f, // Up left
0.0f, 1.0f, // Down right
1.0f, 1.0f  // Up right
};
```

**2.** You now need to declare the vertex colors and associate them with the vertex position array you created in step 1. For this, all you have to do is to declare them in the same order as their counterpart in the POSITION array. As a result, the first vertex will be associated with the first RGBA color, the second vertex with the second color, and so on. Now append this code:

```
static const float COLOR[ 16 ] = {
1.0f /* R */, 0.0f /* G */, 0.0f /* B */, 1.0f /* A */, /* Red */
0.0f, 1.0f, 0.0f, 1.0f, /* Green */
0.0f, 0.0f, 1.0f, 1.0f, /* Blue */
1.0f, 1.0f, 0.0f, 1.0f  /* Yellow */
};
```

**3.** Now that you have all the necessary values required to draw, it's time to start constructing the rendering loop of your application. First, specify which color value will be used to clean the color buffer (in this case, a light gray) by inserting the following code before the glClear function call:

```
glClearColor( 0.5f, 0.5f, 0.5f, 1.0f );
```

**4.** In order to avoid overwriting pixels, you need to tell OpenGL to clear the color buffer every time the templateAppDraw function is called, as follows:

```
glClear( CL_COLOR_BUFFER_BIT );
```

**5.** In step 1, you basically created a 1 by 1 pixel quad, which will be really hard to see onscreen. To make the quad more visible onscreen, all you have to do is scale it on the X and Y axis by adding this code:

```
/* Select the model view matrix. */
GFX_set_matrix_mode( MODELVIEW_MATRIX );
/* Reset it to make sure you are going to deal with a clean
identity matrix. */
GFX_load_identity();
/* Scale the quad to be 100px by 100px. */
GFX_scale( 100.0f, 100.0f, 0.0f );
```

## Drawing the Quad

The next logical step is to start calling the necessary APIs to tell the GPU to actually draw something onscreen. To do this, follow these steps:

**1.** Make sure that you have a valid shader program ID by adding the following if statement:

```
if( program->pid ) {
```

As you might already know, GLES indexes always start at 1, so if the compilation of one of your shaders fails, the program->pid will be 0 and the subsequent code will not be executed.

**2.** Declare two temporary variables that you will use to hold the vertex attribute and uniform locations, as follows:

```
char attribute, uniform;
```

These locations are necessary in order to effectuate the bridge between your application data and the GPU data.

3. Now you have to tell the GPU which program you want to use for drawing; otherwise, the GPU won't know what to do with the data that is sent to it. To do this, call the following:

```
glUseProgram( program->pid );
```

4. Enter the following code to retrieve your uniform variable location from video memory:

```
uniform =
PROGRAM_get_uniform_location( program,
( char * )"MODELVIEWPROJECTIONMATRIX" );
```

Please note that the variable name you wish to retrieve the location for has to be exactly the same as the one you declared in your shader code.

5. The location of the uniform variable has now been retrieved, and it's time to actually update the data on the GPU. To do this, enter the following code:

```
glUniformMatrix4fv(
/* The location value of the uniform. */
uniform,
/* How many 4x4 matrix */
1,
/* Specify to do not transpose the matrix. */
GL_FALSE,
/* Use the GFX helper function to calculate the result of the
current model view matrix multiplied by the current projection matrix. */
( float * )GFX_get_modelview_projection_matrix() );
```

6. Now you'll deal with the vertex attributes in a similar fashion as in the previous step. Retrieve the location of the vertex position by entering the following:

```
attribute =
PROGRAM_get_vertex_attrib_location( program,
( char * )"POSITION" );
```

7. Once you have the location of the POSITION attribute, you can tell GLES to enable this vertex attribute location by using the glEnableVertexAttribArray function as follows:

```
glEnableVertexAttribArray( attribute );
```

Remember that OpenGL ES is a machine state–based implementation, so you have to make sure that everything you want to use is enabled, and everything that you do not need is disabled.

8. Now you need to tell GLES which data to use for this attribute. To do this, use the glVertexAttribPointer function as follows:

```
glVertexAttribPointer(
/* The attribute location */
```

```
    attribute,
    /* How many elements; XY in this case, so 2. */
    2,
    /* The variable type. */
    GL_FLOAT,
    /* Do not normalize the data. */
    GL_FALSE,
    /* The stride in bytes of the array delimiting the elements,
in this case none. */
    0,
    /* The vertex position array pointer. */
    POSITION );
```

**9.** Do the same for the COLOR array by entering the following code:

```
attribute =
PROGRAM_get_vertex_attrib_location( program,
                                ( char * )"COLOR" );
glEnableVertexAttribArray( attribute );
glVertexAttribPointer( attribute,
                    4,
                    GL_FLOAT,
                    GL_FALSE,
                    0,
                    COLOR );
```

**10.** Now call the glDrawArrays function to tell the GPU to draw the data using a specific mode starting from which index in the array and to use how many data:

```
glDrawArrays(
/* The drawing mode. */
GL_TRIANGLE_STRIP,
/* Start at which index. */
0,
/* Start at which index. */
4 );
} /* Close the program->pid check. */
```

**11.** Finally call the GFX_error helper function, as a safety measure. This function will check if a GL error occurs while drawing the current frame (if an error occurs, it will be printed on the console for XCode users or LogCat for Eclipse users).

```
GFX_error();
```

## Cleaning Up

Move to the templateAppExit function and follow these few steps in order to clean up what has been assigned in memory:

**1.** Right after the start bracket of the function, insert a simple print to notify that the application exits:

```
printf("templateAppExit...\n");
```

**2.** Then do a pointer check on the MEMORY structure variable m since it may be still allocated when the execution pointer reaches this line and if it is, simply free it using the mclose function:

```
if( m ) m = mclose( m );
```

**3.** Add the following code to effectuate a similar check as in step 2 but this time on the two SHADER structures as well as for the PROGRAM structure, and free them if necessary:

```
if( program && program->vertex_shader )
    program->vertex_shader = SHADER_free( program->vertex_shader );
if( program && program->fragment_shader )
    program->fragment_shader = SHADER_free( program->fragment_shader );
if( program )
    program = PROGRAM_free( program );
```

You are now ready to run the program, so hit the build and run button! You should have the same result running as shown in Figure 2-3.

This concludes the section on 2D orthographic projections. After reading this section, you are now able to draw a simple colored quad using a 2D orthographic projection where 1 unit equals 1 pixel. As you progress, you will realize that you will be able to reuse this implementation to draw HUD and menus onscreen for your game.

**FIGURE 2-3:** Your first ortho 2D projection

## ORTHOGRAPHIC PROJECTION

In this section, you will learn how to create a scaled orthographic projection that will allow you to use the screen aspect ratio to establish a simple perspective view. In order to explore the orthographic possibilities, you will start by simply modifying the code that you created in the previous section. You will then add a new dimension to your existing coordinate system. Finally, you will create a simple camera using a look-at matrix, which allows you to specify the position and the eye direction of the viewer inside a three-dimensional scene.

## Getting Orthographic

First duplicate the previous project, chapter2-1 (located in the SDK directory), and rename the copy for **chapter2-2**. You are now ready to modify the project to integrate an orthographic projection. Follow these steps:

**1.** Locate the GFX_set_matrix_mode function call inside the templateAppInit function, and remove the block of code between the brackets {}.

**2.** Insert the following lines of code between the {} to replace the previous screen projection with an orthographic projection initialization:

```
/* Clean the projection matrix by loading an identity matrix. */
GFX_load_identity();
GFX_set_orthographic(
```

```
        /* The screen ratio. */
        ( float )height / ( float )width,
        /* The scale of the orthographic projection; the higher to 0,
    the wider the projection will be. */
        5.0f,
        /* The aspect ratio. */
        ( float )width / ( float )height,
        /* The near clipping plane distance. */
        1.0f,
        /* The far clipping plane distance. */
        100.0f,
        /* The rotation angle of the projection. */
        0.0f );
```

Pay attention to the near and far clipping planes — these planes basically control at which distance from the viewer the geometry can be seen. If your vertices after transformation fall behind the far clipping plane or before the near clipping plane, you won't be able to see them onscreen because they will be clipped.

The last parameter of the `GFX_set_orthographic` function allows you to control the rotation angle of the projection. Most modern devices have the ability to flip the screen according to the current orientation of the device. You can then use this parameter to adjust your scene orientation based on your device orientation.

**3.**    Add the following code after the orthographic projection setup call:

```
        glDisable( GL_CULL_FACE );
```

This function tells GLES to not clip backfaces. In order to gain more speed, most modern GPUs automatically analyze triangles to determine whether they are facing the viewer or not, and if not, automatically discard them at an early stage to avoid extra calculations. Later in this tutorial, you will animate the quad, so you have to be sure that it will draw properly onscreen regardless of its rotation angle. You do not want the GPU to discard any vertex data onscreen if the quad becomes inverted.

**4.**    Overwrite the `POSITION` array declaration in the `templateAppDraw` function with the following:

```
        static const float POSITION[ 12 ] = {
         -0.5f, 0.0f, -0.5f, // Bottom left
          0.5f, 0.0f, -0.5f,
         -0.5f, 0.0f,  0.5f,
          0.5f, 0.0f,  0.5f // Top right
        };
```

Notice that you have now added a third dimension to your vertex position data. Since you are now moving from an XY screen coordinate system to an XYZ coordinate system where the positive Z axis represents the up vector, shift the pivot point of your quad to revolve around X:0 Y:0, Z:0.

**5.**    Since the depth buffer and depth mask need to be fully active (not like in the previous example), you have to tell OpenGL ES to clean the depth buffer every frame:

```
        glClear( GL_COLOR_BUFFER_BIT | GL_DEPTH_BUFFER_BIT );
```

6. To begin creating the camera matrix, locate the GFX_scale function call inside the templateAppDraw function and replace it with the following variable declarations:

```
/* The eye position in world coordinates. */
vec3 e = { 0.0f, -3.0f, 0.0f },
      /* The position in world space where the eye is looking. */
      c = { 0.0f,  0.0f, 0.0f },
      /* Use the positive Z axis as the up vector. */
      u = { 0.0f,  0.0f, 1.0f };
```

7. Next, call the GFX_look_at function, use e, c, and u as parameters:

```
GFX_look_at( &e, &c, &u );
```

This GFX_look_at call will create the necessary look-at matrix. For more information about the math behind this function, feel free to consult the source code in SDK/common/gfx.cpp.

8. It's time to animate the quad onscreen! First, you need to create a static float variable that will increment dynamically to animate the Y location of the quad pivot point. To do this, enter the following code:

```
static float y = 0.0f;
      /* Increment the Y location value every frame. */
      y += 0.1f;
```

9. Use the following GFX_translate function to translate the pivot of the quad on the Y axis:

```
GFX_translate( 0.0f /* X */,
               y,
               0.0f /* Z */ );
```

10. Since you already have the variable Y, you can reuse it to also animate the rotation of the quad using the GFX_rotate function:

```
GFX_rotate( /* Boost the angle a bit by multiplying it. */
            y * 50.0f,
            /* X axis */
            1.0f,
            /* Y axis */
            1.0f,
            /* Z axis */
            1.0f );
```

This function takes four parameters: the first one represents the rotation angle in degrees, and the next three represent the axis that should be affected by the rotation angle.

11. In step 4, you modified the size of each POSITION component. In order for GLES to be able to draw the quad properly using the new tri-dimensional vertex position array, you need to adjust the parameter of glVertexAttribPointer from 2 (XY) to 3 (XYZ), as follows:

```
glVertexAttribPointer( attribute,
                       /* 2 */ 3,
```

```
GL_FLOAT,
GL_FALSE,
0,
POSITION );
```

Build and run the program! You should now see the quad rotating on the X, Y, and Z axes (as shown in Figure 2-4), and then disappear after a while when the Y location is above 100 (which means that it has been clipped by the far plane).

Congratulations! You have successfully set up an orthographic projection, used the depth buffer, created a full-fledged 3D object (albeit a very simple object — but hey, that's a start!). You were able to animate it onscreen using translation and rotation, and you have set up a basic look-at matrix to simulate a camera in world space. Quite a lot for a start already!

As you might have already noticed, when the quad is rotating onscreen, the projection does not seem quite right — especially when the quad has a hard angle onscreen. This is because the projection is strictly based on the screen and aspect ratio (no real perspective). However, this type of mode is used by many 3D editing software programs because it provides

**FIGURE 2-4:** Orthographic quad

a straight look at the geometry that the viewer is facing. It is also ideal for some 2D or 2.5D games (since the depth buffer can still be used while drawing) that have a static camera angle looking down at a scene panning left, right, forward, and backward, giving it a true 2.5D aspect.

This concludes this section on orthographic projection. In the next section, you are going to fix the slight perspective problem that occurred in orthographic projection by adding a field of view. This field of view represents the eye angle of the viewer, creating a real 3D projection matrix.

## PERSPECTIVE PROJECTION

In this section, you will learn how to set up a true 3D perspective view. This is basically the last type of projection that this book will teach you, and it will be the type of projection that will be used in almost all examples and exercises in the rest of this book.

Once again, before diving in with more code, simply duplicate the project from the last section (chapter2-2), and for consistency, rename the duplicated project folder for **chapter2-3**.

Since you already have all the necessary code in place, changing from ortho projection to a true 3D perspective projection couldn't be easier! Basically all you have to do is to locate the GFX_set_ orthographic function inside templateAppInit, and replace the function call with the following:

```
GFX_set_perspective(
/* Field of view angle in degree. */
45.0f,
/* The screen aspect ratio. */
( float )width / ( float )height,
/* The near clipping plane. */
```

```
0.01f,
/* The far clipping plane. */
100.0f,
/* The device screen orientation in angle to use. */
0.0f );
```

As you can see, this function is almost the same as GFX_set_orthographic, with the exception of the first parameter, the field of view (FOV). When it comes to FOV, the larger the angle is, the wider the perspective will be; and the smaller the angle, the narrower the projection.

Optionally, before you have a test run at the app, you can also remove or comment the GFX_translate call (located inside the templateAppDraw) to be able to really observe the effect of the 3D perspective on the projection matrix while the quad is rotating.

At this point, build and go! You should see something similar to what's shown in Figure 2-5.

While running the application, observe how the projection matrix created by the GFX_set_perspective function is different from the one you created earlier. The major difference is that the quad looks good from every angle, because the perspective matrix calculation includes the field of view and represents the way someone would look at the quads in the real world.

**FIGURE 2-5:** Quad rendered using a true 3D perspective

## SUMMARY

This chapter showed you how to set up all three primary projection matrices that directly affect the perspective of your drawings. Using those projections, you can now create any type of 2D, 2.5D, or 3D game.

You also learned how to set up and draw a basic shape onscreen, use the depth buffer, manipulate vertex attributes and uniform variables, create a look-at matrix to manipulate the viewer eye location and direction, and a lot more. Pretty good for a start, don't you think?

Even if you don't fully realize it yet, you now have all the basic knowledge that you need to start creating some real games and 3D apps!

Before you move on with the next chapter, I suggest that you go back over this chapter's exercises and make sure that you fully understand everything that has been demonstrated. In addition, you should try to modify some parameters just to get more familiar with the overall program structures and possibilities.

As an extra exercise, try to mix a screen projection with an orthographic or a 3D perspective projection by moving the projection matrix creation code from the templateAppInit function to the templateAppDraw function.

# 3

# Dealing with Complex Geometry

**WHAT'S IN THIS CHAPTER?**

➤ Loading complex geometry from disk using the Wavefront file format

➤ Building VBOs and VAOs using custom geometry data

➤ Handling touch screen events

➤ Loading a PNG file from disk and converting it to a usable texture

➤ Implementing per-vertex lighting calculations

In games, as in graphic programming, it is important to be able to load external mesh data. Hard-coding geometry information inside your apps would just not be practical. From a simple crate to an entire level, every asset used in games has been exported from 2D or 3D software and loaded at initialization.

In this chapter, you will learn how to handle the Wavefront OBJ format using the loader that comes with this book's SDK. In addition to model loading, you will learn how to read the Wavefront material files. You'll also discover how to use the pre-made functions of the book's SDK to load a PNG texture from disk. You will also learn how to handle and work with complex geometry using vertex buffer objects (VBOs) and vertex array objects (VAOs).

By the end of this chapter, you will have built from scratch a 3D viewer, able to load a custom OBJ file along with its associated texture. In addition, your viewer will also be able to support dynamic lighting, and will respond to the user touch to rotate the 3D model in real time.

## THE WAVEFRONT FILE FORMAT

Over the years, the Wavefront file format has almost become a standard for exchanging geometry data between different 3D software. The format is simple, well documented, and open, which makes it perfect for basic 3D data exchanges. For example, the popular Pixologic

ZBrush relies extensively on this format to communicate with other state-of-the-art 3D software such as Autodesk's Maya and 3ds Max, and the free open-source Blender suite.

The Wavefront format consists of two distinct file types: .OBJ and .MTL. The OBJ file contains all vertex positions, vertex normals, and UV coordinates of one or multiple 3D objects. Every time an OBJ file is exported, another file is written along with it: a material (MTL) file.

The MTL file contains the data for all materials that are used by one or multiple objects inside the OBJ file. The MTL file also contains information such as the diffuse and ambient color, texture file names (and on which channel they are assigned), and other material-specific parameters.

For more information about the Wavefront OBJ standards, you can consult http://www.martinreddy.net/gfx/3d/OBJ.spec. For information about the MTL file standards and specifications, go to http://paulbourke.net/dataformats/mtl/.

## Cube.obj

One of the great things about the Wavefront file format is that it's text-based, and you can open it directly using any text editor. This makes it a very good format to start with when it comes to loading complex geometry, because it's very easy to understand and to parse in code. Before jumping right in to the coding part of this section, take a quick look at the following OBJ file in order to understand how it is constructed:

```
mtllib cube.mtl
o Cube
v 1.0 1.0 -1.0
v 1.0 -1.0 -1.0
v -1.0 -1.0 -1.0
v -1.0 1.0 -1.0
v 1.0 1.0 1.0
v 1.0 -1.0 1.0
v -1.0 -1.0 1.0
v -1.0 1.0 1.0
vt 0.0 0.0
vt 1.0 0.0
vt 1.0 1.0
vt 0.0 1.0
vn 0.0 1.0 0.0
vn -1.0 0.0 0.0
vn 0.0 -1.0 0.0
vn 1.0 0.0 0.0
vn 1.0 0.0 0.0
vn 0.0 0.0 1.0
vn 0.0 0.0 -1.0
usemtl Material_diffuse.jpg
f 5/1/1 1/2/1 4/3/1
f 5/1/1 4/3/1 8/4/1
f 3/1/2 7/2/2 8/3/2
f 3/1/2 8/3/2 4/4/2
f 2/1/3 6/2/3 3/4/3
f 6/2/3 7/3/3 3/4/3
f 1/1/4 5/2/4 2/4/4
f 5/2/5 6/3/5 2/4/5
f 5/1/6 8/2/6 6/4/6
```

```
f 8/2/6 7/3/6 6/4/6
f 1/1/7 2/2/7 3/3/7
f 1/1/7 3/3/7 4/4/7
```

With just a quick glance at the file content, you can tell what most lines represent — starting with mtllib, which represents the material library associated with the geometry file. Then you can find an object declaration, represented by the token o, followed by each set of indexed vertex positions (v). Next comes the indexed texture coordinates (vt), also known as UVs, and the vertex normals (vn).

After the vertex data declaration, the usemtl line specifies which material will be used for the incoming faces. Then, for each face, three sets of vertex positions, UV, and normal index are specified (the f lines). Each of these sets basically represents a triangle. Wavefront OBJ also supports a quad (which would be read as four sets); however, since every face representation in GLES has to be defined as a triangle, make sure you triangulate the faces of your meshes before you export them to the OBJ format.

## Cube.mtl

Now take a closer look at the file content for the material file associated with the Cube.obj file that you previously studied.

```
newmtl Material
Ns 96.078431
Ka 0.0 0.0 0.0
Kd 0.64 0.64 0.64
Ks 0.5 0.5 0.5
Ni 1.0
d 1.0
illum 2
map_Kd diffuse.png
```

Once again, this is pretty straightforward. First the material name is specified using the newmtl tag, and then all of the parameters associated with it are listed (very similar to an OBJ mesh). If you are already familiar with lighting calculations, you probably recognize standard terms such as Ka and Kd, which represent the ambient and diffuse color component of a material. As you are progressing, all these variables will be available to you within your code. You can then program your shaders based on these variables.

Finally comes all the textures associated with the material, and which channel they are bound to. In this example, the map_Kd line specifies the diffuse texture. If a texture is associated to the ambient channel, it would be map_Ka; the same goes for the rest of the channels.

## PREPARING THE OBJ VIEWER CODE

Available for download on Wrox.com

Before you start coding, you have to prepare the template project that you will be using for the rest of this chapter. First, create a copy of the template directory and name the copy **chapter3-1**. Then open the related project file for your device. Once this is done, clean up or add to the project file the necessary code to obtain the following structure inside the templateApp.cpp:

```
#include "templateApp.h"

TEMPLATEAPP templateApp = { templateAppInit,
```

```
                              templateAppDraw,
                              templateAppToucheBegan,
                              templateAppToucheMoved };

void templateAppInit( int width, int height ) {
   atexit( templateAppExit );
   GFX_start();
   glViewport( 0.0f, 0.0f, width, height );
}

void templateAppDraw( void ) {
   glClearColor( 0.5f, 0.5f, 0.5f, 1.0f );
   glClear( GL_DEPTH_BUFFER_BIT | GL_COLOR_BUFFER_BIT );
}

void templateAppToucheBegan( float x, float y, unsigned int tap_count ) {
}

void templateAppToucheMoved( float x, float y, unsigned int tap_count ) {
}

void templateAppExit( void ) {
}
```

Notice this time, you are going to use two new function callbacks: `templateAppToucheBegan` and `templateAppToucheMoved`. Later in this chapter, you will use these callbacks to integrate the necessary code to gather the touche location onscreen that you will use to manipulate the rotation of the object inside your OBJ viewer.

## LOADING AN OBJ

In order to get started, link the `model.obj` and `model.mtl` files located inside SDK/data/chapter3-1 to your project.

Since you are now linking assets to your program, also create the two files respectively named **vertex.glsl** and **fragment.glsl**. Now save them on disk inside the SDK/chapter3-1 directory, and link them to your project (as you did before).

Now it's time to start preparing the base program. Follow these steps:

**1.** At the top of the `templateApp.cpp` file, right after the `#include`, create the following defines, globals, and variables:

```
/* The OBJ file name on disk. */
#define OBJ_FILE ( char * )"model.obj"
/* Your vertex and fragment shader files. */
#define VERTEX_SHADER ( char * )"vertex.glsl"
#define FRAGMENT_SHADER ( char * )"fragment.glsl"
#define DEBUG_SHADERS 1
/* The main OBJ structure that you will use to load the .obj. */
```

```
OBJ *obj = NULL;
/* Pointer to an mesh inside the OBJ object. */
OBJMESH *objmesh = NULL;
/* Shader program structure pointer. */
PROGRAM *program = NULL;
```

This is really nothing new, with the exception of the OBJ variables. First there's the OBJ_
FILE, which controls the file that will be loaded by the viewer at loading time. (You can
change this to a different file later on for testing purposes if you like.) Next, the obj and
objmesh variables are declared. The first variable is the main structure that you will be using
for loading complex geometries from a file. The second variable is a pointer to a mesh inside
the obj structure, from which you can gain access to all the vertex data that composes the
geometry as well as the triangle lists created for each material that the mesh is using.

**2.** Right after the TEMPLATEAPP templateApp declaration block, create the following function:

```
void program_draw_callback( void *ptr ) {
}
```

You will use this function later as a callback that will be used by the PROGRAM structure. By
linking it to the structure, this function will be automatically triggered every time you call
PROGRAM_draw (another helper function). This will allow you at runtime to set or update
your uniform variables before the shader program gets bound using glUseProgram.

**3.** Fill in the function code by inserting the following source between the function brackets
({ }):

```
/* Convert the void * in the parameter to a valid PROGRAM pointer. */
PROGRAM *curr_program = ( PROGRAM * )ptr;

/* Loop counter */
unsigned int i = 0;

/* Loop while there are some uniform variables */
while( i != curr_program->uniform_count ) {

    /* Check if the current uniform is the
MODELVIEWPROJECTIONMATRIX. If yes, enter the condition clause
to update the matrix data. */
    if( !strcmp( curr_program->uniform_array[ i ].name,
    "MODELVIEWPROJECTIONMATRIX" ) ) {

        /* Update the matrix. */
        glUniformMatrix4fv(
        /* The uniform location. */
        curr_program->uniform_array[ i ].location,
        /* Number of matrix. */
        1,
        /* Don't transpose the matrix. */
        GL_FALSE,
        /* The result of the current projection matrix multiplied
by the model view matrix. */
        ( float * )GFX_get_modelview_projection_matrix()
```

```
            );
        } /* End if */

        /* Next uniform please... */
        ++i;
    } /* End while */
```

You've just created a dynamic loop that will check for all the uniform variables available in the shader program and gain control to set them independently. You can link this callback to one or multiple shaders and handle all uniform variable updates at one unified point in code. At the moment, you don't have much to handle, but when your programs become more complex, this will become quite handy.

**4.** Now it's time to create the code of `templateAppInit` and set up the 3D projection matrix. To do this, insert the following block right after the `glViewport` call:

```
GFX_set_matrix_mode( PROJECTION_MATRIX );
GFX_load_identity();
GFX_set_perspective( 45.0f,
                     ( float )width / ( float )height,
                     0.1f,
                     100.0f,
                     0.0f );
```

**5.** Create a new shader program using the following `PROGRAM` helper function to automatically load, compile, and link the shader program:

```
program = PROGRAM_create(
/* The shader program name. */
( char * )"default",
/* The vertex shader file. */
VERTEX_SHADER,
/* The fragment shader file. */
FRAGMENT_SHADER,
/* Use relative file path. */
1,
/* Debug program and shaders. */
DEBUG_SHADERS,
/* Not in use for now. */
NULL,
/* The draw function callback that you previously declared in
steps 2 and 3. */
program_draw_callback );
```

**6.** The last piece of code for this section is actually to place the loading call to store the `.obj` file content in memory and parse it using the `OBJ_load` function:

```
obj = OBJ_load( OBJ_FILE, 1 );
```

That's it for now. You've successfully created the code to load an `.obj` file from disk as well as its associated `.mtl` file. You can now access everything using the `obj` variable pointer.

Please note that the OBJ loading implementation itself is around a thousand lines of code, and unfortunately, it cannot be fully covered in this book. However, this book's SDK/common folder includes the `obj.cpp` and `obj.h` files, which you can study and customize in order to load OBJ files inside your own apps.

## BUILDING THE SHADERS

Before you dive into the VBO and VAO creation for the geometry, you first need to create the shader code for this program.

At this point, your goal is to simply draw the geometry. Your shader will have to be able to transform the vertex position. And this time, since the OBJ format doesn't support vertex color, you will be using the vertex normals and convert them to RGB values so you can at least see a color-shaded geometry onscreen.

In addition, since the GLES shading language doesn't provide you with any type of runtime debugging functionalities, it's common practice to convert different types of data (in this case, the vertex normals) to RGB values in order to be able to debug your shaders. Keep in mind that this is the closest way in GLSL to be able to debug data in a similar fashion as you would do with a good old `printf`.

### The Vertex Shader

Open the `vertex.glsl` file that you created earlier, and follow these steps:

**1.** Declare a uniform matrix that you will use to transform the vertex positions:

```
uniform mediump mat4 MODELVIEWPROJECTIONMATRIX;
```

**2.** Declare a vertex attribute to hold the vertex position:

```
attribute mediump vec3 POSITION;
```

**3.** Declare a new vertex attribute for the vertex normals, and a corresponding `varying` to be able to bridge the value to the fragment shader:

```
attribute lowp vec3 NORMAL;
varying lowp vec3 normal;
```

Please take note that you use `lowp` as the precision qualifier. Since the data is a normalized vector in the range of -1 to 1, you can simply save a bit of memory bandwidth, at the cost of precision. Before initializing any type of variables in your shaders, always think about which precision qualifier would be the most appropriate for the variable(s) you are about to declare.

**4.** To finalize the shader, create the `main` function using the following code:

```
void main( void ) {
    normal = ( NORMAL + 1.0 ) * 0.5;
    gl_Position = MODELVIEWPROJECTIONMATRIX * vec4( POSITION, 1.0 );
}
```

Here's a quick note about the normal varying in this code: As mentioned earlier, vertex normal data are always represented by a normalized vector. But in this case, you want to convert the data to RGB, so you have to make sure that the value range is from 0 to 1 (not -1 to 1). To convert the vector to a color, add 1.0, and then divide it by two (or multiply by 0.5).

That's it for the vertex shader (at least for now), so save the file and move on to the next section for instructions on how to create the fragment shader for this program.

## The Fragment Shader

Open the fragment.glsl file in your favorite text editor or inside your IDE.

**1.** Bridge the normal variable as follows:

```
varying lowp vec3 normal;
```

**2.** Create the main function, assigning the normal to the fragment color as follows:

```
void main( void ) {
    gl_FragColor = vec4( normal, 1.0 );
}
```

You now have both your vertex and fragment shader set up. It's time to add the necessary code to start sending vertex data to the shader program. For this, you will first have to create and use a VBO and (optionally) a VAO.

## Vertex Buffer Object

In this section, you'll use the geometry vertex data that you retrieved while loading the OBJ, and actually transform it into a form that GLES understands.

In the previous chapter, all you did was manually declare all the vertex positions and colors and then send them over and over every frame. That works, of course, but it is obviously not as optimized as it should be. Constantly sending the data to the video memory is not the preferred way to save bandwidth or to gain rendering speed.

You might not have noticed any performance drop in the previous chapter examples, because the data sent was fairly small. But if you are sending thousands and thousands of vertex data this way on every frame, you will start seeing drastic performance loss mainly caused by the overuse of the bandwidth. Wouldn't it be great if you could simply initialize the vertex data once, send it over to the video memory, and then reuse it as long as you have to draw the geometry? That's exactly what a vertex buffer object (VBO) will do for you!

In the next exercise, you will learn how to build your own VBO using the vertex data loaded from the OBJ file. You will then use this data to construct the geometry and cache it onto the video memory. From there, all you have to do is refer this data using an index; and you can reuse this index as many times as you need to.

## Storing the Vertex Data

Get back to the `templateAppInit` function and start pasting the code in the following steps right after the `OBJ_load` function call:

**1.** Retrieve the pointer of the first mesh inside the `obj` structure pointer:

```
objmesh = &obj->objmesh[ 0 ];
```

**2.** Declare a few local variables:

```
/* To hold the vertex data. */
unsigned char *vertex_array = NULL,
/* The start position of the vertex data array. */
*vertex_start = NULL;
/* Loop counter. */
unsigned int i = 0,
/* To hold the current vertex index. */
index = 0,
/* Store the size in bytes between each vertex data type. */
stride = 0,
/* The total size in bytes of the vertex data array. */
size = 0;
```

In order to get started, you'll just deal with one mesh for the moment, but please note that the OBJ loader in this book's SDK has full multi-mesh support.

Also, pay attention in the next steps of this section, since a lot of variables are already contained, or already declared inside the `objmesh` structure definition. This is strictly built for your convenience so you don't have to declare them manually every time you want to use the load, and to avoid having to extend this chapter longer than it should be. Do not hesitate to refer to the OBJ implementation (inside the `obj.cpp` and `obj.h` files) if you need more information.

**3.** Calculate the total size of the vertex data array so you can allocate the amount of memory necessary to construct a GLES-friendly vertex data array for your VBO:

```
/* Calculate the total size of the array based on the number of
independent vertex data multiplied by the size of a vertex position
and the size of a vertex normal. */
size = objmesh->n_objvertexdata *
        sizeof( vec3 ) * sizeof( vec3 );
/* Allocate the total amount of bytes in memory. */
vertex_array = ( unsigned char * ) malloc( size );
/* Remember the starting memory address of the vertex array. */
vertex_start = vertex_array;
```

**4.** Construct the vertex data array based on the indexed vertex position and the vertex normals contained in the `objmesh` structure:

```
/* Loop while there is some vertex data. */
while( i != objmesh->n_objvertexdata ) {
/* Get the current vertex data index. */
index = objmesh->objvertexdata[ i ].vertex_index;
```

```
/* Append the vertex position to the vertex data array. */
memcpy( vertex_array,
        &obj->indexed_vertex[ index ],
        sizeof( vec3 ) );

/* Increment the current memory position to move on to
the next insertion point. */
vertex_array += sizeof( vec3 );

/* Insert the vertex normal at the current position. */
memcpy( vertex_array,
        &obj->indexed_normal[ index ],
        sizeof( vec3 ) );

/* Move on to the next insertion point. */
vertex_array += sizeof( vec3 );

/* Request the next vertex data index. */
++i; }
```

GLES has different types of support when it comes to handling VBO and vertex data arrays. You could also have created one separate array for the position and another one for the normals (similar to what you did in the previous chapter). However, what you have right now is a tightly packed vertex data array, where all of the different data types are located near each other. This is the most-optimized type of vertex data array that you could possibly construct. When the driver is going to use this array for drawing, the memory jump to access each position and normal element will be very short. As a result, keeping a tightly pack vertex data array will improve performance, and from a driver standpoint, leave space for internal optimization (if implemented).

## Building the Vertex Data Array VBO

Now that you have the vertex data array constructed in client memory, it's time to build the VBO and send this data to the server memory (the video memory). Starting where you left off at the end of the previous exercise, continue to append the code as described in the following steps:

**1.** Ask the driver to create a new buffer index for a VBO and make it active, as follows:

```
/* Generate a new VBO id. */
glGenBuffers( 1, &objmesh->vbo );

/* Make the id active and tell GLES that it should be represented
as a vertex data array buffer. */
glBindBuffer( GL_ARRAY_BUFFER, objmesh->vbo );
```

**2.** Transfer the vertex data array from local memory to the video memory:

```
glBufferData(
/* The type of data to associate the array with. */
GL_ARRAY_BUFFER,
/* The total size in bytes of the array. */
size,
/* The starting position of the array. */
```

```
        vertex_start,
        /* Since the data will not be updated every frame, tell GLES that
the data is static for internal driver optimization. */
        GL_STATIC_DRAW );

        /* Free the array from the local memory. */
        free( vertex_start );

        /* Deactivate the current VBO id attached as a vertex array buffer. */
        glBindBuffer( GL_ARRAY_BUFFER, 0 );
```

## Building the Element Array VBO

All complex geometry is constructed of one or multiple lists of triangles (basically one triangle list per material). Each vertex position and vertex normal (as well as other types of data) is basically shared by one or more triangles. If you were to draw the array that you've just constructed using `glDrawArrays`, the result would be erroneous. What you have created is an array of unique vertex data from an indexed cache. This means that there are no duplicates. The array you constructed is the smallest possible array that can be used to represent the geometry, which contains a unique combination of vertex position and vertex normal.

In order to be able to draw the mesh properly, you have to use the appropriate set of indices to represent each triangle inside the vertex data array. You will then have to use this array of indices to draw the geometry. This is by far the most optimized way to draw any type of complex geometry. The indices array is fairly small, and as a default limitation of GLES, it has to be specified as `unsigned short` (2 bytes per index, or 16 bits if you prefer).

Of course, you could always pass this index array to the associated GLES drawing instruction (`glDrawElements`), but you will end up sending this array of indices over and over again for every frame. Since the goal of this section is to show you how to build and draw triangle-based geometry as fast and in the most optimized way possible, the following steps introduce you to how to build a VBO for the indices array of this geometry.

1.  Where you left the cursor (inside the `templateAppInit`) in the previous section, add the code to generate a new `id` for the first `objmesh` triangle list and make the current index active, as follows:

    ```
        /* Generate a new VBO id for the indices. */
        glGenBuffers( 1, &objmesh->objtrianglelist[ 0 ].vbo );

        /* Make the current index active, and specify to GLES that the
    index is for an indices array (aka Element Array). */
        glBindBuffer(
        GL_ELEMENT_ARRAY_BUFFER,
        objmesh->objtrianglelist[ 0 ].vbo );
    ```

2.  In a similar fashion as you did for the array buffer, send the indices array to the GPU:

    ```
        glBufferData(
        /* The type of array. */
    ```

```
                GL_ELEMENT_ARRAY_BUFFER,
                /* The total size of the indices array. */
                objmesh->objtrianglelist[ 0 ].n_indice_array *
                sizeof( unsigned short ),
                /* The indices array. */
                objmesh->objtrianglelist[ 0 ].indice_array,
                /* Once again specify that the array is static as the indices
          won't change. */
                GL_STATIC_DRAW );

                /* Deactivate the current VBO id attached as an indices array. */
                glBindBuffer( GL_ELEMENT_ARRAY_BUFFER, 0 );
```

Congratulations! You have now created two fully optimized VBOs: one for your vertex data, and one for the indices data. From now on, every time you want to access these two distinct types of data, all you have to do is to bind them using their respective `ids`.

It's almost time to start drawing! But before that, in order to squeeze every bit of performance that you can get from the hardware, the next section will introduce you to how to create a VAO. This type of object will allow you to save many function calls when you're dealing with any GLES array-like function, and as a result, will save you a lot of bandwidth.

## BUILDING THE VAO

In your endless quest of drawing as much polygons as fast as you can, the vertex array object (VAO) will reveal itself to be quite handy. Before getting started, please note that this functionality is available as a GLES extension, and it is not part of the standard GLES v2.x API specifications. The functionalities of the VAO are only accessible if the `GL_OES_vertex_array_object` extension is present on your device. Fortunately, it is implemented by most of the driver manufacturers, because its effects are quite beneficial for internal optimization purposes and to improve performance.

To give you a quick overview, a VAO enables you to build an "offline" drawing list of all `gl` function calls that affect your vertex data. You can then refer to this list via an index during your actual online drawing.

As a general rule, if the `gl` function or one of its parameters contains the term `array`, it can be used inside a VAO list.

Now you're ready to implement your first VAO. Beginning at the point where you left off in the previous exercise, follow these steps:

**1.** Declare the following local variables and calculate the vertex array stride between the different vertex data:

```
        unsigned char attribute;
        /* Vertex position size in bytes. */
        stride = sizeof( vec3 )+
        /* Vertex normal size in bytes. */
                sizeof( vec3 );
```

In the previous chapter, when you called `glVertexAttribPointer`, you left the stride parameter at 0 since you had two independent arrays. But this time, you will have to use this parameter since there is only one tightly packed vertex data array (also known as interleaved array). The stride parameter tells the driver how many bytes it will have to jump in order to access the next data type.

**2.** Create a new VAO index and make it active as follows:

```
glGenVertexArraysOES( 1, &objmesh->vao );
glBindVertexArrayOES( objmesh->vao );
```

From now on, every array-like function that you call will be added to the VAO "drawing list" until the index is deactivated (set back to 0).

**3.** Start building the VAO list bind including the call to set the array buffer to use:

```
glBindBuffer( GL_ARRAY_BUFFER, objmesh->vbo );
```

**4.** Include the following POSITION vertex attribute call inside the VAO list:

```
/* Get the attribute location from the shader program. */
attribute = PROGRAM_get_vertex_attrib_location( program,
( char * )"POSITION" );
/* Enable the attribute location. */
glEnableVertexAttribArray( attribute );
glVertexAttribPointer(
attribute, /* The location of the attribute. */
3, /* The size of each component (in this case, 3 for XYZ). */
GL_FLOAT, /* The type of data. */
GL_FALSE, /* Do not normalize the vertex data. */
stride, /* The size in bytes of the next vertex position. */
( void * )NULL ); /* No need to pass the vertex position array
because you are using a VBO. */
```

As you can see the declaration slightly changed; besides passing the stride parameter, this time you do not have to pass the vertex position array. When using a VBO as an array or element buffer, the last parameter of `glVertexAttribPointer` now represents the offset in bytes where to find the data. Since the array starts with the vertex position, that explains the NULL value, which basically represents 0 (starting at the first byte of the array).

**5.** Now handle the vertex normals in the same way as you did for the vertex position, with the exception of the last parameter of the vertex attribute pointer call:

```
attribute = PROGRAM_get_vertex_attrib_location( program,
            ( char * )"NORMAL" );
glEnableVertexAttribArray( attribute );
glVertexAttribPointer(
attribute,
3,
GL_FLOAT,
GL_FALSE,
stride,
BUFFER_OFFSET( sizeof( vec3 ) ) );
```

As mentioned in the previous step, you have to specify the offset (in bytes) to the next data type. To do this, use the `BUFFER_OFFSET` macro (declared in `type.h` inside the `common` directory of the SDK) to specify the offset size in bytes. If you had to use other vertex data types, you would need to accumulate the offset between each data type based on the same order that you inserted them inside your VBO vertex data array (more on that later in this chapter).

6. Now bind the array element buffer (your indices) as follows before closing the VAO list:

```
glBindBuffer(
    /* Bind the index as an indices buffer. */
    GL_ELEMENT_ARRAY_BUFFER,
    /* Pass the indices VBO index to activate its usage. */
    objmesh->objtrianglelist[ 0 ].vbo );
```

7. The following function has two effects. It first deactivates the current VAO. Second, it compiles all the array-like commands that have been previously called, associating them to the VAO index.

```
glBindVertexArrayOES( 0 );
```

You've just created your first VAO!

This section covered quite a few key GLES concepts that might be a bit scary and hard to understand at first. I suggest that you review the preceding VBO and VAO exercises to make sure that you fully understand the meaning and the usage of each and every function as well as their parameters.

In addition, you have probably noticed that a lot of variables were coming directly from the `objmesh` structure, so feel free to dig inside the `SDK/common/obj.cpp` and `obj.h` source code if you have problems grasping their meaning.

## RENDERING MOMO

As you've probably already noticed, the learning curve applied in this book is growing exponentially. Fortunately, all the effort you've put into this sample program thus far is about to pay off. It's now time to write the necessary code to actually draw the geometry onscreen.

Locate the `templateAppDraw` function (as usual inside the `templateApp.cpp` source file) and execute the following steps:

1. After the `glClear` function, create a look-at matrix and give a little backward offset on the Y axis to actually be able to see the 3D model (which will obviously be located at 0, 0, 0), as follows:

```
GFX_set_matrix_mode( MODELVIEW_MATRIX );
GFX_load_identity(); {
vec3 e = { 0.0f, -4.0f, 0.0f },
      c = { 0.0f,  0.0f, 0.0f },
      u = { 0.0f,  0.0f, 1.0f };
GFX_look_at( &e, &c, &u ); }
```

**2.** Now bind your VAO as follows:

```
glBindVertexArrayOES( objmesh->vao );
```

By making the VAO index active, all the function calls inside the drawing list that you built earlier are triggered in the background automatically by the driver. Everything that has to be enabled is turned ON, and everything that should be disabled is turn OFF. This saves you the burden of calling each and every one of these functions manually every frame, or even to manually have to check what is ON and what is not in order to avoid saturating the bandwidth with obsolete machine state switches.

**3.** Now set the shader program for drawing as follows:

```
PROGRAM_draw( program );
```

Since you have now linked a draw callback to the `program` pointer, calling this function will automatically bind the shader program using `glUseProgram` and then send the execution pointer inside the `program_draw_callback`. This will then allow you to set all your uniform variables before letting GLES process the drawing call.

**4.** Next comes the actual drawing statement. Since everything is set up, all you have to do is this:

```
/* Function to use when drawing using elements (aka indices). */
glDrawElements(
/* The order in which the indices are listed. */
GL_TRIANGLES,
/* How many indices have to be used for drawing. */
objmesh->objtrianglelist[ 0 ].n_indice_array,
/* The type of indices. */
GL_UNSIGNED_SHORT,
/* The start offset in bytes of the first index; in this case, 0 or
NULL, since you want to start drawing from the first index in the array. */
( void * )NULL );
```

Notice how short this drawing process is compared to the one you used in the previous chapter. You minimized it into literally three lines of code: binding the VAO, binding the shader program, and drawing the triangles.

**5.** Now you're probably asking yourself: "Can I *finally* push the build button and execute the program?!" Well technically, yes, but there's still one last thing that you have to do: You need to clean up everything that has been initialized. To do this, locate the `templateAppExit` function and insert the following code to effectuate the cleanup:

```
SHADER_free( program->vertex_shader );
SHADER_free( program->fragment_shader );
PROGRAM_free( program );
OBJ_free( obj );
```

You did it! Build and run the program and say hello to Momo (shown in Figure 3-1). What you're looking at on your screen is a fully color-shaded "monkey" with vertex normals used as vertex color.

You have now created from scratch a basic OBJ viewer that's able to load an external 3D model from disk, and successfully rendered it onscreen using an advanced data management technique.

Before moving forward with the rest of this chapter, I suggest that you review every step. A lot of material was covered since the beginning of this chapter, and it is important that you grasp it all before moving on. Try, test, modify, experiment — you name it, do it! There's plenty of material here for you to spend another few hours experimenting, so go for it!

## HANDLING TOUCHE

In this section, you will learn how to use the `templateAppToucheBegan` and `templateAppToucheMoved` event callbacks. Before starting with more code, please note that these function callbacks are *not* linked to any GL context. This means that if you directly call any `gl` function inside these callbacks, they will most likely have no effect or will generate an error. If you have to access, modify, or do any other type of operation that requires a `gl` function inside the touche event functions, simply store the event information and process it inside the main loop (the `templateAppDraw` function).

**FIGURE 3-1:** Momo from the Apricot Open Game Project, Yo Frankie

In this section, you'll integrate into your OBJ viewer the necessary code to be able to rotate the object onscreen based on user touch and swipe movement. But before you can do that, create a new project to keep the previous code intact. Duplicate the `chapter3-1` project, rename it **chapter3-2**, and then load it inside your development interface.

At this point, what you want to do is write code that will allow the user to rotate the model on the X and Z axes. So if the user swipes their finger from left to right, the model will rotate on the Z axis; or if swiped from down to up, it will rotate on the X axis.

The steps are fairly easy since you have almost everything already set up.

1. Append the following global variables to the one you previously declared at the top of the `templateApp.cpp` source file:

```
/* Flag to auto rotate the mesh on the Z axis (demo reel style). */
unsigned char auto_rotate = 0;

/* Hold the touche location onscreen. */
vec2 touche = { 0.0f, 0.0f };

/* Store the rotation angle of the mesh. */
vec3 rot_angle = { 0.0f, 0.0f, 0.0f };
```

**2.** Move to the `templateAppToucheBegan` function and add the following code to store the touche location or to toggle autorotate:

```
/* If you receive 2 taps, start/stop auto rotate. */
if( tap_count == 2 ) auto_rotate = !auto_rotate;

/* Remember the current touche position. */
touche.x = x;
touche.y = y;
```

**3.** Paste the following code inside the `templateAppToucheMoved` function callback:

```
/* Stop auto rotate. */
auto_rotate = 0;
/* Calculate the touche delta and assign it to the angle X and Z. */
rot_angle.z += -( touche.x - x );
rot_angle.x += -( touche.y - y );
/* Remember the current touche position. */
touche.x = x;
touche.y = y;
```

Fairly simple and straightforward, right? First you disable autorotate, because it would interfere with the user interaction. Then you simply calculate the touche delta and add the value to the proper axis angle. And finally, you store the last touche location onscreen so the next delta calculation will be up-to-date in case the user continues to swipe the screen.

**4.** The final step consists of setting the rotation angle X and Z to the model view matrix to rotate the model. Insert the following code before the PROGRAM_draw function call inside the `templateAppDraw`; so the model view matrix uniform can be updated properly from the program draw callback function:

```
if( auto_rotate ) rot_angle.z += 2.0f;
GFX_rotate( rot_angle.x, 1.0f, 0.0f, 0.0f );
GFX_rotate( rot_angle.z, 0.0f, 0.0f, 1.0f );
```

The code basically speaks for itself. The first line increments the current Z rotation if autorotate is ON. The next two lines simply rotate the model on the X and Z axes based on their current angle. This will allow the users to move in whatever direction they want the complex geometry rendered onscreen, just like in Figure 3-2.

**5.** Build and run the program. Try dragging Momo around and double-tapping the screen to start and stop the autorotation.

That was a quick-and-dirty example of touche implementation. As you go more deeply into this book, more and more complex interactions will be added inside these touche function callbacks. The purpose of this example was just to show you how simple and easy it is to add code that enables users to interact with your 3D scenes on their touch screens.

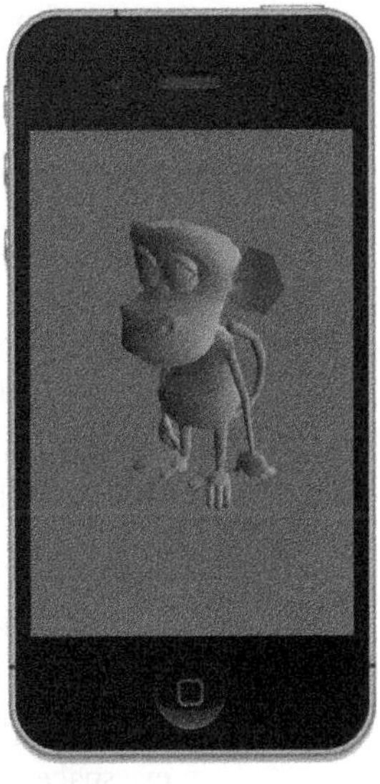

**FIGURE 3-2:** A touchy monkey

# PER-VERTEX LIGHTING

Per-vertex lighting is probably the easiest way to apply basic lighting to your models, and it is actually the default method that is used in OpenGL ES v1.x.

In this section, you will implement a simple directional light source to illuminate the model and learn how to calculate the intensity of the light (aka the Lambert factor) on each vertex. The technique that will be demonstrated here will use the vertex normals that you set up earlier to calculate how much the light direction vector will affect the color based on the current vertex normal.

First start by duplicating the chapter3-2 project folder and rename it **chapter3-3**.

## Vertex Shader Light Calculation

In order to change your existing shader to be able to pass the final light color to the fragment processing phase, open the vertex.glsl shader file (located inside the chapter3-3 directory). Then follow these instructions:

**1.** Replace the MODELVIEWPROJECTIONMATRIX uniform variable declaration line with the following:

```
uniform mediump mat4 MODELVIEWMATRIX;
uniform mediump mat4 PROJECTIONMATRIX;
uniform mediump mat3 NORMALMATRIX;
uniform mediump vec3 LIGHTPOSITION;
```

This time you will handle the model view and projection matrix separately. Your shader also needs to receive the current normal matrix, which is basically the result of the inverse, transposed model view matrix, and finally, another uniform to receive the current light position.

**2.** Declare a new varying variable to be able to bridge the light RGB color of the vertex with the fragment shader:

```
varying lowp vec3 lightcolor;
```

**3.** Remove the varying identifier of the normal variable declaration. You do not need to send it over to the fragment shader, so make it a simple global variable for the current shader.

**4.** Remove the main function declaration completely as well as its content. And start recreating it by adding this code:

```
void main( void ) {
   mediump vec3 position =
   vec3( MODELVIEWMATRIX * vec4( POSITION, 1.0 ) );
```

The code you've just entered declares a new variable to store the result of the vertex position in eye space. Later on, you will send the light position in that same space to the vertex shader, so it's important when it comes to lighting calculations to use the same "space" for each variable that you will use in the equation. Otherwise, the lighting calculation will be wrong.

**5.** Add the following code to multiply the vertex `normal` by the current `NORMALMATRIX`:

```
normal = normalize( NORMALMATRIX * NORMAL );
```

Since your 3D model has the ability to be rotated by the user, it is important to rotate the vertex normal accordingly. In addition, please note that the result is again normalized. This is done as a precautionary measure in case you decide to use `GFX_scale` on the model view matrix. In this case, in order to ensure that the light calculation is correct, you have to make sure that the vertex normal is always normalized.

**6.** Calculate the light direction for the current vertex position as follows:

```
mediump vec3 lightdirection =
normalize( LIGHTPOSITION - position );
```

**7.** Now calculate the intensity of the light for the current vertex position, based on the light direction vector, as follows:

```
lowp float ndotl =
max( dot( normal, lightdirection ), 0.0 );
```

**8.** Multiply the light intensity with the light color as follows:

```
lightcolor = ndotl * vec3( 1.0 );
```

For this example, you've just declared a pure white light (`vec3(1.0)`). But if later on, you want to test another color, simply replace this value with another RGB value, or simply create a new uniform variable to dynamically update the light color from within the C/C++ interface.

**9.** Finally, reuse the eye space position of the vertex calculated in step 4, and multiply it with the projection matrix:

```
gl_Position = PROJECTIONMATRIX * vec4( position, 1.0 );
} /* End of the main function. */
```

Your vertex shader is now ready to calculate the light color based on how "hard" the light direction vector is hitting the vertex position in eye space.

A lot of new uniform variables have been added, and you are going to need to modify the code inside the `templateApp.cpp` to be able to handle them. But right now, let's move on to the next subsection and modify the fragment shader.

## Modifying the Fragment Shader

As usual, the changes in the fragment shader are minimal, and it's a good practice to keep it that way (since every visible fragment onscreen will require you to execute the fragment shader). If you are close to an object, several more calculations will be required from the fragment processing phase, since the object's representation onscreen will require more pixels. Conversely, if you are far from the object, fewer calculations will be handled by the pixel processing phase, because the object does not require many pixels onscreen. Always keep these things in mind while creating your shaders.

Now open `fragment.glsl` and follow these instructions to be able to add the light color to the fragment color calculation:

1. Get rid of the whole line that contains the declaration of the `varying normal` variable. At this point, you don't need it anymore.

2. Create a new `varying` the same way you declared it earlier in the vertex shader for the `lightcolor`:

   ```
   varying lowp vec3 lightcolor;
   ```

3. Next you have to modify the `gl_FragColor` to take into consideration the current value of the light color. Replace the current `main` function of the shader with the following:

   ```
   void main( void ) {
       gl_FragColor = vec4( lightcolor, 1.0 ); }
   ```

4. (As an alternative to step 3) At the moment, the fragment is only affected by the light color and nothing else. In the real world, everything around you is first affected by an ambient color. You could optionally simulate that as well by adding an ambient color to the fragment:

   ```
   void main( void ) {
       gl_FragColor = vec4( lightcolor, 1.0 ) + vec4( 0.1 ); }
   ```

You are now done with modifying shaders. Next, you'll add the necessary code to be able to handle all the new uniforms that you have created.

## More Uniforms

Next, you're going to plug in the necessary code to handle your uniform variables. Open the `templateApp.cpp` file and go to the `program_draw_callback` function. Then follow these steps:

1. Erase the current `if` clause inside the `while` loop — it will be clearer and simpler to just start with a new `if` block.

2. Start the new `if` block with the `MODELVIEWMATRIX` uniform, as follows:

   ```
       /* If the current uniform is the model view matrix send it over to
   the shader .*/
       if( !strcmp( curr_program->uniform_array[ i ].name,
          "MODELVIEWMATRIX" ) ) {
       glUniformMatrix4fv(
       curr_program->uniform_array[ i ].location,
       1,
       GL_FALSE,
       ( float * )GFX_get_modelview_matrix() ); }
   ```

**3.** Now deal with the projection matrix, in a similar way that you did for the model view matrix in step 2:

```
else if( !strcmp( curr_program->uniform_array[ i ].name,
        "PROJECTIONMATRIX" ) ) {
glUniformMatrix4fv(
curr_program->uniform_array[ i ].location,
1,
GL_FALSE,
( float * )GFX_get_projection_matrix() ); }
```

**4.** Now handle the normal matrix:

```
else if( !strcmp( curr_program->uniform_array[ i ].name,
        "NORMALMATRIX" ) ) {
glUniformMatrix3fv(
curr_program->uniform_array[ i ].location,
1,
GL_FALSE,
( float * )GFX_get_normal_matrix() ); }
```

Note that the normal matrix is a 3 by 3 matrix, not 4 by 4 like the projection or model view matrix. It only contains rotation (and possibly a scale factor), but no location.

**5.** Add another `else if` to send the light position in eye space:

```
else if( !strcmp( curr_program->uniform_array[ i ].name,
        "LIGHTPOSITION" ) ) {
/* Set the light position in eye space to be at the same location as
the viewer. */
vec3 l = { 0.0f, 0.0f, 0.0f };
glUniform3fv(
curr_program->uniform_array[ i ].location,
1,
( float * )&l ); }
```

Leave the light position set to 0, 0, 0 in order to keep things simple for the moment — these values represent the center of the screen, aligned to the current viewer position. But do not hesitate later on to try and test different XYZ values to fully understand how the eye space representation works, as in this space the Z is pointing towards the camera.

**6.** Build and run the program.

Once Momo is loaded onto your device, rotate him around and observe how the lighting calculation affects the shading of each vertex position depending on the current direction of the light (see Figure 3-3).

**FIGURE 3-3:** Momo hit by lighting

# MAKING MOMO FURRIER

Momo is indeed a cute little monkey, but right now he does not look as good as he should. He needs a fur coat (in other words, a texture)!

This section is going to teach you how to use the diffuse texture (map_Kd) linked inside the MTL file that you have been using so far. You will learn how to load the texture from disk and how to modify your fragment shader to handle it.

The type of textures that you will be mostly using throughout this book is PNG. Loading functionalities and a lot more can be accessed using the TEXTURE structure implementation available within this book's SDK. Once again, since the implementation is a few hundred lines of code, yours truly doesn't really have the luxury to cover it all in this book.

However, I'll leave it to you as an exercise to dig into the SDK/common/texture.cpp and texture.h source files for more information about PNG loading and how to create textures using OpenGL ES. (There are plenty enough OpenGL texture tutorials available from Google, so no need to go into detail on this.)

The PNG format is basically what I like to call an "all-in-one format" — it has compression, and it supports RGB channels, grayscale, and alpha as well as color palettes. All these features make PNG a very suitable format to use for game textures.

Before starting, do as you normally do every time you are starting a new section, and start by duplicating chapter3-3 and this time, rename it **chapter3-4**.

Now, link the diffuse.png texture file that's located inside SDK/data/chapter3-4 to your project.

## Loading the Texture

In this section, you will learn how to load and use the texture linked by the token map_Kd inside the model.mtl material file.

Before you proceed with the next steps, here's a quick side note about textures. Textures in GLES are expected to have a width and height size of a power of two (2, 4, 8, 16, 32, 64, 128 . . . up to the maximum driver limit). Non–power of two texture (npot) support is either built-in or supported through a GL extension that is usually driver independent. For example, on my Android device. this extension is GL_IMG_texture_npot, but on my iOS devices, it is supported by default. As a general rule, if you want your textures to display correctly on all devices, just insure that the width and height size is a valid power of two that does not exceed the driver limit.

Now follow these few steps to learn how to load and apply a diffuse texture on Momo:

1. Inside the templateApp.cpp, right after the #include statement insert the following variable:

   ```
   TEXTURE *texture = NULL;
   ```

2. Next, you need to load the texture in memory, generate a texture ID, and send over the pixels to OpenGL ES. To do this, insert the following code before the end of the templateAppInit function:

```
texture = TEXTURE_create(
/* Texture name. */
obj->objmaterial[ 0 ].map_diffuse,
/* Texture filename. */
obj->objmaterial[ 0 ].map_diffuse,
/* Use a relative path to find the file. */
1,
/* Generate mipmaps. First time this term is mentioned, if you need more
information on mipmap please visit http://en.wikipedia.org/wiki/Mipmap. */
TEXTURE_MIPMAP,
/* Use a bilinear filter for the mipmaps. */
TEXTURE_FILTER_2X,
/* The anisotropic filtering factor (another new term), if you are not
familiar with it, visit http://en.wikipedia.org/wiki/Anisotropic_filtering.
For the current example, pass the value 0 to keep the texture isotropic. */
0.0f );
```

**3.** Your texture is now fully available for drawing, but before you can actually modify the code to use it for drawing, you have to make sure that the memory will be deallocated properly. Jump to the `templateAppExit` function and paste the following code before the end of the function:

```
TEXTURE_free( texture );
```

## Adjusting the Vertex Data

Since you're planning on using texture, you will need UVs and as a result you have to modify the VBO and VAO accordingly. Locate the VBO creation code (it's right after the `OBJ_load` function call inside the `templateAppInit`). Then follow these steps to modify the existing code to add UVs support:

**1.** Modify the total size in bytes of the vertex data array. Locate the following line:

```
size = objmesh->n_objvertexdata *
        sizeof( vec3 ) *
        sizeof( vec3 );
```

And replace it with this:

```
size = objmesh->n_objvertexdata *
        sizeof( vec3 ) * /* Vertex position. */
        sizeof( vec3 ) * /* Vertex normals. */
        sizeof( vec2 ); /* Texture UVs. */
```

**2.** At the end of the `while( i != objmesh->n_objvertexdata )` block, right before incrementing the loop (the line that contains `++i`), insert the following code to handle the insertion of the UV data in the array:

```
memcpy( vertex_array,
    /* Get the index UV data for the current index attached to the
current vertex and insert it into the vertex_array. */
    &obj->indexed_uv[ objmesh->objvertexdata[ i ].uv_index ],
    sizeof( vec2 ) );

    /* Move on to the insertion point. */
    vertex_array += sizeof( vec2 );
```

**3.** Since you modified the structure of the vertex data array, you will have to adjust the stride. Locate the following line:

```
stride = sizeof( vec3 ) +
         sizeof( vec3 );
```

And replace it with this:

```
stride = sizeof( vec3 ) + /* Vertex position. */
         sizeof( vec3 ) + /* Vertex normal. */
         sizeof( vec2 ); /* Vertex UV. */
```

**4.** Finally all you have to do is to add another vertex attribute inside the VAO list. Append the following code on the line just before the last glBindBuffer( GL_ELEMENT_ARRAY_BUFFER call of the templateAppInit function:

```
attribute = PROGRAM_get_vertex_attrib_location( program,
            ( char * )"TEXCOORD0" );

glEnableVertexAttribArray( attribute );
glVertexAttribPointer(
attribute,
/* Vertex UV contains 2 float, one for the U and one for the V
(obviously). */
2,
GL_FLOAT,
GL_FALSE,
stride,
/* The number of bytes to jump to gain access to the UV. */
BUFFER_OFFSET(
sizeof( vec3 ) + /* Vertex position. */
sizeof( vec3 ) ) ); /* Vertex normal. */
```

You've now updated your VBO and VAO so they can handle the vertex UVs that are necessary to "map" the texture on Momo.

## Adding UV Support to the Vertex Shader

In this section, you will learn how to modify your existing shader program to support texture UVs.

In order to be able to actually see a texture inside your OBJ viewer, you first have to create an attribute and the necessary varying variables to bridge the UV data over to the fragment processing phase. Follow these two easy steps to learn how to add texture coordinate support to your vertex shader:

**1.** At the top of the vertex.glsl file, declare a new vertex attribute for the texture coordinate along with a varying, like this:

```
attribute mediump vec2 TEXCOORD0;
varying mediump vec2 texcoord0;
```

**2.** Inside the main function, affect the attribute value to the varying as follows:

```
texcoord0 = TEXCOORD0;
```

You are now able to process the UVs coordinate on a vertex basis and send the data over to the fragment shader.

## Adding Texture Support to Your Fragment Shader

Follow these steps to learn how to handle the texture unit, and texture coordinates to use for your diffuse texture:

**1.** Declare the following variable at the top of the fragment.glsl file:

```
varying mediump vec2 texcoord0;
```

**2.** In order for OpenGL ES to be able to execute a UV based "pixel fetch" operation on your texture, you have to tell it on which texture unit (or channel) to execute it. To do this, you first need to create a uniform variable to handle the texture channel number that you will be using. There is a variable identifier called sampler2D built into the GLSL language that's specifically reserved to do just that. To use this built-in variable, declare the following:

```
uniform sampler2D DIFFUSE;
```

**3.** Replace the line that contains the gl_FragColor affectation by the following code to be able to get the current pixel on the texture and modulate the resulting RGBA with the light and ambient color:

```
gl_FragColor =
/* Fetch the pixel on the texture specified by the current UV data. */
texture2D( DIFFUSE, texcoord0 ) *
vec4( lightcolor, 1.0 ) + /* The light color. */
vec4( 0.1 ); /* The ambient color. */
```

The process that you just created can be reused for any type of texture UVs and texture channels. You can either use this code with a separate set of UVs, or use the same set on multiple texture channels. Each texture has to match the unit that it has been assigned to (which you will learn about in a moment).

In addition, by default, GLES 2.x requires driver manufacturers to make sure that at least eight active texture units can be used. This is a physical limit, so keep it in mind while building your shaders and applications.

## Binding the Texture

Two small things are left in order to see the texture on your 3D model: First bind the texture to a texture channel (or texture unit if you prefer), and second pass this channel number to the DIFFUSE uniform variable.

1. In the `templateApp.cpp` file, just before the `PROGRAM_draw` call, paste the following code to bind the texture to the first unit:

```
/* Activate the first texture unit. */
glActiveTexture( GL_TEXTURE0 );

/* Bind a texture to a specific texture channel; in this case,
0 (GL_TEXTURE0). */
glBindTexture(
/* Since your texture is a 2D texture, GL_TEXTURE_2D = sampler2D in your
fragment shader. */
GL_TEXTURE_2D,
/* Use the built-in variable tid (texture id) of the TEXTURE structure,
which represents the id for the texture that has been automatically
generated by GLES. */
texture->tid );
```

2. Move on to the `program_draw_callback` and append the following `else if` to the existing `if` statement to be able to send the `DIFFUSE` texture channel id 0 (`GL_TEXTURE0`) to the shader program:

```
else if( !strcmp( curr_program->uniform_array[ i ].name,
        "DIFFUSE" ) &&
        !curr_program->uniform_array[ i ].constant ) {
    /* Specify that the uniform is constant and will not change over
time, in order to always have to bind the same value over and over. */
    curr_program->uniform_array[ i ].constant = 1;
    glUniform1i(
    curr_program->uniform_array[ i ].location,
    0 );
} /* The first texture channel. */
```

3. Your screen should now display something similar to what's shown in Figure 3-4.

Before moving on to the next chapter, make sure you extensively test the different parameters to get a feel for what is possible with what you have learned.

In the next chapter, you will start getting deeper and deeper into hardcore game and graphics programming; so make sure you grasp everything covered in this chapter!

## SUMMARY

In this chapter, you learned how to load and handle complex geometries using any optimized VBO and VAO. You also learned how to use texture loading and how to do basic per-vertex lighting.

**FIGURE 3-4:** Momo with a coat

You have now been introduced to most of the core concepts that you're going to need to deal with on a daily basis as a game graphics programmer. But of course, there's still a lot to learn, so keep reading!

In the next chapter, you will learn how to handle the different types of objects commonly found in a scene, as well as how to adjust their rendering sequence to draw them correctly onscreen.

# Building a Scene

**WHAT'S IN THIS CHAPTER?**

➤ Handling a scene with multiple objects

➤ Classifying objects based on their material properties

➤ Mixing solid, alpha tested, and transparent objects and rendering them correctly

➤ Creating and using Uber Shaders

➤ Handling double-sided semitransparent objects, and other alpha tricks

➤ Implementing per-pixel lighting inside your fragment shaders

So far you have been rendering single objects. Whether it is in 2D or in 3D, it has been pretty straightforward until now. In this chapter, you will learn how to handle a scene with multiple objects of different types, including how to sort and draw these objects using a correct rendering sequence.

You will progressively go through each aspect of rendering a complex scene. And you'll fix each and every drawing issue as you go in order to end up with a perfectly rendered scene.

This chapter will also show you how to move the lighting calculation from the vertex to the fragment shader in order to obtain a more realistic lighting effect.

You will also learn about the Uber Shader concept, which allows you to have multiple effects contained inside one giant vertex and fragment shader file. And you'll discover how to make full use of this popular technique inside you own games and 3D apps.

## HANDLING MULTIPLE OBJECTS

Until now, you have been handling only a single object. Whether it's a simple quad or a furry monkey, it's still just one set of vertex data drawn over and over again. In this chapter, you will progressively discover how to handle and manage a simple, but relatively challenging, scene that contains multiple objects, materials (shaders), and textures.

## THE CODE STRUCTURE

As usual at the beginning of each chapter, start by duplicating the `template` project and rename it **chapter4-1**. Now open the project file for your designated platform, and then modify the code of the `templateApp.cpp` in order to start working with the following structure:

```
#include "templateApp.h"
#define OBJ_FILE ( char * )"scene.obj"
OBJ *obj = NULL;

TEMPLATEAPP templateApp = { templateAppInit,
                            templateAppDraw };

void program_bind_attrib_location( void *ptr ) {
   PROGRAM *program = ( PROGRAM * )ptr;
}

/* This time you will use the material draw callback instead of the
program draw callback, since in this chapter you will work on a
material basis, not on a shader program basis. */
void material_draw_callback( void *ptr ) {
   OBJMATERIAL *objmaterial = ( OBJMATERIAL * )ptr;
   PROGRAM *program = objmaterial->program;
   unsigned int i = 0;
   while( i != program->uniform_count ) {
      ++i;
   }
}

void templateAppInit( int width, int height ) {
   atexit( templateAppExit );

   GFX_start();

   glViewport( 0.0f, 0.0f, width, height );

   GFX_set_matrix_mode( PROJECTION_MATRIX );
   GFX_load_identity();
   GFX_set_perspective( 45.0f,
   ( float )width / ( float )height,
   0.1f,
   100.0f,
```

```
    -90.0f ); /* This time you will use a landscape view, so rotate the
projection matrix 90 degrees. */

    obj = OBJ_load( OBJ_FILE, 1 );
}

void templateAppDraw( void ) {
    glClearColor( 0.5f, 0.5f, 0.5f, 1.0f );
    glClear( GL_DEPTH_BUFFER_BIT | GL_COLOR_BUFFER_BIT );

    GFX_set_matrix_mode( MODELVIEW_MATRIX );
    GFX_load_identity();
    vec3 e = {  0.0f, -6.0f, 1.35f }, /* The location of the camera. */
         c = {  0.0f, -5.0f, 1.35f }, /* Where the camera is looking. */
         u = {  0.0f,  0.0f, 1.0f  };
    GFX_look_at( &e, &c, &u );
}

void templateAppExit( void ) {
    unsigned i = 0;
    while( i != obj->n_objmaterial ) {
        SHADER_free( obj->objmaterial[ i ].program->vertex_shader );
        SHADER_free( obj->objmaterial[ i ].program->fragment_shader );
        PROGRAM_free( obj->objmaterial[ i ].program );
        ++i;
    }
    OBJ_free( obj );
}
```

## LOADING AND DRAWING THE SCENE

By now you are already familiar with most of the code, with the exception of the 90-degree flip of the projection matrix to draw in landscape mode.

In addition, notice that this time you will be using an OBJ file named scene.obj. You can find it inside the SDK/data/chapter4-1 directory. Now link both the .obj and .mtl files along with all the PNGs located in the same directory to your project.

In addition, you will need a vertex and fragment shader for this section. Create two new shader files named **vertex.glsl** and **fragment.glsl**, save them inside the SDK/chapter4-1 folder, and link them to your project. Then follow these steps to start implementing the necessary code to draw the scene onscreen:

1. Inside the templateAppInit function, locate the call to OBJ_load, and then add the following code right after it to build the VBOs and VAO for all meshes contained in the OBJ file:

   ```
   /* Initialize the counter. */
   unsigned int i = 0;
   /* While there are some objects. */
   while( i != obj->n_objmesh ) {
   /* Generate the VBOs and VAO for the current object. */
   ```

```
OBJ_build_mesh( obj, /* The OBJ structure to use. */
                     i ); /* The object index inside the OBJ structure. */
        /* Free all the vertex data related arrays. At this point, they have
    all been transferred to the video memory by the OBJ_build_mesh call. */
        OBJ_free_mesh_vertex_data( obj, i );
        ++i; } /* Move to the next object. */
```

The OBJ_build_mesh function basically wraps all the VBO and VAO calls that you manually coded in the previous chapter. (Don't worry about the attribute locations — you will be handling them a bit later in this section.)

2.  Load all the textures linked inside the MTL file and generate their texture IDs as follows:

```
i = 0;
while( i != obj->n_texture ) {
OBJ_build_texture( obj,
i,
/* By default the same as where the .mtl is located. */
obj->texture_path,
TEXTURE_MIPMAP,
TEXTURE_FILTER_2X,
0.0f );
/* Next texture. */
++i;
}
```

3.  Now use the following code to link all textures to their respective materials and manually create a shader program for each of them using the two shader files that you created previously:

```
i = 0;
while( i != obj->n_objmaterial ) {
/* Link all textures to the material(s). */
OBJ_build_material( obj,
                 i,
   /* No need to pass a PROGRAM pointer. You'll create one. */
                    NULL );

    /* Use the following helper function to create a shader program for
each material using the same vertex and fragment shader file. */
    obj->objmaterial[ i ].program =
    PROGRAM_create( ( char * )"default",
                    ( char * )"vertex.glsl",
                    ( char * )"fragment.glsl",
                    1, /* Use a relative path. */
                    1, /* Debug the shaders and program linking. */
                    /* Custom callback to be able to specify the
attribute location before the linking phase of the shader program. */
                    program_bind_attrib_location,
                    /* Do not link the draw callback this time */
                    NULL );

    /* Set the material draw callback to have direct access to the
material data before drawing. */
```

```
OBJ_set_draw_callback_material( obj,
                                i,
                                material_draw_callback );

        /* Next material. */
        ++i;
    }
```

4. Move on to the `templateAppDraw` function and insert on the next line right after the `GFX_look_at` call the following block of code to loop through all the objects and draw them onscreen:

```
        /* Initialize a counter. */
        unsigned int i = 0;

    /* Loop for each OBJMESH. */
    while( i != obj->n_objmesh ) {

        /* Push the current model view matrix down. */
        GFX_push_matrix();

        /* Translate the model view matrix use the location XYZ of the
    current mesh. */
        GFX_translate( obj->objmesh[ i ].location.x,
                       obj->objmesh[ i ].location.y,
                       obj->objmesh[ i ].location.z );

        /* Draw the mesh and its associated material(s) onscreen. */
        OBJ_draw_mesh( obj, i );

        /* Pop the model view matrix back. */
        GFX_pop_matrix();

        /* Next mesh. */
        ++i;
    }
```

5. Now move to the `material_draw_callback` function and insert inside the `while` loop block the following block on the line just before the loop incrementation (++i):

```
        if( !strcmp( program->uniform_array[ i ].name,
            "DIFFUSE" ) ) {
            /* If a diffuse texture is specified inside the MTL file, it will
        always be bound to the second texture channel (GL_TEXTURE1). */
            glUniform1i(
            program->uniform_array[ i ].location,
            1 );
        }

        else if( !strcmp( program->uniform_array[ i ].name,
                "MODELVIEWPROJECTIONMATRIX" ) ) {
            /* Send over the current model view matrix multiplied by
        the projection matrix. */
            glUniformMatrix4fv(
```

```
        program->uniform_array[ i ].location,
        1,
        GL_FALSE,
        ( float * )GFX_get_modelview_projection_matrix() );
    }
```

Since you let the `OBJ_build_material` call handle the texture linking work for you, the function is using predefined texture channels for each type of texture found inside the MTL file material definition. Table 4.1 lists the texture channels available for each material and which texture unit they will bind to.

**TABLE 4-1:** Default Texture Unit Attribution

| MTL TEXTURE MAP | TYPE | CHANNEL | SAMPLER2D |
|---|---|---|---|
| map_Ka | Ambient | GL_TEXTURE0 | 0 |
| map_Kd | Diffuse | GL_TEXTURE1 | 1 |
| map_Ks | Specular | GL_TEXTURE2 | 2 |
| disp map_disp map_Disp | Displacement map | GL_TEXTURE3 | 3 |
| bump map_bump map_Bump | Bump map | GL_TEXTURE4 | 4 |
| map_Tr | Translucency | GL_TEXTURE5 | 5 |

**6.** Similar to the previous step, the `OBJ_build_mesh` function has handled the attributes generation for you. You now have to tell the shader program which attributes location you will be using. Please note that this can only be done before the linking phase of the shader program. To do this, go to the `program_bind_attrib_location` function and add the following before the end of the function bracket:

```
        glBindAttribLocation( program->pid, 0, "POSITION" );
        glBindAttribLocation( program->pid, 2, "TEXCOORD0" );
```

Refer to Table 4.2 for the full list of predefined attribute locations supported by the OBJ loader that comes with the SDK.

**TABLE 4-2:** Default OBJ Loader Attribute Location

| ATTRIBUTE TYPE | ATTRIBUTE LOCATION | AUTO-GENERATED DATA |
|---|---|---|
| POSITION | 0 | No |
| NORMAL | 1 | Yes |

| ATTRIBUTE TYPE | ATTRIBUTE LOCATION | AUTO-GENERATED DATA |
|---|---|---|
| TEXCOORD0 | 2 | No |
| TANGENT0 | 3 | Yes |
| FNORMAL | 4 | Yes |

You now have all the necessary code to load and draw your scene. As you can see, by using the helper functions that come with the book's SDK, you are drastically decreasing the number of lines of code. At this point, all that's left to be done is to write the necessary vertex and fragment shaders.

## THE SHADERS CODE

Open the vertex shader file `vertex.glsl`, insert the following code, and then save the file:

```
uniform mediump mat4 MODELVIEWPROJECTIONMATRIX;
attribute mediump vec3 POSITION;
attribute mediump vec2 TEXCOORD0;
varying mediump vec2 texcoord0;
void main( void ) {
    texcoord0 = TEXCOORD0;
    gl_Position = MODELVIEWPROJECTIONMATRIX * vec4( POSITION, 1.0 );
}
```

Next, open `fragment.glsl` and insert the following fragment shader code, and then save the file:

```
uniform sampler2D DIFFUSE;
varying mediump vec2 texcoord0;
void main( void ) {
    gl_FragColor = texture2D( DIFFUSE, texcoord0 );
}
```

Now build and run the application and you should now have the same as Figure 4-1 drawn onscreen.

As you can see, all the objects and textures are properly applied. However, there are some obvious major issues. The tree leaves are not transparent — they completely cover the face of our beloved monkey. In addition, if you take a look at the material definition inside the `scene.mtl` file, you will discover that the balloon material should be semitransparent due to the dissolve value (aka alpha).

**FIGURE 4-1:** Your first scene using multiple objects

In order to handle a proper drawing for all the objects, you will have to create multiple shaders in order to handle all of the effects set in their material settings. However, before moving to more shader creation code, you have to first learn about the different object types that are commonly found in all 3D scenes.

# THE DIFFERENT OBJECT TYPES

Basically, the few oddities mentioned at the end of the last section come to the fact that depending on the type of objects that you are dealing with, you have to treat them differently — not only from a shader point of view, but also from the drawing sequence that has to be used to draw them properly.

There are basically three main types of objects that require your attention. Each of them can be identified based on their material settings. The term *object* is used at this stage to keep things clear and simple. However, as you start to dive deeper into advanced game and graphic programming, you will find that a more appropriate term would be *triangle list*, because one object can contain multiple materials and each of them has to be drawn using a separate triangle list.

At this stage, you can think of an object as a single mesh that has one material applied onto its whole surface, keeping in mind that each distinct material will have a direct impact on the category that object belongs to. The three main object categories that should be identified at loading time are as follows:

➤ **Solid object** — This is the common object type. The object material does not have any alpha value in its material properties. The textures associated with the material do not contain any alpha channel; they are all either RGB or grayscale.

➤ **Alpha-tested object** — This type is most commonly used for foliage or to represent eroded surfaces such as rusty metal. You can identify this type if at least one of the textures of the material has an alpha channel and an alpha test threshold to be used to exclude pixels from being rendered.

➤ **Transparent object** — A transparent object is basically the opposite of a solid object. An object is considered transparent if an alpha other than 1.0 is specified inside its material property, or if at least one of the textures assigned to the material contains an alpha channel. As a result, blending will need to be turned ON when drawing this type of object.

# THE DRAWING SEQUENCE

At loading time, you need to be able to identify the type of each object. An object's rendering order will be directly affected by the object category it belongs to.

For example, if you have a semitransparent surface, you need to make sure that all objects behind it are drawn first. Otherwise, the rendering will look weird, because objects or parts of objects will be missing or simply invisible.

That said, it basically comes down to a universal sequence for drawing each and every object type. The simplest and most recommended sequence of rendering is as follow:

**1.** Draw all your solid objects as they appear. Alternatively, you can sort the objects from front to back (based on their distance from the viewer) to gain a bit of speed using an early Z test with the depth buffer. This technique can help you avoid "overdrawing" smaller objects that are occluded by larger ones, but it requires a bit more CPU for sorting the objects.

2. Draw all the alpha-tested objects. As with the solid objects, you can order alpha-tested objects from front to back to avoid processing unnecessary pixels in the fragment shader. And for the sake of better performance at the cost of machine state changes, you can optionally integrate them inside your solid object drawing list. This is assuming that the pixels of the alpha-tested objects are not semitransparent (which are dealt with in the next step).

3. Draw all your semitransparent objects, ordered from back to front based on their distance from the current viewer location. Sorting them in this order will ensure that your semitransparent surfaces are always drawn correctly.

This rendering sequence will help you avoid a lot of machine state switches while ensuring that your scenes are rendered properly. You should be able to use this sequence for most of your 3D scenes.

In the next section, you'll implement the necessary code to categorize every object in order to properly fix the drawing sequence of your current scene.

## FIXING THE SCENE

Duplicate the project file from the previous section and rename it **chapter4-2**. Then open this new project file.

Let's start by analyzing the scene the way it is right now, and categorize each object. Momo, the tree bark, the background, and the ground are rendering just fine with the current shader. All of these belong to the solid objects category and do not require any other special care at the moment.

The balloon object has a dissolve (aka alpha) value of 0.65 in its material definition. This means that you will have to turn on alpha blending and use the alpha value of the material to affect the whole object opacity, making it semitransparent. As you might have already guessed, this object belongs to the transparent object type. Since there are no other transparent objects at the moment, there's no point sorting it by distance. You will simply plug its drawing into a good location inside your rendering sequence.

The only objects left to categorize are the tree leaves. Since their texture has an alpha channel, what you want to do at the moment is to simply get rid of the alpha pixels in order to only keep the contour of the leaves. For this, you will have to use alpha testing. This makes the leaves an alpha-tested object.

Now that you have successfully classified your objects, you will need to create the necessary shaders for each type. Right now, you need two extra shaders: one for the balloon, and one for the tree leaves (which is in fact one object).

You haven't worked with many shader files so far, but once again, as the complexity of your scene grows, you will require more and more shader files. It can be quite a burden to maintain two different files for each different material and their variants. However, in the next section, you'll learn how to maintain multiple effects inside one vertex and fragment shader file.

## Uber Shader

Wouldn't it be nice to simply have a single shader program that can be dynamically adjusted to handle *all* the effects that you want? That's exactly what an Uber Shader will do for you.

Uber Shaders use pre-processor macro definitions (#define) to toggle ON or OFF part of the GLSL ES code contained in your vertex and fragment shader file(s). In your application, you can then dynamically toggle only the part of the source you need before compilation time. This allows you to re-use the same shader files to achieve a single effect or a combination of multiple effects.

This technique is very practical and enables you to avoid branching (if, else if, else) directly inside your shaders. Vastly used by most of the modern game engines, this approach still has some downsides. First, you will still need to bind ON and OFF multiple shader program IDs at drawing time. In addition, as your Uber Shader grows in complexity, it might be become more and more difficult to maintain.

Let's first start fixing your app by adding the necessary code to your shader program so you can use the Uber Shader method on the solid, semitransparent, and alpha tested objects of your scene.

At the moment, the vertex shader will stay the same for all your objects. So open the fragment .glsl file and replace its content with this code:

```
uniform sampler2D DIFFUSE;
varying mediump vec2 texcoord0;
void main( void ) {
    lowp vec4 diffuse_color = texture2D( DIFFUSE, texcoord0 );

    #ifdef SOLID_OBJECT
        gl_FragColor = diffuse_color;
    #endif

    #ifdef ALPHA_TESTED_OBJECT
        /* NEW! If the alpha value of the texture diffuse color is
less than 0.5, discard the fragment. */
        if( diffuse_color.a < 0.5 ) discard;
        else gl_FragColor = diffuse_color;
    #endif

    #ifdef TRANSPARENT_OBJECT
        gl_FragColor = diffuse_color;
        /* NEW! Override the texture diffuse color alpha value (if any) with
the one contained in the material (you only have one at the moment, so you
can hardcode the value in the shader for now). */
        gl_FragColor.a = 0.65;
    #endif
}
```

Now you have three different effects contained inside the same fragment shader. Of course, this is a pretty simple example, but as you begin creating more complex scenes with many objects and materials, this approach will enable you to handle larger shaders with many effects and variants.

## Using Your Uber Shader

What's left to be done in order for you to be able to use the appropriate block of code that you plug inside your Uber fragment shader is to trigger the necessary #define tag before compilation.

Open the `templateApp.cpp` file and find the following `while` loop inside the `templateAppInit` function:

```
i = 0;
while( i != obj->n_objmaterial ) {
    /* Loop Code */
    ++i; }
Replace that code block completely with the following:
i = 0;
/* Load the global vertex shader that you are going to use for all the
material shader programs. */
MEMORY *vertex_shader = mopen( ( char * )"vertex.glsl", 1 );
while( i != obj->n_objmaterial ) {
    ++i;
}
```

This loop structure will enable you to initialize and create your shader program. Next, you have to dynamically enable the necessary shader code of your fragment shader, depending on the type of object you're dealing with. To do this, follow these steps:

**1.** For each material that you will be creating in the loop, you will need to access a clean copy of the fragment shader. Insert the following code on the next line after the `while` loop start bracket:

```
MEMORY *fragment_shader = mopen( ( char * )"fragment.glsl", 1 );
```

**2.** To make things easier, declare a local `OBJMATERIAL` pointer to handle the current material you are dealing with and build the material as follows:

```
OBJMATERIAL *objmaterial = &obj->objmaterial[ i ];
OBJ_build_material( obj, i, NULL );
```

**3.** Now insert the following code block to analyze the value of the dissolve parameter for the current material and take the proper action in order to toggle the necessary `#define` inside your fragment shader code:

```
/* The material has no alpha, so it is considered a solid object.
In addition, please note that the current and following conditions are
strictly based on the dissolve value. However, in a real-world scenario,
an extra check has to be made on the number of bits of the texture to
analyze if it contains an alpha channel. And modifications in the shaders
are required to handle this type of scenario. */
/* If dissolve is equal to one it means that the material you are
dealing with will be applied on solid objects. */
    if( objmaterial->dissolve == 1.0f )
        /* This function will insert the appropriate #define code at an
arbitrary position in the current fragment shader memory stream that you
loaded in the previous step. */
        minsert(
        /* The memory stream. */
        fragment_shader,
        /* The code to insert. */
```

```
        ( char * )"#define SOLID_OBJECT\n",
        /* The character position in the stream to insert the code. In this
case, it's 0, which represents the beginning of the stream. This way, only
the block of the marked the #ifdef SOLID_OBJECT will be enabled. */
        0 );

    /* There's no real way in an OBJ material file to tag an object for
alpha test. Simply use the 0.0 value on the dissolve parameter to tag the
object as an alpha-tested object. */
    else if( !objmaterial->dissolve )
        /* Insert the necessary code to enable the ALPHA_TESTED_OBJECT code
block of the shader by manually inserting the definition. */
        minsert( fragment_shader,
                ( char * )"#define ALPHA_TESTED_OBJECT\n",
                0 );

    /* Same as above except that if the object does not fall between
the two previous conditions, you have to treat it as a transparent
object. */
    else {
        minsert( fragment_shader,
                ( char * )"#define TRANSPARENT_OBJECT\n",
                0 );
    }
```

4.  You have now dynamically enabled the appropriate block of code for each object type. It's now time to compile the shader for the current material using the modified source code as follows:

```
        /* Use the objmaterial program pointer to initialize the
shader program. */
        objmaterial->program = PROGRAM_init( objmaterial->name );

        /* Create the vertex shader. */
        objmaterial->program->vertex_shader =
        SHADER_init( ( char * )"vertex",
                GL_VERTEX_SHADER );

        /* Create the fragment shader. */
        objmaterial->program->fragment_shader =
        SHADER_init( ( char * )"fragment",
                GL_FRAGMENT_SHADER );

        /* Compile both the vertex and fragment programs. */
        SHADER_compile( objmaterial->program->vertex_shader,
                    ( char * )vertex_shader->buffer,
                    1 );

        SHADER_compile( objmaterial->program->fragment_shader,
                    ( char * )fragment_shader->buffer,
                    1 );

        /* Link the bind attribute location callback BEFORE the linking phase
of the shader program to insure that the location of the attribute that you
```

```
specify will be taken into consideration. */
        PROGRAM_set_bind_attrib_location_callback(
        objmaterial->program,
        program_bind_attrib_location );

        /* Link the shader program so you can use it for drawing. */
        PROGRAM_link( objmaterial->program, 1 );

        /* Assign the draw callback to the material so you can receive
live feedback before drawing in order to update your uniform variables
based on the current material data. */
        OBJ_set_draw_callback_material( obj,
                                        i,
                                        material_draw_callback );

        /* Close and free the memory stream. */
        mclose( fragment_shader );
```

**5.** And finally, paste the following code below the `while` loop end bracket to flush the vertex shader code from memory:

```
mclose( vertex_shader );
```

## Render Loop Objects Categorization

You are almost there! Basically at this point, the only thing that's left to be done is to implement the same kind of categorization code inside your render loop. Locate the `while` loop block that's being used to render all the objects inside the `templateAppDraw` function, and get rid of it completely.

In the following steps, you will be replacing it with three different loops, one for each type of object that you are going to draw.

**1.** Start by re-implementing a new `while` loop, right after the `unsigned int i = 0;` declaration, but this time for the solid objects only:

```
/* Solid Objects */
while( i != obj->n_objmesh ) {
        /* Get the material pointer of the first triangle list of the
current mesh. All your objects are using a single material, so only
one triangle list is available. By getting access to the first
triangle list, you can now gain access to the material used by your
current mesh. You can then use the material dissolve property as you
did earlier to classify your object at render time. */
        OBJMATERIAL *objmaterial =
        obj->objmesh[ i ].objtrianglelist[ 0 ].objmaterial;

        /* Is it a solid object? */
        if( objmaterial->dissolve == 1.0f ) {
        GFX_push_matrix();
        GFX_translate( obj->objmesh[ i ].location.x,
                        obj->objmesh[ i ].location.y,
                        obj->objmesh[ i ].location.z );
```

```
        OBJ_draw_mesh( obj, i );
        GFX_pop_matrix(); }
        ++i;
    }
```

**2.**  Now run another type of condition to evaluate if it is an alpha-tested object (dissolve = 0):

```
/* Alpha-Tested Objects */
i = 0;
while( i != obj->n_objmesh ) {
    OBJMATERIAL *objmaterial =
    obj->objmesh[ i ].objtrianglelist[ 0 ].objmaterial;

    if( !objmaterial->dissolve ) {
    GFX_push_matrix();
    GFX_translate( obj->objmesh[ i ].location.x,
                   obj->objmesh[ i ].location.y,
                   obj->objmesh[ i ].location.z );
    OBJ_draw_mesh( obj, i );
    GFX_pop_matrix(); }
    ++i;
}
```

Note that since you only have one alpha-tested object (the leaves of the tree), there's no real need to sort the object by distance. However, keep in mind that if you have multiple alpha-tested objects, the performance gain of sorting them from front to back based on their distance from the viewer can be quite beneficial.

**3.**  Now apply the same structure for the last object type to be drawn onscreen: the transparent objects. But this time, you will have to tell the video card to enable blending and to use the alpha value of the texture for the blend operation on each visible pixel, as follows:

```
/* Tell the GPU to enable blending. */
glEnable( GL_BLEND );
/* Specify which source and destination function to use for
blending. In this case, all you want is the alpha value of the
fragment to be used by the blending operation to make your object
semitransparent. */
glBlendFunc( GL_SRC_ALPHA, GL_ONE_MINUS_SRC_ALPHA );

/* Transparent Objects */
i = 0;
while( i != obj->n_objmesh ) {
    OBJMATERIAL *objmaterial =
    obj->objmesh[ i ].objtrianglelist[ 0 ].objmaterial;
    /* If the current dissolve value doesn't fit the conditions of
the solid or alpha tested objects, the current object has to be
transparent, so draw it onscreen. */
    if( objmaterial->dissolve > 0.0f &&
        objmaterial->dissolve < 1.0f ) {
    GFX_push_matrix();
    GFX_translate( obj->objmesh[ i ].location.x,
                   obj->objmesh[ i ].location.y,
```

```
                        obj->objmesh[ i ].location.z );
        OBJ_draw_mesh( obj, i );
        GFX_pop_matrix(); }
        ++i;
    }
    /* Every time you enable a machine state, remember to turn it
back OFF when you don't need it. This way, you won't have any
surprises when drawing the next frame. */
    glDisable( GL_BLEND );
```

Well, that was quite a bit of code that you just wrote, but it's all to your advantage. You now have all the necessary knowledge to be able to draw a scene containing multiple object types.

Go ahead and build and execute your program. You should see what's shown in Figure 4-2 on your screen.

It's already better — at least you can see that you get the alpha test and semitransparent object right. But there are obviously still some issues. Since the balloon is semitransparent, you should

**FIGURE 4-2:** Your scene rendered with object classification

be able to see its back faces before seeing the leg and belly of Momo. And as for the leaf of the tree, unless a hurricane passed right through it, it should look a lot more bulky than that!

Do a quick review of the section code to make sure you grasp all the key concepts, and then jump to the next section of this chapter to learn how to fix your scene by implementing double-sided rendering.

## Double-Sided

Before implementing the key concept that will be demonstrated in this section, duplicate the last section's project and rename it **chapter4-3**.

When dealing with partially transparent or semitransparent geometry, you will have to determine if the back face of the object should be visible.

Simply turning off GL_CULL_FACE (which allows you to control if either the front or back face should be culled) wouldn't do the trick.

You never know in which order the triangles will be sent to be drawn. And sorting all triangles in real time based on their distance from the viewer (to ensure proper triangle rendering order) is too expensive in terms of calculation and therefore out of the question.

Alternatively, you have to rely on another trick that will allow you to draw in the right order both the front face and back face of an object that is semitransparent or partially transparent.

The most efficient and best performing trick is to invert the side of the cull face and render the geometry twice. Let's start by implementing double-sided rendering on the balloon.

Locate the `OBJ_draw_mesh` function call inside the `while` loop where you render the transparent objects, and replace the function call with the following:

```
glCullFace( GL_FRONT );
OBJ_draw_mesh( obj, i );
glCullFace( GL_BACK );
OBJ_draw_mesh( obj, i );
```

What you just coded was a two-step drawing approach: First you tell the GPU to get rid of all the front face of the mesh, and then you send the draw call. At this point, only the back faces are processed. Then you invert the condition and render all the front faces (remember that it has to be done from back to front for correct alpha sorting).

Congratulations! You have now implemented double-sided rendering of semitransparent objects. That was easy, right?

To visualize the result, build and execute the program. You should notice right away that the balloon is now rendered properly, as shown in Figure 4-3.

**FIGURE 4-3:** Balloon rendered double-sided

Obviously this technique can only work with hollow objects that are semitransparent or on alpha-tested objects that are not using semitransparency. Since the alpha test is done on a pixel basis, there's no problem using this technique, because only the visible pixel will be written in the depth buffer and color buffer.

To implement this method on your alpha-tested objects, locate the `while` loop where you render this kind and replace the `OBJ_draw_mesh` function the same way you did for the transparent object. Then build and run the program. You should now see what's shown in Figure 4-4.

**FIGURE 4-4:** Alpha-tested tree leaves using the double-sided drawing approach

Your scene basically renders fine at the moment. However, as you might have already noticed, the contour of the leaves is pretty jaggy.

Let's now use a different approach, and consider the alpha-tested object as a sub-class of the transparent objects to be able to achieve a new range of effects. Since simply tweaking the alpha-test threshold will only get rid of more or less pixels (depending on the value you are using), the following technique can be used to properly handle smooth alpha-blended overlapping triangles and can be used on foliage, just like the leaves of the tree.

To demonstrate how you can use this method, start by duplicating the last project and rename it **chapter4-4**. Then follow these steps to change the rules of the game a bit:

1. Get rid of the whole `while` loop rendering block for the alpha-tested objects, or simply comment it.

2. Inside the transparent object `while` loop, change the `if` condition to the following:

```
if( objmaterial->dissolve != 1.0f )
```

3. Change the alpha-test value inside the `fragment.glsl` file. Since you are now using the alpha channel of the texture in conjunction with alpha blending, the alpha-test threshold doesn't have to be as dramatic as 0.5.

```
if( diffuse_color.a < 0.1 ) discard;
```

4. Now build and run your program. You will now see how much smoother the leaves of the trees are, as demonstrated in Figure 4-5.

**FIGURE 4-5:** Smooth tree leaves using alpha testing and blending

## PER-PIXEL LIGHTING

Let's now use the power of the Uber Shader and implement per-pixel lighting! So far, you have been implementing per-vertex lighting, where all the calculations were done inside the vertex shader. As the name of the technique implies, you will now move the lighting calculations to the fragment shader. Note that once again you will be using a directional light (basically simulating the sun).

This section will introduce you to the Phong lighting model. In addition, this time you will directly use the material values that you have been extracting from the MTL file and will directly plug them inside the lighting equation.

### Making the Vertex Shader Even Fatter

Start by duplicating the last section project and rename it **chapter4-5**. Then open the project file and let's get this show on the road!

1. Open the `vertex.glsl` shader file and replace

```
uniform mediump mat4 MODELVIEWPROJECTIONMATRIX;
```

with the following code:

```
/* Declare a new entry inside your Uber Shader */
#ifdef LIGHTING_SHADER
    uniform mediump mat4 MODELVIEWMATRIX;
    uniform mediump mat4 PROJECTIONMATRIX;
    uniform mediump mat3 NORMALMATRIX;
```

```
attribute lowp vec3 NORMAL;

/* Since the lighting calculation will be done inside the
fragment shader, declare two variables to bridge the vertex normal
and the vertex position to send them over. */
    varying lowp vec3 normal;
    varying mediump vec3 position;
#else
    uniform mediump mat4 MODELVIEWPROJECTIONMATRIX;
#endif
```

**2.** Now replace the following `gl_Position` affectation code:

```
gl_Position = MODELVIEWPROJECTIONMATRIX * vec4( POSITION, 1.0 );
```

with this:

```
#ifdef LIGHTING_SHADER
    /* Calculate the vertex position in eye space. */
    position = vec3( MODELVIEWMATRIX * vec4( POSITION, 1.0 ) );
    /* Adjust the current vertex normal with the normal matrix. */
    normal = normalize( NORMALMATRIX * NORMAL );
    /* Multiply the eye position with the projection matrix to be
able to position the vertex onscreen. */
    gl_Position = PROJECTIONMATRIX * vec4( position, 1.0 );
#else
    gl_Position = MODELVIEWPROJECTIONMATRIX * vec4( POSITION, 1.0 );
#endif
```

## Getting the Fragment Shader More Uber

As you can see, not much has changed compared to the approach that you studied in Chapter 3.
Only the value of the vertex normal and the vertex position are sent over to the fragment shader.
And using the power of the Uber Shader, you can now toggle ON or OFF whether or not to use
lighting calculation on top of the current effects that you have been using for each object.

Now save the `vertex.glsl` file (if you have not already done so) and open `fragment.glsl`. Then
follow these steps:

**1.** At the top of the `fragment.glsl` file, insert the following code:

```
#ifdef LIGHTING_SHADER
    uniform mediump vec3 LIGHTPOSITION;
    uniform lowp vec3 AMBIENT_COLOR;
    uniform lowp vec3 DIFFUSE_COLOR;
    uniform lowp vec3 SPECULAR_COLOR;
    uniform mediump float SHININESS;
    uniform lowp float DISSOLVE;
    varying mediump vec3 position;
    varying lowp vec3 normal;
#endif
```

There are lots of new uniforms here, but you already had *all* of these values available. So far, you have been ignoring all these parameters contained in the MTL file, but from now on, you will make full use of them! All you have to do is tag the current material that you're going to be using to draw and send over the data. It couldn't be easier, and you already have all the structure to do so.

**2.** On the next line right after you declare the `diffuse_color` variable (`lowp vec4 diffuse_color = texture2D( DIFFUSE, texcoord0 );`), insert the following code to handle the lighting calculation:

```
#ifdef LIGHTING_SHADER
    /* Remember the alpha value of the texture. */
    lowp float alpha = diffuse_color.a;
    /* Use the light position in eye space with the vertex
position in eye space to calculate the light direction vector. */
    mediump vec3 L = normalize( LIGHTPOSITION - position );
    /* Invert the eye position vertex. */
    mediump vec3 E = normalize( -position );
    /* Calculate the reflection vector of the light direction and
the current vertex normal that will be used for specular color
calculation. */
    mediump vec3 R = normalize( -reflect( L, normal ) );
    /* Assign the ambient color. */
    mediump vec4 ambient  = vec4( AMBIENT_COLOR, 1.0 );
    /* Calculate the final diffuse color. This calculation is
based on the multiplication of the material diffuse color with the
diffuse texture color and finally adjusted by the light intensity
calculation. */
    mediump vec4 diffuse  = vec4( DIFFUSE_COLOR *
                                  diffuse_color.rgb, 1.0 ) *
                                  max( dot( normal, L ), 0.0 );
    /* Calculate the final specular color. This calculation is
based on the specular color of the material affected by the
reflection vector of the light and boosted by the shininess of the
material. */
    mediump vec4 specular = vec4( SPECULAR_COLOR, 1.0 ) *
                                  pow( max( dot( R, E ), 0.0 ),
                                  SHININESS * 0.3 );
    /* Calculate the final fragment color by adding together all
the different colors that you have calculated above. */
    diffuse_color = vec4( 0.1 ) + /* Scene Color. */
                    ambient +
                    diffuse +
                    specular;
    /* In the calculation above, you lose the original alpha of the
texture, so you have to make sure to reassign it. */
    diffuse_color.a = alpha;
    #endif
```

**3.** Finally, since you now have the uniform variable `DISSOLVE` available, simply modify the `gl_FragColor.a` affectation inside the `TRANSPARENT_OBJECT` block definition with the following code:

```
gl_FragColor.a = DISSOLVE;
```

## Wrapping Up the Implementation

You are done modifying the shader files. (Did you notice how easy it was?) Now it's time to modify your current source code to handle all these new uniforms and send them over to your shader program from within your app.

Open templateApp.cpp and follow the next few steps to finalize the implementation of the per-pixel lighting:

1. Start off by locating the line where you are initializing the vertex shader memory variable (MEMORY *vertex_shader). Select it, cut it, and paste it on the next line right after the MEMORY *fragment_shader initialization code. From now on the vertex shader will also need to receive a dynamic macro definition, so you need to have access to a fresh copy for every material.

2. On the line before the PROGRAM_init function call, insert another condition based on the illumination model of the material to determine whether or not the current material should have lighting enabled.

```
if( objmaterial->illumination_model ) {
  minsert( vertex_shader,
           ( char * )"#define LIGHTING_SHADER\n", 0 );
  minsert( fragment_shader,
           ( char * )"#define LIGHTING_SHADER\n", 0 ); }
```

The illumination model value found inside the MTL file determines if a material should be part of the lighting calculation or not. If you open the .mtl file for the scene, you will find that every material has an illumination model (illum) value of 2, with the exception of the background material, which is 0 because it represents a shadeless material.

3. Locate the mclose( vertex_shader ); line, select it, cut it, and paste it on the next line right after the mclose( fragment_shader ); call. This way, the vertex_shader variable will be freed for each material and won't leak.

4. Since your vertex and fragment shaders are now using the vertex normals (when lighting is ON), insert the following vertex attribute location affectation inside the program_bind_attrib_location function:

```
glBindAttribLocation( program->pid, 1, "NORMAL" );
```

5. All that's left to be done is to pass all the uniforms based on the current material values. Jump to the material_draw_callback function and append the following else if (one for each uniform) to the current condition block:

```
/* The material dissolve (alpha) value. */
else if( !strcmp( program->uniform_array[ i ].name,
         "DISSOLVE" ) ) {
glUniform1f( program->uniform_array[ i ].location,
             objmaterial->dissolve );
}

/* The ambient color of the material. */
```

```
            else if( !strcmp( program->uniform_array[ i ].name,
                    "AMBIENT_COLOR" ) ) {
        glUniform3fv( program->uniform_array[ i ].location,
                    1,
                    ( float * )&objmaterial->ambient );
    }       ·

    /* The material diffuse color. */
    else if( !strcmp( program->uniform_array[ i ].name,
            "DIFFUSE_COLOR" ) ) {
        glUniform3fv( program->uniform_array[ i ].location,
                    1,
                    ( float * )&objmaterial->diffuse );
    }

    /* The specular color. */
    else if( !strcmp( program->uniform_array[ i ].name,
                    "SPECULAR_COLOR" ) ) {
        glUniform3fv( program->uniform_array[ i ].location,
                    1,
                    ( float * )&objmaterial->specular );
    }

    /* The specular exponent (aka shininess) of the material. */
    else if( !strcmp( program->uniform_array[ i ].name,
            "SHININESS" ) ) {
        /* MTL range for specular exponent is in the range of 1 to 1000.
Convert it to the OpenGL standard shininess range of 1 to 128. */
        glUniform1f( program->uniform_array[ i ].location,
                    objmaterial->specular_exponent * 0.128f );
    }
```

**6.** Now append more `else if` cases to the code to be able to send the appropriate matrices to the shader program, as follows:

```
    else if( !strcmp( program->uniform_array[ i ].name,
            "MODELVIEWMATRIX" ) ) {
        glUniformMatrix4fv(
        program->uniform_array[ i ].location,
        1,
        GL_FALSE,
        ( float * )GFX_get_modelview_matrix() );
    }

    else if( !strcmp( program->uniform_array[ i ].name,
            "PROJECTIONMATRIX" ) ) {
        glUniformMatrix4fv(
        program->uniform_array[ i ].location,
        1,
        GL_FALSE,
        ( float * )GFX_get_projection_matrix() );
    }

    else if( !strcmp( program->uniform_array[ i ].name,
```

```
                        "NORMALMATRIX" ) ) {
            glUniformMatrix3fv(
            program->uniform_array[ i ].location,
            1,
            GL_FALSE,
            ( float * )GFX_get_normal_matrix() );
            }
```

**7.** In the final `else if`, you have to pass the light position in eye space in order to follow the OpenGL standard. To convert an arbitrary position specified in world space to eye space, simply multiply it with the current model view matrix. At this point in the code, when the execution point reaches the following code, the current model view matrix will be the one used for the current object. So in order to calculate the appropriate eye position, you will have to use the previous matrix in the stack, the one that is used for the camera. To do this, insert the following code block:

```
    else if( !strcmp( program->uniform_array[ i ].name,
            "LIGHTPOSITION" ) ) {

        /* The light position in world space coordinates. */
        vec3 position    = { 0.0f, -3.0f, 10.0f };
        vec3 eyeposition = { 0.0f,  0.0f,  0.0f };

        /* Convert the light position to eye space. */
        vec3_multiply_mat4(
        &eyeposition,
        &position,
        /* The current pushed matrix represents the transformation of
    the object. You have to access the look-at matrix. For this, simply
    specify to use the previous model view matrix. */
        &gfx.modelview_matrix[ gfx.modelview_matrix_index - 1 ] );

        glUniform3fv(
        program->uniform_array[ i ].location,
        1,
        ( float * )&eyeposition ); }
```

**8.** Build and run your application. As you can see in Figure 4-6, the scene is fully lighted by a directional light (with the exception of the background, of course).

Each surface is using its appropriate material values extracted right from its corresponding MTL file entry. Feel free to tweak and modify these values to achieve better coloring, a crisper shininess, or whatever you want. Try and test as many different values as you can — this is the best way to learn and to be able to predict how things are going to appear onscreen.

**FIGURE 4-6:** Scene using per-pixel lighting based on the Phong model

However, be aware that what you have been doing in this section is really heavy on the GPU! The frame rate of your app has taken a drastic hit. You really have to be careful — even a small scene with 5.5k of triangles requires a lot of fragment calculations as this scene occupies the whole screen.

You can test the current FPS (frames per second) by inserting the following code at the beginning of each render loop (the first block of instructions in `templateAppDraw`) used in this chapter:

```
static unsigned int start = get_milli_time(),
                    fps = 0;
if( get_milli_time() - start >= 1000 ) {
   console_print( "FPS: %d\n", fps );
   start = get_milli_time();
   fps = 0;
}
++fps;
```

As you are progressing and adding more effects, you can see how drastically the FPS rate is going down. While you're building your own apps, keep in mind that every instruction costs, so you should constantly monitor the FPS while developing.

At the moment, you are still learning and no real optimization has been done, which explains the performance hit. As you are going through this book, you'll learn about different optimization techniques, so you can return to this section and apply what you have learned to increase the FPS.

On a side note, the best way to test optimization is by using a static scene (just like the one you built), where the camera and the number of objects and effects are constant. Keep in mind that even an increase of 5 FPS is a major gain on a mobile device!

## SUMMARY

You now have all the necessary knowledge to be able to start building more complex scenes. From now on, you should be able to spot and handle different object types and render them correctly onscreen. You can adjust their rendering sequence, and render semitransparent, alpha-tested, and blended objects double-sided if necessary.

Using the Uber Shader technique inside your own apps, you can now start building more and more complex shaders and multiple combinations of effects. You have also been introduced to complex per-pixel lighting, which allows you to add another level of realism to your scenes by simulating real-life lighting calculation.

Before moving on to Chapter 5, where you are going to improve rendering performances, make sure that you fully grasp all the techniques demonstrated in *this* chapter. And test, test, test, and test again, as many parameters as you can before moving on to the next chapter. Trial and error is the key to improvement and success!

# 5

# Optimization

**WHAT'S IN THIS CHAPTER?**

➤ Optimizing your indices data by converting them from triangles to triangle strips

➤ Optimizing your textures and saving video memory

➤ Implementing bump mapping to fake details and improve visual quality

➤ Implementing geometry and shader levels of detail

➤ Using a texture atlas

➤ Conceptualizing how to manage machine states in software to avoid unnecessary GL calls

➤ Using the Automatic Shader Optimizer that comes with the SDK

In the previous chapter, you noticed how much the frame rate was dropping as you were adding more and more effects. Many factors affect performance, whether it is the size of your textures, the memory usage, the amount of polygons, or the complexity of your shaders — you need to be able to optimize each of them.

Always keep in mind that you are dealing with a portable device that has a pretty limited amount of resources compared to desktop PCs. However, that doesn't mean that you should call it a day — there are still many tricks that can be done to improve performance.

This chapter will introduce you to many different optimization techniques that you can easily integrate inside your own games and 3D applications.

## THE BASE APP

In this chapter, you will first take a step backward in order to go forward! Instead of creating a new full-fledged scene with many objects, you are going to work with one single object and progressively add the necessary code to optimize it in full.

Now to speed things up a bit, this time you will start with a base program. Instead of duplicating the good old `template` project, duplicate the `template_chapter5` project located at the root of the SDK and rename it **chapter5-1**. Then open it with Eclipse or XCode (depending on which mobile platform you are working on) and briefly study the code. It should look familiar to you, since this base code is just a mix of the code you wrote in Chapter 3 (touche movement) and Chapter 4 (textures and material data).

Now build and execute the code. First say hi to Ramy (as in Figure 5-1) and then make him do some little turns so you can analyze the geometry you are dealing with. Also study the shaders used by the template and the MTL file property.

**FIGURE 5-1:** Say "Hi" to Ramy!

## TRIANGLES TO TRIANGLE STRIPS

So far what you have been doing is what I like to call *stacking*, which means that you haven't really cared about anything else except stacking triangles, textures, and all the necessary code to just make it work.

This approach is okay for testing or learning purposes, but it won't work in a real game scenario. The performance loss was not noticeable at first, because you were working with a single object, but you witnessed it in full at the end of the previous chapter when you started assembling a more complex scene.

Thus far, you have only learned how to build and use optimized VBO vertex data and VAO to deal with the vertex data attributes, so you can rest assured that this is already as optimized as it can be.

But what about your triangle indices? In this section, you will learn how to optimize them and, as a result, drastically reduce the amount of triangle indices that have to be used for drawing.

The only mode of drawing that you have been handling up until now for complex geometry is triangles (`GL_TRIANGLES`). However, OpenGL ES offers a more optimized and alternate route to triangle drawing called `GL_TRIANGLE_STRIP` (which you briefly used to draw the quad in Chapter 2). Using this mode, you will be able to reuse the last two indices of a triangle and will simply have to specify an extra index to create a new triangle.

In other words, instead of sending six indices to draw a quad, only four are needed, just as you did before in Chapter 2. And as the strip is progressing, only one extra index is required to draw the next triangle, and the next, and so on, as demonstrated in Figure 5-2.

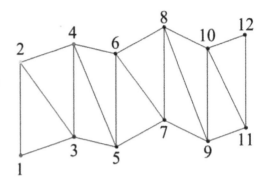

This is, of course, in an ideal world, where all triangles and their edges are aligned in a way that it would be easy for you to build a single strip out of it. However, that will most likely never happen on a real geometry; instead, the strip will have to be stopped and then restarted by creating a degenerated triangle. This process is called *stitching*.

**FIGURE 5-2:** Progressive triangle strip

Depending on the optimization, you may end up with more indices by using triangle strips than by using good old triangles. If this happens, my suggestion is to simply fall back to triangles. But in most cases, if your geometry is properly built, that won't happen.

## BUILDING TRIANGLE STRIPS

Now that you have learned the mechanics behind this optimization process, you can implement them in your code. This book's SDK includes the NvTriStrip library from NVIDIA (http://www.nvidia.com/object/nvtristrip_library.html). This library allows you to send an arbitrary set of triangle indices to the library, and then an algorithm is used internally by the API, based on a vertex cache size that you can specify.

The higher the vertex cache size specified, the lower the resulting indices array will be. Vertex cache on modern mobile device GPUs is nonexistent, so the smaller the number of indices, the faster the geometry will be drawn.

Now back to the chapter5-1 project, more precisely inside the templateApp.cpp source file, just before calling the OBJ_build_mesh function add the following lines of code:

```
console_print( "%s: %d: GL_TRIANGLES\n",
obj->objmesh[ i ].name,
obj->objmesh[ i ].objtrianglelist[ 0 ].n_indice_array );

    /* Built-in method that implements the NvTriStrip library.
For more information, check the obj.cpp source code in order to implement
it inside your own apps. */
    OBJ_optimize_mesh(
    obj, /* The main OBJ pointer. */
    i, /* The index of the mesh to optimize */
    0 ); /* The vertex cache size to use (0 = default), which is
automatically set to 16 inside the NvTriStrip library. */

    console_print( "%s: %d: GL_TRIANGLE_STRIP\n",
    obj->objmesh[ i ].name,
    obj->objmesh[ i ].objtrianglelist[ 0 ].n_indice_array );
```

Now build and run the program. Check the system console inside XCode or the LogCat inside Eclipse to monitor the number of indices before and after optimization. You should now see the following values on your console:

```
ram: 8730: GL_TRIANGLES

ram: 5371: GL_TRIANGLE_STRIP
```

As you can see, even using the default vertex cache size optimizes the indices quite a bit. As a result, about 40-percent fewer indices will be required to draw the same geometry.

For the sake of this example, the optimization is done at initialization time, which will obviously increase the loading time. However, in a real game or engine scenario, this optimization should be done offline when you export your objects(s) using custom-made command-line tools.

As mentioned earlier, the cache size will have a direct impact on the final number of indices the strips will contain. To try this out, change the cache size value from 0 to 64 and run the program again. You should now see the following values on your console:

```
ram: 8730: GL_TRIANGLES

ram: 4727: GL_TRIANGLE_STRIP
```

With this new vertex cache size, you were able to optimize the resulting indices even more, and this time hit 46 percent. You can continue to increase the number only up to a certain point. In Ramy's case, a vertex cache of 128 is about the most that you can use to optimize the mesh, which will result in an optimization of nearly 48 percent. This is not much of a gain, but it's the best that the library can do for you. Even with a higher cache number, it would only take longer to process for a very little or no percentage increase.

With this optimization done, you can now draw almost two Ramys for the price of one (in terms of indices that is). What a good deal!

## TEXTURE OPTIMIZATION

Portable-device GPUs have a pretty limited amount of video memory compared to desktop cards. Always remind your artists to keep their texture resolution as small as they can to save as much memory as possible.

In order to have smooth textures from any distance away from the viewer, you (and your artists) need to use *mipmaps*. And of course, the size of these mipmaps directly affects the necessary space required in memory.

For example, even a simple RGBA texture of 512 by 512 (which represents absolutely no problem on a desktop card) with full mipmaps generated will require up to 1,398,100 bytes in memory!

When the video memory is around 24 MB, the available amount of memory will go down *really* fast. And the larger the texture, the slower the fetch operation will take to pick and interpolate pixels.

The best solution to optimize the video memory usage is to first resize your textures and then convert them to 16 bits. OpenGL ES has prebuilt pixel types especially reserved for storing 16-bit textures:

```
GL_UNSIGNED_SHORT_4_4_4_4,
GL_UNSIGNED_SHORT_5_5_5_1, and
GL_UNSIGNED_SHORT_5_6_5.
```

Depending on the type of texture you are dealing with, you have to choose which pixel type is the most appropriate to suit your needs. For example, an RGB texture should always be converted to 5_6_5 in order to keep the maximum color resolution for each color component.

When it comes to an RGBA texture, it depends on the way it is constructed. If your alpha channel is only built of 255 and/or 0, the 5_5_5_1 type is the most appropriate (because the alpha value will be either 1 or 0). If your alpha channel has multiple values ranging from 255 to 0, the 4_4_4_4 type is mandatory to keep the desired alpha effect.

## ADDING 16-BIT TEXTURE CONVERSION

It's time to learn how to convert your 24- and 32-bit textures to 16 bits and save up to half of the memory normally used on the video memory!

Inside the templateAppInit function, locate the OBJ_build_texture call and replace it with the following lines:

```
OBJ_build_texture(
obj,
i,
obj->texture_path,
/* Automatically convert the texture to 16 bits. */
TEXTURE_MIPMAP | TEXTURE_16_BITS,
TEXTURE_FILTER_2X,
0.0f );
```

Now build and run your program! For the type of RGB texture that Ramy is using, the loss of texture quality is barely noticeable. However, if you have a texture that contains some sort of pronounced gradient, the loss will be a lot more noticeable. But this is still quite acceptable considering that you are literally using up to half of the memory size originally required to draw the same texture.

For more information about the 16-bit conversion code, check the TEXTURE_convert_16_bits function source located inside texture.cpp.

By default, when the OBJ_build_texture function receives the TEXTURE_16_BITS parameter, it will analyze the type of texture that has to be converted. If the texture is RGB, this function will automatically convert it to 5_6_5; or if the texture is RGBA, the function will convert it to 4_4_4_4. Alternatively, you could force an RGBA texture to be converted to 5_5_5_1 by adding TEXTURE_16_BITS_5551 to the texture parameter flags. Then your function call will look like this:

```
OBJ_build_texture(
 obj,
 i,
 obj->texture_path,
 /* Force RGBA textures to be converted to 5_5_5_1 */
 TEXTURE_MIPMAP | TEXTURE_16_BITS | TEXTURE_16_BITS_5551,
 TEXTURE_FILTER_2X,
 0.0f );
```

Once again, the process of converting and optimizing your textures should be done offline during export in order to minimize the loading time of your apps.

## PVR TEXTURE COMPRESSION

Unfortunately, when it comes to 16-bit textures, there is no popular graphics format that is especially built for or even supports them. You can either build your own, or if you have access to the GL_IMG_texture_compression_pvrtc extension, you can use the PVR compression format for your texture.

Developed by Imagination Technologies, the PVR format uses a proprietary compression scheme that allows you to use 4 bits per pixel or 2 bits per pixel. This will reduce the memory size of your texture to a ratio of 8:1 (PVRTC4bpp) or 16:1 (PVRTC2bpp).

On top of the awesome compression ratio, you can also pre-generate mipmaps offline and offload this work at export time. To convert your PNGs (as well as other formats) to PVR, you will first need to grab a copy of the PowerVR Insider SDK from http://www .imgtec.com. Under the Utilities folder, you have the choice of using either a GUI (as shown in Figure 5-3) or a command-line tool (perfect for offline automatic line conversion) to automatically convert your texture to PVR.

If you do have access to this extension (you can verify this by checking your system console for the GL extension previously mentioned), duplicate the chapter5-1 project and rename it **chapter5-2**; then

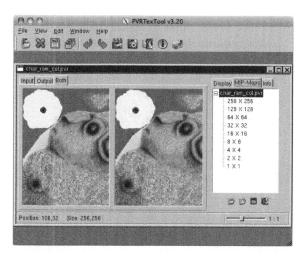

**FIGURE 5-3:** Imagination Technologies PVRTexTool

follow the rest of the instructions in this section. Otherwise, skip this part and jump directly to the next section.

First remove the PNG and MTL files from the Resources directory (for XCode users) or the assets folder (Eclipse users). Then link the .PVR and .MTL files from SDK/data/chapter5-2 to your project, and build and run the program.

If you compare the original 32-bit image to the image you get now, you will notice quite a difference in quality. But with an 8:1 compression ratio in memory (or more), it's a good compromise.

For more information about how to implement the PVR texture loader that comes with the SDK in your own games, check the TEXTURE_load_pvr function inside the texture.cpp source file.

## FAKING DETAILS

Another good way to improve the visual of your scene is to use a technique called *bump mapping*. This technique uses a pre-generated texture that contains vertex normal information that is baked from a high-detail polygon model. By applying this normal map on the low polygon model, it becomes virtually identical to the high polygon model, as shown in Figure 5-4.

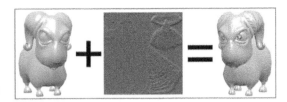

**FIGURE 5-4:** Bump mapping using GLSL ES

## Bump Mapping Implementation

In order to implement simple bump mapping within your current app, duplicate the chapter5-1 project and rename it **chapter5-3**. Then open the project file within your favorite IDE and link the char_ram_nor.png texture (located in SDK/data/chapter5-3) to your project.

The following steps will guide you through the full implementation of this technique:

**1.** Open the templateApp.cpp file and locate the program_bind_attrib_location function. Before the end of the function bracket, integrate the two following lines to bind the normal and tangent attributes:

```
glBindAttribLocation( program->pid, 1, "NORMAL" );
glBindAttribLocation( program->pid, 3, "TANGENT0" );
```

You are already familiar with the normal attribute, but not the tangent. What it represents is the direction vector of the UVs on the X axis. Since you have the normal and the tangent, all that's left to be done is to calculate their cross product to obtain the bi-tangent allowing you to reconstruct a 3 by 3 matrix. You can then use this rotation matrix to convert your data to tangent space. (If you are not familiar with the terms, visit http://en.wikipedia.org/wiki/Normal_mapping.)

**2.** Jump to the material_draw_callback function and append the following new else if to the existing if block to be able to bind the normal map (the bump map) to the fourth texture channel:

```
else if( !strcmp( program->uniform_array[ i ].name,
        "BUMP" ) &&
        !program->uniform_array[ i ].constant ) {
    program->uniform_array[ i ].constant = 1;
    glUniform1i( program->uniform_array[ i ].location, 4 );
}
```

**3.** Insert the following else if to be able to send the light position in eye space:

```
else if( !strcmp( program->uniform_array[ i ].name,
        "LIGHTPOSITION" ) ) {
    vec3 position   = { 0.0f, -3.0f, 4.0f };
    vec3 eyeposition = { 0.0f,  0.0f, 0.0f };
```

```
                        vec3_multiply_mat4(
                        &eyeposition,
                        &position,
                        &gfx.modelview_matrix[ gfx.modelview_matrix_index - 1 ] );

                        glUniform3fv(
                        program->uniform_array[ i ].location,
                        1,
                        ( float * )&eyeposition );
                    }
```

**4.** Finally, set up the necessary code to send over the current normal matrix, like this:

```
                    else if( !strcmp( program->uniform_array[ i ].name,
                            "NORMALMATRIX" ) ) {
                        glUniformMatrix3fv( program->uniform_array[ i ].location,
                                            1,
                                            GL_FALSE,
                                            ( float * )GFX_get_normal_matrix() );
                    }
```

## Precision Qualifiers Optimization

You are now about to attack the vertex shader portion of this program. Since this chapter is about optimization, pay close attention to the qualifiers used for each variable. Setting the best qualifiers can drastically increase the performance of your shaders.

While creating vertex or fragment shaders, always try to write the smallest amount of code necessary to achieve the best possible effect. Always think about which instructions would be the fastest for the GPU to execute.

To keep things simple in this example, instead of dividing a variable by 2, multiply it by 0.5, or avoid normalization when the two vectors that you multiply are already normalized.

Every microsecond or millisecond that you can save will pay off on a large scale, because microseconds will become milliseconds and will let you gain more frames.

Now it's time to write some code! Open the vertex.glsl file and then follow these steps:

**1.** On the line after the PROJECTIONMATRIX uniform declaration, insert the following code to handle the normal matrix and the light position uniforms:

```
        /* This matrix is already normalized (since you do not use scale),
        so there's no need to use any other precision qualifier than lowp. */
        uniform lowp mat3 NORMALMATRIX;
        /* The light position is not normalized, so you have no choice but to
        use at least mediump. */
        uniform mediump vec3 LIGHTPOSITION;
```

**2.** On the line after the TEXCOORD0 declaration, insert the following vertex attribute data:

```
        /* Always use lowp when dealing with the normal attribute, because it
        should always be normalized outside the shader. */
        attribute lowp vec3 NORMAL;
```

```
/* As with the normal, the tangent should always be normalized. */
attribute lowp vec3 TANGENT0;
```

As you might have noticed, this time you are using a `lowp` qualifier with the `TEXCOORD0` attribute. The texture UVs for Ramy are in the range of 0 to 1, so there's no need to use a `mediump` qualifier since you are not tiling the texture.

**3.** On the line right after the varying variable `texcoord0` declaration, insert the follow varyings:

```
/* The current vertex position in tangent space. */
varying mediump vec3 position;
/* The light direction in tangent space. */
varying lowp vec3 lightdirection_ts;
```

**4.** Replace the whole content of the `main` function with the following code:

```
mediump vec3 tmp; /* Temp variable. */

/* Rotate the normal and the tangent by the current normal matrix. Since
the normal, tangent, and normal matrix are all normalized, you can save two
normalize instruction calls.*/
lowp vec3 normal   = NORMALMATRIX * NORMAL;
lowp vec3 tangent  = NORMALMATRIX * TANGENT0;

/* Calculate the binormal (or bi-tangent if you prefer) based on the
current normal and tangent. The cross-product of two normalized vectors
will always be normalized, which explains the lowp precision qualifier.*/
lowp vec3 binormal = cross( normal, tangent );

/* Calculate the current vertex position in eye space. */
position = vec3( MODELVIEWMATRIX * vec4( POSITION, 1.0 ) );

/* Since you just calculated the position in eye space, you can
use the current value and multiply it by the projection matrix to be
able to see the current vertex on screen. */
gl_Position = PROJECTIONMATRIX * vec4( position, 1.0 );

/* Calculate the light direction in eye space and normalize it. */
lowp vec3 lightdirection_es =
normalize( LIGHTPOSITION - position );

/* Transform the light direction in eye space to tangent space. */
lightdirection_ts.x = dot( lightdirection_es, tangent );
lightdirection_ts.y = dot( lightdirection_es, binormal );
lightdirection_ts.z = dot( lightdirection_es, normal );

/* Since the light calculation will be done in tangent space,
also convert the current position in eye space to tangent space and
invert it. */
tmp.x = dot( position, tangent );
tmp.y = dot( position, binormal );
tmp.z = dot( position, normal );
```

```
position = -normalize( tmp );

/* Bridge over the texture coordinate. */
texcoord0 = TEXCOORD0;
```

As you can see, you did quite a bit of optimization on this vertex shader already, that otherwise would be somewhat heavy to execute. You used as many `lowp` qualifiers as you possibly could, and avoided a lot of unnecessary normalization.

If you always keep in mind the best possible precision qualifiers for each variable and use as few instructions as necessary, you will see a drastic performance gain on a large scale.

## The Normal Map Lighting Calculation

You now have all the necessary data calculated within your vertex shader, and you have bridged the sensitive variables to be accessible from your fragment shader. Next, open the `fragment.glsl` file and include the following modifications:

**1.** Start off by declaring the normal map sampler at the top of your shader file. To do this, insert the following code on the line right after the DIFFUSE `sampler2D` declaration:

```
uniform sampler2D BUMP;
```

**2.** Now insert the varying variables that you declared earlier on the line right after the `texcoord0` varying declaration, like this:

```
/* Notice that originally in the vertex shader, this variable
precision qualifier was declared as mediump. But since you
normalized it before sending it to the fragment shader, you can now
declare it here as lowp. */
varying lowp vec3 position;
varying lowp vec3 lightdirection_ts;
```

**3.** To see how the pixel values that you will convert to normal data will affect the visual of the model, you'll begin with the first stage of the lighting calculation. To visualize this technique, replace the content of the `main` function with the following:

```
    /* Get the current RGB data from the bump map and convert it into
a normal value. */
    lowp vec3 normal = texture2D( BUMP, texcoord0 ).rgb * 2.0 - 1.0;

    /* Now calculate the intensity (aka Lambert factor) based on the
light direction vector and the normal, which are now both in tangent
space. */
    lowp float intensity = max( dot( lightdirection_ts, normal ), 0.0 );
    /* Set the default ambient color. */
    gl_FragColor = vec4( 0.1 );
    /* Check if you have an intensity. */
    if( intensity > 0.0 ) {
    /* Add to the current fragment the result of the intensity with the
current diffuse color of the material. */
    gl_FragColor += vec4( DIFFUSE_COLOR, 1.0 ) * intensity; }
```

**4.** Build and run the program. Your screen should now display what's shown in Figure 5-5.

Observe how the normal map that you applied really accentuates details that are basically nonexistent! Using this technique, you can add more details to your scenes — at a relatively low cost compared to what it would take to actually build geometry with this many polygons.

The purpose of the preceding exercise was to introduce you to what this technique is really all about under the hood. You can now replace the last gl_FragColor affectation with the following in order to apply the diffuse texture in the equation:

```
gl_FragColor +=
texture2D( DIFFUSE, texcoord0 ) *
vec4( DIFFUSE_COLOR, 1.0 ) * intensity;
```

Build and run the program again. You will get the screen display shown in Figure 5-6.

This technique works quite well with specularity. Adding the specular component to the formula will make the details really stand out, as you'll learn in the next section.

**FIGURE 5-5:** Normal mapping

## Adding Specularity

Start by duplicating the chapter5-3 project directory and rename it **chapter5-4**. Not much code will be added to this project, but by completing this exercise, you will be able to compare the result with and without specularity.

**1.** Open the templateApp.cpp source file and insert the following else if statements inside the loop of the material_draw_ callback function:

```
/* Send over the specular color of the material. */
else if( !strcmp( program->uniform_array[ i ].name,
        "SPECULAR_COLOR" ) ) {
glUniform3fv( program->uniform_array[ i ].location,
        1,
        ( float * )&objmaterial->specular ); }
/* Set the shininess of the material. */
else if( !strcmp( program->uniform_array[ i ].name,
        "SHININESS" ) ) {
glUniform1f( program->uniform_array[ i ].location,
        objmaterial->specular_exponent * 0.128f ); }
```

**FIGURE 5-6:** Normal mapping + diffuse texture

2.   Open the `fragment.glsl` shader file and add the following uniform variable after the `DIFFUSE_COLOR` declaration:

```
/* Receive the specular color of the material. */
uniform lowp vec3 SPECULAR_COLOR;
/* Receive the shininess of the material. */
uniform mediump float SHININESS;
```

3.   Replace the final fragment affectation (the one set inside the `if` clause) with the following:

```
    /* Calculate the reflection vector in order to determine the
specular intensity of the fragment. */
    lowp vec3 reflectionvector =
    normalize( -reflect( lightdirection_ts, normal ) );

    /* Calculate the final fragment color including the specularity. */
    gl_FragColor +=
    texture2D( DIFFUSE, texcoord0 ) *
    vec4( DIFFUSE_COLOR, 1.0 ) *
    intensity
    +
    vec4( SPECULAR_COLOR, 1.0 ) *
    pow( max( dot( reflectionvector, position ), 0.0 ), SHININESS );
```

4.   Build and run the program.

You should be able to notice right away a huge visual difference from the previous program. By adding specularity to the final fragment calculation, you've made Ramy look a lot better, and the details really stand out, just like in Figure 5-7.

Mastering this technique will allow you to use more-advanced techniques based on the same concept, such as specular mapping, parallax mapping, and relief mapping among others.

This concludes the section on faking details. You have learned how to implement simple bump mapping to add better details to your models at a fairly low cost on GPU. You also have learned how to evaluate the precision qualifiers of each variable, trading precision for faster calculations (and less storage).

Ready for more? Keep reading to discover other optimization techniques that you'll be able to use on a daily basis to improve the performance of your scenes!

**FIGURE 5-7:** Shiny Ramy

## GEOMETRY AND SHADERS LOD

This technique consists of using different levels of detail (LODs) for a specific geometry or shader based on the current distance of the object from the camera.

To implement geometry LOD, you will have to create a different mesh for each level of detail that you wish to use, where each level has fewer polygons than the previous one. You can create the geometry for each level manually, or you can use your favorite 3D software to do it, or implement manually some polygon reduction algorithm to generate them automatically.

At render time, you will need to calculate the object's distance from the camera and analyze which LOD to use. By implementing this technique, if a geometry is very close to the camera, it will be very detailed, and as it goes far away from the camera, it will become less and less detailed.

You can also implement this same mechanism for your shaders, regardless if you choose to use geometry LOD or not. Objects that are very close to the camera could use a bump mapping shader, and as they move far away, they could progressively transition from per-pixel lighting to per-vertex lighting. From there, you can use an Uber shader and create multiple versions of the shader program inside one shader file, and then reassign them in real time to your materials. Or you could use branching (if) inside your shader and pass the current level of detail calculated on your CPU as a uniform variable.

When used wisely, these two approaches, either combined or used separately, can really improve the rendering time of each frame (albeit at the cost of more memory usage).

## TEXTURE ATLAS

This is a technique that can be used to optimize the texture usage and avoid multiple texture switches at run time. A *texture atlas* is a large texture that contains multiple smaller textures. With it, you can simply bind your texture once and draw all the objects that are using it. Then you can move on to another set of objects that are using another atlas.

Atlases are great for GUIs as well as for objects that have a UV range from 0 to 1. With some tweaks, they can also be used for tiled textures. To create a texture atlas, you can either use your favorite image-manipulation program or use a pre-made script for your preferred 3D software. When drawn, an atlas can look like the one displayed in Figure 5-8 (which was used for a video player GUI).

To optimize the result of this technique, you should try to put all the non-alpha textures together in one atlas, and all the textures that use an alpha channel into another atlas. By batching objects of the same type and using the same atlas, you will avoid a lot of unnecessary machine-state switching, which will have a direct impact on your frame rate.

**FIGURE 5-8:** Video player GUI texture atlas

# MANAGING STATES IN SOFTWARE

As you know, OpenGL ES is a machine-state API, meaning that it is basically acting like a crane carrying boxes to a dock. You tell it which boxes to pick up, and it will deliver them. But what if the boxes have already been picked up or have already been delivered?

Switching machine states costs processing time, and some more than others. In fact every instruction that you send to the driver costs!

For example, why would you ask the driver to turn blending ON when it is already ON, or to bind a texture, a shader, a VBO or VAO that is already bound?

Some might think that using commands such as `glIsEnabled` or `glGet` variant to check or get a specific state might be more convenient. However, on a large scale it will result in performance drop.

By asking multiple times per frame what the current state is or what resources are bound, you are going to overflow the bandwidth between the client and the server with unnecessary calls that might even stall the pipeline. The trick is to do this on the client side, and leave the GPU (server side) to do what it is doing best: drawing!

This will require that you build a structure containing all of the flags, states, and IDs to keep track of everything that you set on or off or bind. When designing your games, always try to centralize all the GL calls in one place. For example, create one dynamic function that receives as parameters the texture ID and the texture channel to bind it to. By using this function everywhere in your code, you can then know exactly which texture ID is attached to which texture channel at any time. This way, you can easily determine, on the client side, whether the texture should be bound or if it is already bound.

Once again, when used wisely and on a large scale, maintaining machine states on the client side will have a direct impact on the performance of all sorts of 3D apps.

# AUTOMATIC SHADER OPTIMIZATION

As the complexity and the size of your shaders grow (especially in the case of an Uber shader), it will become difficult to manually optimize your shader code. Fortunately there are tools available that will automatically perform generic optimization directly on your GLSL ES code.

One such tool is the GLSL optimizer, which is a free downloadable open source package that you can download from `https://github.com/aras-p/glsl-optimizer`. This package contains a C++ library that receives GLSL or GLSL ES shader files, executes a GPU-independent optimization on them, and outputs back the optimized source code. It allows you to automatically strip dead code and optimize arithmetic operations, along with many other code goodies.

For your convenience, this book's SDK includes pre-built libraries in both Windows (32 bits) and MacOS (32 bits and 64 bits) formats. In addition, I created a simple command-line program for you that wraps around the main library functionalities. Please note that if your current operating system version differs from the one I compiled, you'll need to download the library source files from `https://github.com/aras-p/glsl-optimizer` and re-compile it for your platform.

To test the optimizer, first create a copy of the `chapter5-4` directory and rename it **chapter5-5**. Then open the project file for your current platform under the `SDK/glsloptimizerCL/` directory and compile the executable.

Once the program is compiled, open either an MS-DOS (Windows) or a Terminal (MacOS) console and browse to the directory where the executable is located.

If you are a Windows user, execute the following in your MS-DOS command prompt:

```
glsloptimizerCL.exe -in <pathtothesdk>/SDK/chapter5-5/vertex.glsl -out
<pathtothesdk>/SDK/chapter5-5/vertex.glsl -profile GL_VERTEX_SHADER

glsloptimizerCL.exe -in <pathtothesdk>/SDK/chapter5-5/fragment.glsl -out
 <pathtothesdk>/SDK/chapter5-5/fragment.glsl -profile GL_FRAGMENT_SHADER
```

If you are a MacOS (or Linux) user, run the following in a Terminal window:

```
./glsloptimizerCL -in <pathtothesdk>/SDK/chapter5-5/vertex.glsl -out
<pathtothesdk>/SDK/chapter5-5/vertex.glsl -profile GL_VERTEX_SHADER

./glsloptimizerCL -in <pathtothesdk>/SDK/chapter5-5/fragment.glsl -out
<pathtothesdk>/SDK/chapter5-5/fragment.glsl -profile GL_FRAGMENT_SHADER
```

Now open the `chapter5-5` project file and view the `vertex.glsl` and `fragment.glsl` code. You can see how much the code has changed compared to the original version that you manually created in the previous section.

To insure that the optimization was in fact generated without any errors, build and run the application. (If you're an Eclipse user, remember to update the new shader files and copy and paste them into the `assets` directory.)

You now have vertex and fragment shader source code that is fully independent and GPU-optimized. It runs the exact same way as the shader you created in `chapter5-4` — but technically faster!

Once again, on a large scale, optimizing each and every shader used in your application will allow you to gain crucial render time and will boost overall performance.

This concludes the chapter on optimization. You have been given a gold mine of tips and tricks! Please review the different concepts and key techniques demonstrated in this chapter, and make sure you grasp them all before moving on to the next chapter.

## SUMMARY

Optimization is a never-ending quest! This chapter guided you through a few primary techniques of optimization. You learned how to convert triangles to triangles strips, optimizing the indices data by almost 50 percent! You also discovered how to economize memory by converting your 24- and 32-bit textures to 16 bits, and how to use the PVR texture compression format.

You can now fully use bump mapping in conjunction with a normal map generated in tangent space to make a low polygon model look virtually the same as a high polygon model. With a bit of extra coding, you can now integrate geometry and shader LOD within your app, trading speed at the cost of more memory usage. On top of that, by converting multiple textures into one atlas, you can now batch objects that use the same texture and avoid unnecessary texture binding.

In addition, you have been given all the necessary basics to start implementing your client-based machine state system in order to avoid sending useless machine-state switches on your GPU. This will save you bandwidth so you can crank up the realism of your scenes by adding more effects and more polygons!

And finally, you learned how to automatically optimize your shaders, saving you the burden of trying to figure out how every GLSL ES of each GPU is built (if such information exists). You can now use a command-line program that does all this for you, and integrate it inside your game development pipeline.

Having as much fun as I have so far? Stay tuned for the next chapter which is about real-time physics.

# 6

# Real-Time Physics

**WHAT'S IN THIS CHAPTER?**

➤ Introducing the different types of physics objects

➤ Learning about the most popular physics shapes supported by the Bullet physics library

➤ Setting up a 3D physical world

➤ Understanding how collision callbacks are working and how to use them for game logic code

➤ Implementing a 2D physics game similar to Angry Birds (a popular game developed by Rovio Mobile Ltd.)

➤ Learning about the .bullet file format and how to export it from Blender

➤ Implementing a 3D physics-based pinball machine using physics constraints

Since the beginning of this book, you have been focusing only on graphics. It is indeed an important part of your app, but games are not all about graphics! In this chapter, you will learn how to integrate real-time 2D and 3D physics inside your apps.

You will discover how to use the Bullet physics library for collision detection as well as for rigid and soft body dynamics. Bullet is open source and cross-platform, and can freely be used for commercial software. You can find more information about Bullet at http://bulletphysics.org, where you can also download the full SDK and have access to the latest API and documentation.

## TYPES OF PHYSICAL OBJECTS

Bullet supports multiple physical object types, which will allow you to make your geometries respond in a specific way during real-time physics simulation. Before adding any type of physical body to your scene, you should first analyze what type of physical object it is in order to ensure that it behaves properly inside your physical world.

The physics library includes the following object types for each of your collision objects:

➤ **Rigid Body** — This type of object will respond to gravity and rolling physics.

➤ **Dynamic Body** — This type is similar to Rigid Body, except the object does not respond to rolling physics.

➤ **Soft Body** — This type is typically used for cloth simulation or to represent soft volumetric objects that can be bended and deformed. This type of physical body is extremely CPU-intensive, and should be used with care on mobile devices.

➤ **Static** — This type should be used to represent objects that cannot be moved, such as the ground, walls, or similar motionless boundaries.

In each of the scenes where you integrate physics, you will use a combination of these object types. Select them with care, depending on the way you want your objects to behave inside your 2D or 3D world.

## PHYSICS SHAPES

For each object that will be part of your physics simulation, you will have to assign a specific physics shape. This is referred to as a *bound*.

When choosing which bound would be the most appropriate for the object you are dealing with, you need to be able to evaluate which basic shape would represent it the best. Figure 6-1 introduces you to some of the collision bounds that Bullet supports, along with the data that has to be provided at initialization time for each shape.

As you can see, you have the flexibility to select between enough shapes to fit with all types of geometry outlines. Basic shapes don't require explanations; however, if the bound of your geometry doesn't match any of them, you will have to choose either Triangle Mesh or Convex Hull.

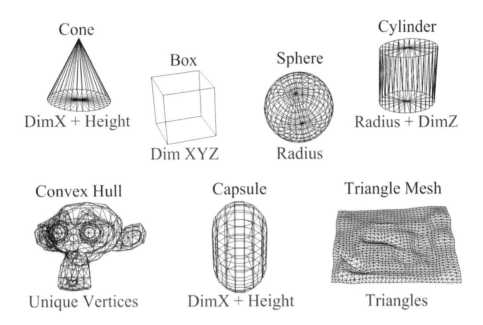

**FIGURE 6-1:** Physics collision shapes

As demonstrated in Figure 6-1, a triangle mesh will use the triangle's index information to build the collision shape for your geometry. This type works effectively on large static surfaces (such as a terrain or irregular walls,) and can be used as a base representation for other more optimized collision shapes such as BVH triangle mesh (which is a tree representation of bounding volumes) to make them more performant.

For more complex shapes that have a small amount of vertices and that are not static in the scene — no matter if it's a dynamic shape or a rigid shape — you should use a convex hull represented by an array of non-duplicated vertices. This way, you can avoid any extra calculations on the CPU for all the vertices that are redundant.

When you're selecting the collision boundaries for your geometry, you should always try to approximate them to the most basic shapes. A triangle mesh or convex hull will obviously require more processing time on the CPU than a box, sphere, or cylinder.

Another alternative to triangle mesh and hull is compound shapes, which are also fully supported in Bullet. This type of collision bound allows you to merge multiple basic shapes into one. For example, if you are dealing with a car, you could use a box for the frame and two large cylinders for the front and back wheels.

In addition, always keep in mind that you should tag your geometry as physical objects *only* if they are going to interact with either the player or with other objects as part of the physics simulation. For example, adding physics properties to a skybox would be pointless and would only require more processing for nothing — especially if the player in your game can't even fly!

## USING BULLET

Working with Bullet is quite easy. In order to integrate physics simulation inside your apps, the first thing that you will have to do is to initialize a physical world. Once initialized, you have to add the different collision shapes that this world is built of and link these shapes to their designated physical bodies.

The task can be done either by directly using the Bullet C++ API or by using the Bullet (`.bullet`) file format. The Bullet file format can be automatically generated by most popular 3D software programs that have Bullet support, or if an exporter is available.

Keep in mind that Bullet is only responsible for driving the physics simulation and basically has no idea (graphics-wise) about the scene that you are drawing.

Once your physical world is created and your shapes are added, you will have to link the transformation matrix of each physical body to the 2D or 3D geometry associated with it. As you increment the simulation step, Bullet will return a 4 by 4 transformation matrix that will represent the current model view matrix of the object (in world-space coordinates).

At this point, if you need to modify the transformation of an object, you will have to use the Bullet API (discussed later in this chapter), because your geometry is now fully driven by it.

## HELLO PHYSICS

**Available for download on Wrox.com**

Now it's time for you to start diving into the necessary code in order to learn how to create a physical world and set up some basic collision shapes. First, duplicate `template_chapter6` located at the root of the SDK and rename it **chapter6-1**. Once that's done, open the project inside your IDE and build and run it. You should now see what's shown in Figure 6-2.

**FIGURE 6-2:** Hello Physics base program

Before starting, have a quick look at the code of this base program. The program loaded the `Scene.obj` file located in `SDK/data/chapter6-1` and used the same shader that you created in `chapter3-1` when you were converting vertex normals to vertex color. This will be the base program that you will start with for the exercises in this section.

Follow these steps to modify the base program in order to add physics:

**1.** At the top of `templateApp.cpp`, where you declare the global variables, add the following definitions:

```
/* The collision world configuration. */
btSoftBodyRigidBodyCollisionConfiguration *collisionconfiguration = NULL;
/* The collision dispatcher to use for the collision world. */
btCollisionDispatcher *dispatcher = NULL;
```

```
/* Contain the algorithm to use to quickly calculate and maintain the
list of objects that are colliding, as well as the information about
the objects that intersect but are not close enough to collide. */
btBroadphaseInterface *broadphase = NULL;
/* Contain the algorithm to use to solve the physics constraints added to
the world (if any). */
btConstraintSolver *solver = NULL;
/* Declare a physical world variable capable of dealing with rigid and
soft bodies and their interactions. */
btSoftRigidDynamicsWorld *dynamicsworld = NULL;
```

**2.** On the line just before the `program_bind_attrib` function declaration, create a new
function to be able to initialize the physical world:

```
void init_physic_world( void ) {
  /* Initialize a new collision configuration. */
  collisionconfiguration =
  new btSoftBodyRigidBodyCollisionConfiguration();

  /* Initialize the collision dispatcher. */
  dispatcher =
  new btCollisionDispatcher( collisionconfiguration );

  /* Determine which broad phase algorithm to use for the current
physical world. The btDbvtBroadphase is the one that gives the best result
(from what I've observed) on most of the mobile devices for generic
physical world. However Bullet offers many others; check the Bullet SDK
for more information.*/
  broadphase = new btDbvtBroadphase();

  /* Initialize the constraint solver. */
  solver = new btSequentialImpulseConstraintSolver();

  /* Now that you have all the necessary variables and algorithms
initialized, you are ready to create your physical world */
  dynamicsworld =
  new btSoftRigidDynamicsWorld(
  dispatcher,
  broadphase,
  solver,
  collisionconfiguration );

  /* And finally, set up the world gravity direction vector using the
same value as the gravity on earth by assigning it on the -Z axis. */
  dynamicsworld->setGravity( btVector3( 0.0f, 0.0f, -9.8f ) ); }
```

**3.** Declare a new function that is able to receive an OBJMESH pointer and a mass as parameters
in order to be able to create a new collision shape and rigid body:

```
void add_rigid_body( OBJMESH *objmesh, float mass ) {

  /* Create a new Box collision shape for the current mesh. */
  btCollisionShape *btcollisionshape =
```

```
    /* Use half of the dimension XYZ to represent the extent of the box
relative to its pivot point, which is already centered in the middle of
its bounding box. */
    new btBoxShape( btVector3( objmesh->dimension.x * 0.5f,
                               objmesh->dimension.y * 0.5f,
                               objmesh->dimension.z * 0.5f ) );


    /* Declare a btTransform variable to be able to contain the
transformation matrix of the object in a form that Bullet will understand. */
    btTransform bttransform;


    /* Declare a 4x4 matrix. */
    mat4 mat;
    /* Set up the identity matrix to make sure the matrix is clean. */
    mat4_identity( &mat );
    /* Declare 3 vectors to be able to hold the rotation of the mesh on
the XYZ axis. */
    vec4 rotx = { 1.0f, 0.0f, 0.0f, objmesh->rotation.x },
         roty = { 0.0f, 1.0f, 0.0f, objmesh->rotation.y },
         rotz = { 0.0f, 0.0f, 1.0f, objmesh->rotation.z };
    /* Translate the matrix. */
    mat4_translate( &mat, &mat, &objmesh->location );
   /* Rotate the matrix using a ZYX order. */
    mat4_rotate( &mat, &mat, &rotz );
    mat4_rotate( &mat, &mat, &roty );
    mat4_rotate( &mat, &mat, &rotx );


    /* Assign the current transformation matrix that you create using the
standard "OpenGL way" and send it over to the Bullet transform variable. */
    bttransform.setFromOpenGLMatrix( ( float * )&mat );


    /* Create a new motion state in order for Bullet to be able to
maintain and interpolate the object transformation.*/
    btDefaultMotionState *btdefaultmotionstate =
    new btDefaultMotionState( bttransform );


    /* Create a Bullet vector to be able to hold the local inertia of
the object. */
    btVector3 localinertia( 0.0f, 0.0f, 0.0f );
    /* If a mass greater than 0 is passed in a parameter to the function,
use it to calculate the local inertia. If a mass is equal to 0, it means
that the object is static and you do not need to execute this calculation. */
    if( mass > 0.0f )
        btcollisionshape->calculateLocalInertia( mass, localinertia );


    /* Create a new rigid body and link the information that you have
calculated above. Note that you are using the btRigidBody pointer already
contained in the OBJMESH structure to initialize the class. This way, when
you're drawing, you can easily query the pointer in order to gain access to
its transformation matrix, which is from now on maintained by Bullet
internally. */
    objmesh->btrigidbody =
    new btRigidBody( mass,
                     btdefaultmotionstate,
```

```
                        btcollisionshape,
                        localinertia );
```

/* Built inside the btRigidBody class, there is a void * variable that allows you to associate a user-defined pointer to the rigid body. By associating the current objmesh pointer to this data, you can then have direct access to the OBJMESH structure at any time inside any Bullet-driven functions and callbacks. */

```
    objmesh->btrigidbody->setUserPointer( objmesh );
```

/* Add the new rigid body to your physical world. */

```
    dynamicsworld->addRigidBody( objmesh->btrigidbody ); }
```

**4.** Now build a new function to free the collision world as well as all the rigid bodies that it contains:

```
void free_physic_world( void ) {
    /* Loop while you've got some collision objects. */
    while( dynamicsworld->getNumCollisionObjects() ) {
    /* Get the first collision object in the list. */
    btCollisionObject *btcollisionobject =
    dynamicsworld->getCollisionObjectArray()[ 0 ];

    /* Try to upcast it to a rigid body. */
    btRigidBody *btrigidbody =
    btRigidBody::upcast( btcollisionobject );

    /* If the upcast is successful, the pointer will be != than NULL,
so you know that you are dealing with a valid btRigidBody. */
    if( btrigidbody ) {
    /* Delete the collision shape. */
    delete btrigidbody->getCollisionShape();
    /* Delete the motion state. */
    delete btrigidbody->getMotionState();
    /* Remove the rigid body from the collision world. */
    dynamicsworld->removeRigidBody( btrigidbody );
    /* Remove the collision shape from the collision world. */
    dynamicsworld->removeCollisionObject( btcollisionobject );
    /* Delete the rigid body from the memory. */
    delete btrigidbody; }
    }
    /* Delete all the pointers that you have initialized inside the
init_physic_world. */
    delete collisionconfiguration; collisionconfiguration = NULL;
    delete dispatcher; dispatcher = NULL;
    delete broadphase; broadphase = NULL;
    delete solver; solver = NULL;
    delete dynamicsworld; dynamicsworld = NULL; }
```

**5.** Move on to the `templateAppInit` function and insert the following on the next line after the GFX_start call:

```
init_physic_world();
```

**6.** Locate the `OBJ_build_mesh` function call and add the following code on the next line:

```
/* Get the current mesh pointer. */
OBJMESH *objmesh = &obj->objmesh[ i ];
/* Test the current mesh name to check if it is the Cube. If yes,
give it a rotation of 35 degrees on the XYZ axis; and then call the
add_rigid_body
function using the mesh pointer and passing in a mass of 1kg as a
parameter. */
if( !strcmp( objmesh->name, "Cube" ) ) {
   objmesh->rotation.x =
   objmesh->rotation.y =
   objmesh->rotation.z = 35.0f;
   add_rigid_body( objmesh, 1.0f ); }
/* If it's not the Cube, it must be the plane. Add it as a new rigid body
using a mass of 0 since you want it to be a static object. */
else add_rigid_body( objmesh, 0.0f );
```

**7.** Inside `templateAppDraw`, locate the following code:

```
GFX_translate( objmesh->location.x,
objmesh->location.y,
objmesh->location.z );
```

And replace it with the following to be able to query the current matrix maintained by Bullet for the current object and multiply it with the current model view matrix:

```
mat4 mat;
objmesh->btrigidbody->getWorldTransform().getOpenGLMatrix(
( float * )&mat );
GFX_multiply_matrix( &mat );
```

**8.** Before the end of the `templateAppDraw` function, add the following line of code to increase the physics simulation step based on a static time of 60fps:

```
dynamicsworld->stepSimulation( 1.0f / 60.0f );
```

**9.** At this point, your program is ready to rock and roll. However, in order to keep your code clean, add the following call inside the `templateAppExit` function:

```
free_physic_world();
```

**10.** Build and run your application.

You should now be able to visualize the physics simulation in real time. You can observe the cube falling down and landing on the plane, and finally becoming steady — like in the real world — as demonstrated in Figure 6-3.

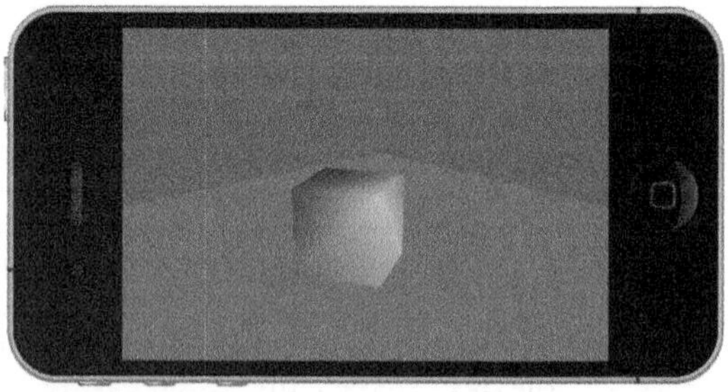

**FIGURE 6-3:** Hello Physics in action!

## COLLISION CALLBACKS, TRIGGERS, AND CONTACTS

Having real-time physics running within your apps is great! However, in order to be able to add logic code, you need to get some sort of feedback about what is happening in the simulation. That's where the collision callbacks, triggers, and contacts come in!

Using one of these approaches, you'll be able to actually code the necessary logic that you want your game to respond to, based on either the collision of two objects, or if their bounding boxes overlap (near callback), or directly on the contact point(s) between two or more collision objects.

Bullet is pretty flexible when it comes to collision callbacks and provides a multitude of different ways to handle them. In this section, I will introduce you to the most useful and popular way of getting feedback on collisions, as well as the method to loop through all contact points of your physical world, so you can then use them within your applications. Because these triggers can be called multiple times per frame, and the logic code that you'll implement can become quite complex, you'll have to determine which one is the most appropriate for your needs.

For more information and other callbacks and Bullet trigger techniques, do not hesitate to refer to the official Bullet Wiki at `http://www.bulletphysics.org/mediawiki-1.5.8/`.

## Contact-Added Callback

The first type of callback that you'll get familiar with is `gContactAdded`. This type will occur every time a new contact point is added or updated. When the implementation triggers the function, you can then get information about which collision shapes collide and the data of the manifold point (the contact itself).

Now it's time to implement this in code. First, duplicate the `chapter6-1` project directory and rename it **chapter6-2**. Open the project and jump right away to the `add_rigid_body` function. Then follow these steps:

1. In order for the contact-added callback to be triggered when a rigid body collision shape collides with another, you have to mark it for custom material callback. Making all physics objects respond to callback is not recommended. Only mark the objects that absolutely need to receive callback to avoid unnecessary processing. To do this for the current tutorial, insert the following lines before the end bracket of the function:

```
/* Only mark the object name "Cube" to receive a contact-added
callback. */
   if( !strcmp( objmesh->name, "Cube" ) ) {
   /* Adjust the collision flags of the rigid body to tell Bullet to
trigger the callback function for this body by adding
CF_CUSTOM_MATERIAL_CALLBACK to the current flags. */
   objmesh->btrigidbody->setCollisionFlags(
   objmesh->btrigidbody->getCollisionFlags() |
   btCollisionObject::CF_CUSTOM_MATERIAL_CALLBACK ); }
```

**2.** Create a new function before the `program_bind_attrib_location` function declaration. This function will be used later on as the contact-added callback function, so it has to be declared prior to the assignment.

```
bool contact_added_callback(
/* The current contact point info. */
btManifoldPoint &btmanifoldpoint,
/* The first collision object */
const btCollisionObject *btcollisionobject0,
/* The part number and index of the collision object (if using
multipart or compound collision shape). */
int part_0, int index_0,
/* The second collision object involved in the collision. */
const btCollisionObject *btcollisionobject1,
/* The part and index number of the second collision object. */
int part_1, int index_1 ) {

/* Remember the user pointer (setUserPointer) that you set up earlier?
It is now time to retrieve it to check which geometry you are dealing with.
To do this, first extract which rigid body is associated to the current
collision object. Then cast the user pointer back to an OBJMESH pointer.
This way, all the variables and functions of the OBJMESH can be called or
manipulated within the callback. Very convenient! */
OBJMESH *objmesh0 = ( OBJMESH * )
( ( btRigidBody * )btcollisionobject0 )->getUserPointer();

OBJMESH *objmesh1 = ( OBJMESH * )
( ( btRigidBody * )btcollisionobject1 )->getUserPointer();

/* Print the name of the first mesh. */
console_print("Object #0: %s\n", objmesh0->name );
/* Print the XYZ location on the mesh where the contact point is added. */
console_print("Point  #0: %.3f %.3f %.3f\n",
                btmanifoldpoint.m_positionWorldOnA.x(),
                btmanifoldpoint.m_positionWorldOnA.y(),
                btmanifoldpoint.m_positionWorldOnA.z() );

/* Same as above for the second mesh. */
console_print("Object #1: %s\n", objmesh1->name );
console_print("Point  #1: %.3f %.3f %.3f\n",
                btmanifoldpoint.m_positionWorldOnB.x(),
                btmanifoldpoint.m_positionWorldOnB.y(),
                btmanifoldpoint.m_positionWorldOnB.z() );

/* Print the normal vector at the current location of the contact point on
the second geometry. */
console_print("Normal   : %.3f %.3f %.3f\n",
                btmanifoldpoint.m_normalWorldOnB.x(),
                btmanifoldpoint.m_normalWorldOnB.y(),
                btmanifoldpoint.m_normalWorldOnB.z() );
console_print( "%d\n\n", get_milli_time() );

/* Return true only if you change any variables of the contact point
(such as the friction). */
return false; }
```

**3.** Link the global contact-added collision callback function. To do this, add the following line inside the `templateAppInit` function, right after the `init_physic_world` call:

```
gContactAddedCallback = contact_added_callback;
```

**4.** Now build and run the program, and look at the console (if you are using XCode) or at the LogCat (if you are using Eclipse).

As the collision between the two objects occurs, the collision information is printed in real time. When the object (the cube) becomes stable, the callback simply stops being called, because no new contact points are added or updated.

## Near Callback

Another type of callback is called *near callback*. This type is triggered when the bounding box of two collision objects overlap. Based on which objects are about to collide, you can then add the appropriate logic code. What I also personally like about this callback is that it can be used to prevent objects from colliding when special cases occur — by making the collider act like a ghost.

Similar to the contact-added callback demonstrated in the previous exercise, the near callback is also very easy to implement. Start by duplicating `chapter6-1` and rename it **chapter6-3**. Then follow these steps:

**1.** Right before the `program_bind_attrib_location` function declaration, create a new function as follows:

```
void near_callback( btBroadphasePair &btbroadphasepair,
                    btCollisionDispatcher &btdispatcher,
                    const btDispatcherInfo &btdispatcherinfo ) {
    /* Retrieve the 2 meshes that are part of the collision. */
    OBJMESH *objmesh0 = ( OBJMESH * )( ( btRigidBody * )
    ( btbroadphasepair.m_pProxy0->m_clientObject ) )->getUserPointer();

    OBJMESH *objmesh1 = ( OBJMESH * )( ( btRigidBody * )
    ( btbroadphasepair.m_pProxy1->m_clientObject ) )->getUserPointer();

    console_print("Object #0: %s\n", objmesh0->name );
    console_print("Object #1: %s\n", objmesh1->name );
    console_print("%d\n\n", get_milli_time() );

    /* Let Bullet continue to deal with the collision by sending the
    information to the default near-callback function maintained internally. */
    btdispatcher.defaultNearCallback( btbroadphasepair,
                                      btdispatcher,
                                      btdispatcherinfo ); }
```

**2.** Inside `templateAppInit`, on the line after the `init_physic_world` call, insert the following code line to link the callback directly to the dispatcher:

```
dispatcher->setNearCallback( near_callback );
```

**3.** Now build and run the program and monitor the console. You can instantly notice that, unlike the previous callback you implemented, this one is continuously called, even if the object becomes deactivated.

You have to be careful when using this callback, because the trigger will occur as long as the two objects are near or touching each other.

However, this type is very convenient for multiple purposes. As mentioned earlier, in addition to using this trigger to determine when the two bounding boxes of the objects collide, you can use it to prevent collision between objects. You can test this by simply commenting the last call of the function, like this:

```
/*
btdispatcher.defaultNearCallback( btbroadphasepair,
                                  btdispatcher,
                                  btdispatcherinfo );
*/
```

Then build and go! Observe how the collision between the cube and the plane is completely omitted. You can use this trick inside your own games to avoid collisions between certain objects based on logic.

## Contact Points

The technique that will be demonstrated inside this section can be inserted anywhere in your code. It consists of enumerating through all the contact points of all the physical objects that are currently in contact with each other. Obviously, this can be quite expensive, especially if you have a lot of objects.

To discover what you can do with this technique, start by duplicating the chapter6-1 project directory and rename it **chapter6-4**. Then launch it within your IDE. Now add the following structure before the end bracket of the templateAppDraw function:

```
/* Retrieve the total amount of manifold points. */
unsigned int n_manifolds =
            dynamicsworld->getDispatcher()->getNumManifolds();
i = 0;
/* Loop while there are some manifolds */
while( i != n_manifolds ) {
/* Get the current manifold based on its index. */
btPersistentManifold *manifold =
dynamicsworld->getDispatcher()->getManifoldByIndexInternal( i );

/* Retrieve the two mesh pointers for the first and second rigid bodies. */
OBJMESH *objmesh0 = ( OBJMESH * )
( ( btRigidBody * )manifold->getBody0() )->getUserPointer();
OBJMESH *objmesh1 = ( OBJMESH * )
( ( btRigidBody * )manifold->getBody1() )->getUserPointer();

/* Initialize a counter and extract the number of contact point(s) the
current manifold contains. */
```

```
        unsigned int j = 0,
        n_contacts = manifold->getNumContacts();

    /* Loop while there are some contact points. */
    while( j != n_contacts ) {
        /* Retrieve the current contact point information using the index. */
        btManifoldPoint &contact = manifold->getContactPoint( j );
        /* Print the current manifold index. */
        console_print("Manifold : %d\n", i );
        /* Print the current contact point index. */
        console_print("Contact  : %d\n", j );
        /* Print the two rigid body names and the contact point's world
position for each of them. */
        console_print("Object #0: %s\n", objmesh0->name );
        console_print("Point  #0: %.3f %.3f %.3f\n",
                    contact.getPositionWorldOnA().x(),
                    contact.getPositionWorldOnA().y(),
                    contact.getPositionWorldOnA().z() );

        console_print("Object #1: %s\n", objmesh1->name );
        console_print("Point  #1: %.3f %.3f %.3f\n",
                    contact.getPositionWorldOnB().x(),
                    contact.getPositionWorldOnB().y(),
                    contact.getPositionWorldOnB().z() );

        /* Print some miscellaneous information about the current contact point. */
        console_print("Distance : %.3f\n", contact.getDistance() );
        console_print("Lifetime : %d\n"  , contact.getLifeTime() );
        console_print("Normal   : %.3f %.3f %.3f\n",
                    contact.m_normalWorldOnB.x(),
                    contact.m_normalWorldOnB.y(),
                    contact.m_normalWorldOnB.z() );

         console_print("%d\n\n", get_milli_time() );
        /* Next contact point. */
        ++j; }
    /* Next manifold. */
    ++i; }
```

Build and run the application, and monitor the console to follow in real time the data related to every collision and contact point.

You now have the ability to create higher-level logic based on the information you extracted using this method. Whether it's multiple contacts on a single geometry, or a single contact on multiple geometries, you now have full control over everything that is happening inside your physical world!

This concludes the section on collision callbacks and contact points. There are, of course, many more callbacks available, so check the Bullet website! However, with just the callbacks presented to you in this section, you can get light collision feedback (contact-added) to full control (contact points). And by using one or more of the three methods that you learned in this section, you can create virtually everything that you can possibly imagine and implement the necessary logic for it.

Now it's time to move on to some *real* in-game implementation using the knowledge that you've gained since the beginning of this chapter!

## 2D PHYSICS

Thus far in this chapter, you've received a good overview of how to set up a physical world, how to add collision shapes and rigid bodies, and link collision callbacks. Now let's wrap it all up into a small 2D game like the one shown in Figure 6-4.

I'm sure you recognize the style — it is very similar to the popular mobile-device game Angry Birds developed by Rovio Mobile Ltd. In this section, you'll discover how easy it is to create such a game with what you've learned so far in this book.

**FIGURE 6-4:** 2D physics game featuring Momo

For this example, you will still be using the default Bullet implementation (which can be used for both 2D and 3D). However, embedded inside the library, you also have access to an implementation especially built for 2D physics simulation: *Box2d*. If you are planning to only create 2D physics-based games, I suggest that you take a look at the `Box2dDemo` inside the Bullet SDK.

Enough said — let's get started! First, duplicate the `template_chapter6-5` directory from the SDK root and rename it **chapter6-5**. (Please note that all of the assets that have been linked for this game are available to you and located in `SDK/data/chapter6-5`.) Open the project, and study the code structure implemented inside `templateApp.cpp`.

You are already familiar with all the code in this project, so there's nothing new here. However, you can still take a look at all the assets and shaders that have already been linked to this project to get familiar with what you're going to be working with.

Now build and run the program. You should get the result shown in Figure 6-5.

In the following subsections, you'll modify the existing code to turn the application into a basic 2D game with logic and physics!

**FIGURE 6-5:** Game Over already!?

## More Shapes!

First let's handle the creation of the physics shapes. Follow these steps:

**1.** Locate the `add_rigid_body` function and add the following constant declaration on the line just before the function initialization:

```
enum {
    BOX = 0,
    SPHERE = 1,
    CYLINDER = 2 };
```

As you might have already noticed, the add_rigid_body function now contains new parameters in addition to the ones you have been handling so far. In the previous section, you only worked with a box shape, but this time you will be passing to the function more specific parameters such as bounds (the one you just defined) and the parameter to define whether the physical body should be rigid or dynamic (in other words, whether it should respond to rolling physics or not).

2.  Inside the add_rigid_body function, insert the following code to be able to handle multiple collision shapes as well the other parameters received by the function:

```
/* Initialize a blank collision shape pointer. */
btCollisionShape *btcollisionshape = NULL;
/* Create a conditional switch based on the type of bound. */
switch ( bound ) {
/* If the current bound is a box, do the same as in the previous
sections. */
case BOX: {
btcollisionshape =
new btBoxShape( btVector3( objmesh->dimension.x * 0.5f,
                           objmesh->dimension.y * 0.5f,
                           objmesh->dimension.z * 0.5f ) );
break; }
/* If it's a sphere, initialize a new sphere shape, passing in as a
parameter the radius of the mesh (which is automatically pre-calculated
when OBJ_mesh_build is called). */
case SPHERE: {
btcollisionshape =
new btSphereShape( objmesh->radius );
break; }
/* Handle the cylinder shape, which is initialized the same way as a
Box shape, by passing the bounding box extend to the constructor. */
case CYLINDER: {
btcollisionshape =
new btCylinderShapeZ( btVector3( objmesh->dimension.x * 0.5f,
                                objmesh->dimension.y * 0.5f,
                                objmesh->dimension.z * 0.5f ) );
break; }
}
```

3.  Prepare the transformation to be assigned to the motion state. However, this time, use the btTransform API to set the location of the mesh as follows:

```
btTransform bttransform;
bttransform.setIdentity();
/* Set the origin location of the transformation, which is basically
the pivot XYZ location of the object. Note that the origin should always be
the center of the bounding box of the object in world space coordinates. */
bttransform.setOrigin( btVector3( objmesh->location.x,
                                  objmesh->location.y,
                                  objmesh->location.z ) );
```

**4.** Initialize the motion state and a new rigid body, as follows:

```
btDefaultMotionState *btdefaultmotionstate = NULL;
btdefaultmotionstate = new btDefaultMotionState( bttransform );
btVector3 localinertia( 0.0f, 0.0f, 0.0f );
/* If the function receives a positive mass, calculate the local inertia
tensor of the object. */
if( mass > 0.0f )
    btcollisionshape->calculateLocalInertia( mass, localinertia );
    objmesh->btrigidbody =
    new btRigidBody( mass,
                     btdefaultmotionstate,
                     btcollisionshape,
                     localinertia );
```

**5.** It's time to handle the constraint on the XZ axis for the collision objects that have a positive mass (non-static objects). Since your game is basically in 2D, and you are using an orthographic projection, you want the physics simulation to occur only on these two axes. In order to do this, add the following code:

```
if( mass > 0.0f ) {
/* Constraint the linear velocity (the movement of the object) to the
XZ axis by setting 0 to the Y linear factor. */
    objmesh->btrigidbody->setLinearFactor(
    btVector3( 1.0f, 0.0f, 1.0f ) );

/* Check to see if the object is not a dynamic object. If it's not,
you have to prevent the object from rolling on the XZ axis. To do this,
in the same way you handled the linear factor, pass 0 as the XZ value of
the angular factor of the rigid body. This way, all your non-dynamic
objects will roll only on the Y axis. */
    if( !dynamic_only )
        objmesh->btrigidbody->setAngularFactor(
        btVector3( 0.0f, 1.0f, 0.0f ) );
    /* If the object is a fully dynamic object, set the XYZ angular factor
to 0, so the object (such as the bananas) won't respond to rolling physics
at all. */
    else objmesh->btrigidbody->setAngularFactor( 0.0f );
    }
```

**6.** Add the newly created rigid body to your physical world, and link the OBJMESH pointer to the rigid body user pointer as follows so you can reuse this data later on in the contact added callback:

```
objmesh->btrigidbody->setUserPointer( objmesh );
dynamicsworld->addRigidBody( objmesh->btrigidbody );
```

That's it for the add_rigid_body function. You have learned how to add new types of collision shapes and you are now able to constrain movement and rotation on a particular axis. Not bad for a start!

## Building the Physical Objects

Your function to add a new rigid body is ready to be used. Now it's time to actually send the mesh from the scene to be dispatched to this function in order to start dynamically creating the collision objects of your world.

**1.** Locate the `OBJ_build_mesh` function call and insert the following code on the line after the function invocation:

```
/* For each momo, create a sphere shape, with a mass of 2kg that
responds to rolling physics. */
   if( strstr( objmesh->name, "momo" ) )
     add_rigid_body( objmesh, SPHERE, 2.0f, 0 );

   /* For the barrels, create a cylinder shape with a mass of 1kg
(so Momo can bash them easily) that also responds to rolling physics. */
   else if( strstr( objmesh->name, "barrel" ) )
     add_rigid_body( objmesh, CYLINDER, 1.0f, 0 );

   /* Initialize each plank as a box, with a mass of 1kg that also responds
to angular velocity. */
   else if( strstr( objmesh->name, "plank" ) )
     add_rigid_body( objmesh, BOX, 1.0f, 0 );

   /* Create a static box for the ground. */
   else if( strstr( objmesh->name, "ground" ) )
     add_rigid_body( objmesh, BOX, 0.0f, 0 );

   /* Create a static cylinder for the steel barrel. */
   else if( strstr( objmesh->name, "steel" ) )
   add_rigid_body( objmesh, CYLINDER, 0.0f, 0 );
```

In this code, you reused what you learned in the previous exercise to handle the collision shapes, and used an `if`/`else if` clause (based on the object names) to dynamically dispatch them to the `add_rigid_body` function and create their collision shapes.

**2.** Now you need to add another `else if` to handle the fruits. In addition to adding the bananas to the physical world, you have to specify that when a new contact point is created, the `contact_added_callback` function should be triggered (just like you did previously in the "Contact-Added Callback" section). To do this, add the following code block:

```
   else if( strstr( objmesh->name, "banana" ) ) {
     /* Create a sphere shape for each banana that has a mass of 1kg
and that does not respond to rolling physics. You do not want the bananas
to start rolling around! */
     add_rigid_body( objmesh, SPHERE, 1.0f, 1 );
     /* Add to the rigid body collision flags that appropriate tags to
respond to custom material callbacks (contact added) */
     objmesh->btrigidbody->setCollisionFlags(
     objmesh->btrigidbody->getCollisionFlags() |
     btCollisionObject::CF_CUSTOM_MATERIAL_CALLBACK );
```

**3.** You also do not want the bananas to respond to physics right away and start falling down. You need to force the rigid body to be deactivated so it won't be affected by the gravity of the world right away, but will instead start responding to gravity only when another collision object hits it. To do this, add the following lines:

```
objmesh->btrigidbody->forceActivationState
( ISLAND_SLEEPING ); }
```

**4.** Since you are already looping and analyzing each object name, this is the best time to hide the `"gameover"` object. You will specify when this object should be visible later, when you're implementing the logic part of the game. But for right now, to prevent the object from being rendered, simply add the following:

```
else if( strstr( objmesh->name, "gameover" ) ) {
    objmesh->visible = 0;
}
```

**5.** In order to be able to update the matrices of your meshes, you need to insert the code to query Bullet about the current OpenGL matrix states that the library is maintaining. To do this, locate the line that calls `GFX_translate` and replace it with the following code:

```
/* Check if the current mesh has a valid rigid body pointer. */
if( objmesh->btrigidbody ) {
    mat4 mat;
    /* Get the current transformation matrix from Bullet. */
    objmesh->btrigidbody->getWorldTransform().getOpenGLMatrix(
    ( float * )&mat );
    /* Update the X location based on the current OpenGL matrix value. */
    objmesh->location.x = mat.m[ 3 ].x;
    /* Multiply it with the current model view matrix. */
    GFX_multiply_matrix( &mat ); }

    /* If the current object does not have a rigid body pointer, simply call
the GFX_translate function to position the object inside the world, as you
normally do. */
    else
        GFX_translate( objmesh->location.x,
                       objmesh->location.y,
                       objmesh->location.z );
```

Now build and run the application. Observe that "Game Over" is not rendering anymore, and that the barrel and planks smoothly balance and align to create a stable stack of physics objects.

## Camera Tracking

In this section, you will implement the necessary code to be able to track the current Momo in action. You will first have to establish a mechanism that is able to focus a specific mesh and use a linear interpolation to follow it as it moves inside the 2D world. To do this, follow these steps:

**1.** At the top of the `templateApp.cpp`, on the line after the `vec2 start_pos`, declare the following variables:

```
/* Index of the current Momo. Since the momo objects are named respectively
momo1, momo2, and so on, keeping an index enables you to easily retrieve
the current OBJMESH pointer for the current index by dynamically creating
the name of the mesh in code. */
unsigned int momo_index = 0;
/* Pointer to the current Momo mesh. */
OBJMESH *momo = NULL;
```

**2.** You now have the necessary variables in place, so create a new function right before the `load_game` function declaration to get the next mesh named "momo" on demand:

```
void get_next_momo( void ) {
    /* Temp. characters to dynamically create the mesh name. */
    char tmp[ MAX_CHAR ] = {""};
    /* Loop counter. */
    unsigned int i = 0;
    /* Reset the global momo mesh pointer. */
    momo = NULL;
    /* Increase the current momo index. */
    ++momo_index;
    /* Dynamically create the mesh name based on the current index. */
    sprintf( tmp, "momo%d", momo_index );
    /* Loop while you've got some mesh to be able to find the mesh
with the corresponding name. */
    while( i != obj->n_objmesh ) {
        if( strstr( obj->objmesh[ i ].name, tmp ) ) {
            /* You found the good mesh, so assign the OBJMESH pointer to the
global momo variable. */
            momo = &obj->objmesh[ i ];
            /* Disable the deactivation of the rigid body. Since the object
will be thrown in the air, it has to be active in order to respond to the
linear velocity movement that you are going to assign it. If the rigid body
is disabled, the object won't respond, even if you affect the velocity.
By calling the line above, you can be sure that the object will stay
"alive" and ready to be thrown. */
            momo->btrigidbody->setActivationState( DISABLE_DEACTIVATION );
            /* You found the mesh return. */
            return;
        }
        /* Next mesh please... */
        ++i;
    }
}
```

**3.** Now call the function you created in step 2 as the last instruction of the `load_game` function:

```
get_next_momo();
```

**4.** Move on to the `templateAppDraw` function and locate the line where you call `GFX_look_at`. Then on the previous line, insert the following code to be able to track the current Momo:

```
/* If you got an active momo. */
if( momo ) {
    /* Linearly interpolate the camera eye position with the current
location of momo on the X axis. */
    eye.x = eye.x * 0.98f + momo->location.x * 0.02f;
    /* Clamp the camera X position to be between the range of -2 to 3.5.
This way, even if Momo is going off screen, you will stop tracking it. */
    center.x =
    eye.x = CLAMP( eye.x, -2.0f, 3.5f ); }
```

**5.** Execute the program to visualize what you have done in code. Notice how smoothly the camera interpolates to the left side of the screen where your army of Momo is located, focusing on the first one in the row.

This kind of camera interpolation can be used for multiple situations, it is fast and easy to implement, and it makes movements behave pretty smoothly based on a customizable factor.

## User Interactions

Everything is now set up for you to start throwing some Momos around! All you have to do right now is add the following code inside the `templateAppToucheEnded` function:

```
/* Make sure you've got an active momo first. */
if( momo ) {
    /* Force the activation state from DISABLE_DEACTIVATION to
ACTIVE_TAG. This way, as soon as the object is thrown in the air, it can
then become deactivated when it lands and becomes immobile. */
    momo->btrigidbody->forceActivationState( ACTIVE_TAG );
    /* Use the direction vector created by the swipe of the user to
assign the linear velocity of the object. In addition, to avoid a very high
velocity (since the vector is in pixels, and Bullet is working in meters),
adjust the value by multiplying it by 0.1f and clamping it in the range of
0 to 10. Note that the X and Y values are inverted because you are in
landscape mode. */
    momo->btrigidbody->setLinearVelocity(
    btVector3( CLAMP( ( y - start_pos.y ) * 0.1f, 0.0f, 10.0f ),
            0.0f,
            CLAMP( ( x - start_pos.x ) * 0.1f, 0.0f, 10.0f ) ) ); }
```

You can now start to have a glimpse of the game play for this simple physics-based puzzle game. Start it and swipe your finger on the screen. Observe how the first Momo is affected by your movement as it gets thrown in the air. Please note that you haven't yet fully coded the game logic for the game to behave as it should. In other words, only the basic mechanism has been implemented so far — so don't worry if you feel the current execution is not correct (for example, Momo is not taking the banana). You will be implementing the full game workflow and complete the game logic in the next section.

## The Game Logic

There's only one part left: the game logic! This section will show you how to implement and how to handle the win/loose condition and how to restart the game. You will also fix a few things, such as preventing the player from continuously swiping the screen to give extra boosts to Momo. In addition, you will learn how to determine and evaluate whether the current object is inactive or out of bounds, along with other small fixes that will make this basic game a bit more like a real game. Follow these steps:

**1.** Locate the line where you declare OBJMESH *momo, and then, beginning on the next line, insert the following declarations:

```
OBJMESH *gameover = NULL; /* To remember the gameover object. */
unsigned char restart_game = 0, /* Flag to restart the game. */
               momo_launch  = 0, /* Flag to let momo be throw. */
               banana       = 0; /* Banana counter. */
```

**2.** Inside the contact_added_callback function, on the line after the two OBJMESH * declarations, paste the following code to insert the necessary logic to accumulate bananas and remove them from the physical world:

```
/* Check if one of the two objects involved in the collision is
a momo. */
   if( ( strstr( objmesh0->name, "momo" ) ||
        strstr( objmesh1->name, "momo" ) )
      &&
      /* Check if one collision object is a banana. */
      ( strstr( objmesh0->name, "banana" ) ||
        strstr( objmesh1->name, "banana" ) ) ) {

      /* Declare an empty mesh pointer. */
      OBJMESH *objmesh = NULL;
      /* Declare an empty collision object pointer. */
      btCollisionObject *btcollisionobject = NULL;

      /* Check if the first mesh is a banana. If yes, it means that
the other is obviously a momo. Store the objmesh pointer and the collision
object for the first collision object. */
      if( strstr( objmesh0->name, "banana" ) ) {
         objmesh = objmesh0;
         btcollisionobject =
         ( btCollisionObject * )btcollisionobject0; }
      /* If not, it means that the first one is the momo and the
second one is the banana. Store the pointer information of the second
collision object and the mesh. */
      else {
         objmesh = objmesh1;
         btcollisionobject =
         ( btCollisionObject * )btcollisionobject1; }

      /* Make the banana mesh invisible.*/
      objmesh->visible = 0;

      /* Decrease the banana counter. Don't worry, you will implement
```

```
        the incrementation of this variable in a moment. */
            --banana;

            /* The following lines will remove the banana from the physical
    world. First delete the collision shape of the rigid body. */
            delete objmesh->btrigidbody->getCollisionShape();
            /* Delete the motion state. */
            delete objmesh->btrigidbody->getMotionState();
            /* Remove the rigid body from the physical world. */
            dynamicsworld->removeRigidBody( objmesh->btrigidbody );
            /* Remove the collision object from the physical world. */
            dynamicsworld->removeCollisionObject( btcollisionobject );
            /* Delete the rigid body from memory. */
            delete objmesh->btrigidbody;
            /* Reset the pointer to NULL, just to be clean. */
            objmesh->btrigidbody = NULL; }
```

At this point, just for testing purposes, you could execute the game and check the logic code that you have just added. Momo can start eating bananas in real time! Try it!

**3.** Inside the `if` clause brackets of the `get_next_momo` function, insert the following line at the beginning of the block to reset the launch state for the next Momo (if any):

```
        momo_launch = 0;
```

**4.** Move to the `load_game` function and locate the `else if` block where you are handling the bananas physics properties. Then right before the end of the code block, add the following code to increase the total number of bananas:

```
        ++banana;
```

By adding this line, every time you add a new banana to the physics world, you increase the counter. This way, you can evaluate the counter later on, and if it reaches 0, the game is over and the player needs to restart the game.

**5.** Inside the `"gameover"` block (the next `else if` after step 4), add the following line before the end bracket to be able to remember the `gameover` object pointer:

```
        gameover = objmesh;
```

**6.** On the line just before you call `get_next_momo`, insert the following code to reset the current Momo index number and reset the camera to its original position:

```
        momo_index = 0;
        momo_launch = 0;
        center.x =
        eye.x    = 3.5f;
```

This will enable you to call the `load_game` function over and over, and all the game states will be reset.

**7.** Inside the `templateAppDraw`, on the line right after the `glClear` call, paste the following lines:

```
/* If the restart flag is != than 0, call the templateAppExit function
to clear the scene, and then reload it using the load_game function.
Finally, reset the restart_game flag back to 0 to avoid loading again and
again if the flag is raised. */
   if( restart_game ) {
   templateAppExit();
   load_game();
   restart_game = 0; }
```

**8.** At the end of the `templateAppDraw` function, insert the following logic code to determine if you should request another Momo or if the current one is still active in the world:

```
if(
/* Make sure that you got a valid momo pointer. */
momo &&
/* Check the current velocity of the rigid body. If the speed is
greater than 20, it means that momo is falling out of bounds. */
   ( momo->btrigidbody->getLinearVelocity().length() > 20.0f ||
   /* If the speed is less than 20, maybe the rigid body has stalled
somewhere, so this check is done to confirm that the current rigid body is
deactivated .*/
   momo->btrigidbody->getActivationState() == ISLAND_SLEEPING ) )
      /* If either of the conditions above is true, select a new momo. */
      get_next_momo();
```

Note that, in order to keep things simple in this tutorial, you simply requested the next object index. However, in case the current Momo is out of bounds, you should also remove it from the physical world (like you did for the bananas) and make it invisible for rendering. That way, you will avoid extra calculations on the CPU and GPU.

**9.** You are currently at the perfect location in code to determine if the player wins or loses. The condition for the player to win is if the number on the `banana` counter reaches 0. The losing condition is if the `momo` variable is equal to NULL (the player already threw all the available Momos) but there are still some bananas left (the index number increments, but the mesh wasn't found by the `get_next_momo` function). Append the following code to interpret these conditions:

```
if( !momo || !banana ) {
/* Put the gameover object visible. */
gameover->visible = 1;
/* Change the X and Z location of the gameover object to be in front of
the camera. */
   gameover->location.x = eye.x;
   gameover->location.z = eye.z; }
```

**10.** If the game is over, the player has to be able to restart it. To set this up, simply add the following lines at the beginning of the `templateAppToucheEnded` function:

```
/* Check if the gameover object is visible and if the restart game state
is equal to 0. If yes, raise the restart flag and exit the callback. */
   if( gameover->visible && !restart_game ) {
    restart_game = 1;
    return; }
```

**11.** To prevent the player from giving the current Momo an extra boost for free, simply replace the following `if` statement in `templateAppToucheEnded`:

```
if( momo ) {
```

with this statement:

```
/* Make sure that you have a momo, and the momo has not been launched.
If it has, enter the condition and prevent any extra launches until
the next momo is selected by your game logic. */
if( momo && !momo_launch) { momo_launch = 1;
```

**12.** Build and run the game. You should now have the complete game running on your mobile device, with real-time 2D physics, physics logic, and user interaction fully implemented — just like what was shown previously in Figure 6-4.

Wow! In less than 500 lines of code, you reproduced the base code of a multi-million dollar game! (Just a few hundred more, and you'll be able to compete against both iOS and Android in the touch-screen game world!) And you are only on Chapter 6 of this book — pretty cool!

Already thinking about taking over the App Store and the Android Market with your game? Well maybe you should finish reading this book first — you still have a lot to learn from it, believe me!

Enjoy the moment for a bit while playing your game. Then move on to the next section, where I will demonstrate how to handle more-complex 3D physics.

**FIGURE 6-6:** 3D pinball game

## 3D PHYSICS

At this point, you have all the necessary basics to crank things up a notch and apply what you have learned so far in a 3D environment. In this section, you will code a simple pinball machine like what's shown in Figure 6-6, and discover how to use the Bullet file format.

The knowledge that you will receive in this section will allow you to build full-fledged 3D physical worlds with collision shapes as well as static, dynamic, or rigid bodies and constraints. You will also learn how to save them on disk and load them directly inside your own apps so you can interact with them in code.

## The Bullet File Format

The Bullet file format (files usually saved with the extension `.bullet`) allows you to export your physical world along with all the collision object settings into one file that can then be loaded at initialization time. The Bullet website provides downloadable plug-ins that will enable you to export the physics settings that you create with your 3D editor to the Bullet file format.

In Blender, this feature is built into the Blender Game Engine. And since Blender has full Bullet support, everything that you set in the Game Engine Physics property panel can be exported to the Bullet file format; however, in the case of physics constraints, only Rigid Body Joint is supported by Bullet.

If you want to do a test to see how to export a .bullet file from Blender, follow these steps:

1. Switch the engine type from Blender Render (located in the top bar) to Blender Game.

2. Select any mesh object in your scene and click the Physics button under the Properties panel (located on the right side by default). You can then set all the physics properties of the currently selected mesh just the way Bullet is expecting it. Repeat this process for every physical object in your scene.

   In addition, you can create physics constraints by clicking the Object Constraints button on the property panel and then selecting Rigid Body Joint from the Add Constraint combo box. From there, you can set up constraint properties and object relations, along with other physics-based settings, and get direct visual feedback from your operations in the 3D viewport.

3. Once your physics properties and constraints of your world are all set, all you have to do is to insert the following lines inside a new Python script (under the Scripting layout):

```
import PhysicsConstraints;
PhysicsConstraints.exportBulletFile("<fullpath>/filename.bullet")
```

4. To call the script in order to save your .bullet file, you can create a Sensor. To do this, select an object (such as the camera or any other object in your scene), and switch the layout to Game Logic. Then create a new Sensor that links the script filename to the Script field of the controller, like the one shown in Figure 6-7.

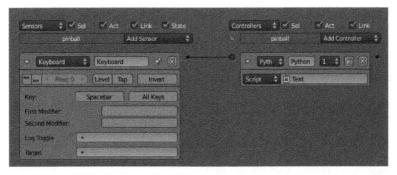

**FIGURE 6-7:** Sensor to export a .bullet file

5. To export the .bullet file, simply start the Blender Game Engine (by pressing P on your keyboard when your mouse is over the 3D viewport), and then hit the spacebar to save the file at the location that you specify in the script. Every time you change a physics property, you have to repeat this step in order to update the .bullet file with the latest changes.

By using this approach, you can save a lot of time and lines of code, and you can even test your physical world right inside the Blender Game Engine. From there, all you have to do is to link the rigid body pointers back to your objects. All properties (including the transformation matrix) will automatically be restored to the way you set them inside Blender.

Before you start building the pinball machine code (which you'll be doing next), open the SDK/ data/chapter6-6/pinball.blend file (along with the different assets located in that same directory) in Blender and study the physics properties and constraints for the Bullet physical world.

If you need more information about how to use Blender, just do a Google search and you'll find lots of resources that will get you up-and-running in no time!

# 3D Pinball Game

Begin by duplicating the template_chapter6-6 project directory and rename it **chapter6-6**. Open the project within your IDE, and then build and run at it. Your screen should now display what was shown previously in Figure 6-6.

Now open the project and select the templateApp.cpp to have a quick look at the code before getting started. The code and the structure look pretty much like the structure that you ended up with at the end of the last section. However, this time you will be using a near callback and have a new function to fill: the load_physic_world function, which is called by the load_game function and where you are going to load the .bullet.

## Bullet World Importer

Insert the following code to load the pinball.bullet inside the load_physic_world function. Please note that the filename is declared and defined by the variable PHYSIC_FILE created at the top of this source file.

```
    /* Declare the necessary class to be able to import a .bullet file and
link it to your current dynamic world that you have initialized in the
init_physic_world function. */
    btBulletWorldImporter *btbulletworldimporter =
    new btBulletWorldImporter( dynamicsworld );

    /* Now create a new in-memory stream and load pinball.bullet from disk. */
    MEMORY *memory = mopen( PHYSIC_FILE, 1 );

    /* Send over the file content to the world importer. */
    btbulletworldimporter->loadFileFromMemory(
    ( char * )memory->buffer, memory->size );

    /* Close and free the memory stream. */
    mclose( memory );

    /* At this point all the rigid bodies and constraints have been
re-created and are now present inside your dynamic world. All you have to
do now is loop through the rigid bodies and link their pointers to the
appropriate mesh. To do this start off by creating a new counter.*/
    unsigned int i = 0;
```

```
/* Loop while there are some rigid bodies. */
while( i != btbulletworldimporter->getNumRigidBodies() ) {
/* Get a OBJMESH pointer based on the name of the current rigid body.
Since you have exported your .obj and .bullet from Blender (presumably)
each mesh and rigid body has the same name. */
OBJMESH *objmesh =
OBJ_get_mesh( obj,
/* Get the name of the current rigid body. */
btbulletworldimporter->getNameForPointer(
btbulletworldimporter->getRigidBodyByIndex( i ) ), 0 );

/* If you get a valid pointer it means that you have a match. */
if( objmesh ) {
/* Link the btRigidBody pointer to the mesh. */
objmesh->btrigidbody =
( btRigidBody * )btbulletworldimporter->getRigidBodyByIndex( i );
/* Set the user pointer so you can get back access to the OBJMESH
structure within any Bullet function callback (in this case the near
callback). */
objmesh->btrigidbody->setUserPointer( objmesh );

/* Tweak the restitution of the current rigid body. Since you are
working on a pinball, everything should be very bouncy. */
objmesh->btrigidbody->setRestitution( 0.75f ); }

/* Next rigid body please... */
++i; }
/* At this point everything has been loaded and linked. Get rid of the
world importer in the memory. */
delete btbulletworldimporter;
```

Build and run the app, and as it starts, pay attention to the balls located on the right side of the screen. As you can see, they don't fall down in space. This means that you now have all the pinball table physics set up and your balls are ready to roll!

## Getting a Ball

To animate your pinball, you first have to be able to launch it on the table based on the user's touch. Follow these steps to set this up:

**1.** At the top of the source file, on the line right above the `btSoftRigidDynamicsWorld` variable declaration, insert these new variables:

```
/* Represent the current ball index. Since the ball objects
are named ball1, ball2, ball3, and so on, you will use this variable to
implement a mechanism that is similar to the one you used in the previous
section with the Momo faces. */
unsigned char ball_index = 0,
/* Flag to use to restart the game when all the balls
are depleted. */
restart_game = 0;

/* Variable to use to contain the current ball mesh pointer. */
OBJMESH *ball = NULL;
```

**2.** Create a new function before the declaration of the `near_callback` function to be able to get the next ball mesh pointer based on the next index:

```
void get_next_ball( void ) {
    /* String variable to dynamically create the current ball name
based on the current index. */
    char tmp[ MAX_CHAR ] = {""};
    /* Increment the index. */
    ++ball_index;
    /* Generate the name of the current ball. */
    sprintf( tmp, "ball%d", ball_index );
    /* Get the ball pointer based on the mesh name. */
    ball = OBJ_get_mesh( obj, tmp, 0 );
}
```

**3.** Move to the `templateAppToucheBegan` function and add the following code to launch a new ball:

```
    /* Check if you got a valid ball pointer first. If not, request a
new ball. */
    if( !ball ) {
        get_next_ball();
        /* If you got a valid ball pointer. */
        if( ball ) {
        /* Activate the rigid body. */
        ball->btrigidbody->setActivationState( ACTIVE_TAG );
        /* Give it a boost on the Y axis to launch the ball using the
setLinearVelocity function. */
        ball->btrigidbody->setLinearVelocity(
        btVector3( 0.0f, 30.0f, 0.0f ) ); }
    }
```

To test the code you've just added, build and run the application. Then tap anywhere on the screen to launch the first ball on the pinball table.

## Animate the Flippers

When you studied the blend file earlier, you probably noticed that the two flippers are using a hinge constraint. In addition to preventing them from simply falling down, this will allow their rotation to be constrained to a specific axis (in this case, the Z axis).

To be able to play the game, as soon as a new ball is launched on the table, the control should allow the player to control the flipper.

Still inside the `templateAppToucheBegan`, append the following code before the end bracket of the function to be able to give an angular velocity to the flippers when the user touches the screen:

```
    /* If you already have a valid ball pointer, you need to give control
over to the flippers. */
    else {
        /* Get the first flipper by querying the name. */
        OBJMESH *objmesh = OBJ_get_mesh( obj, "flipper1", 0 );
```

```
        /* Activate the rigid body. Since you are about to assign a new
angular velocity to it, it has to be alive first. */
        objmesh->btrigidbody->setActivationState( ACTIVE_TAG );
        /* Set a negative angular velocity (since the first flipper is
located on the right side and will respond to a negative rotation on the
Z axis). */
        objmesh->btrigidbody->setAngularVelocity(
        btVector3( 0.0f, 0.0f, -30.0f ) );

        /* Do the same as above, but this time on the left flipper, assigning
a positive angular velocity on the Z axis. */
        objmesh = OBJ_get_mesh( obj, "flipper2", 0 );
        objmesh->btrigidbody->setActivationState( ACTIVE_TAG );
        objmesh->btrigidbody->setAngularVelocity(
        btVector3( 0.0f, 0.0f, 30.0f ) );
    }
```

Execute the program and tap once to launch a new ball, and then tap again to activate the flippers.
You almost have a working pinball machine already! However, as soon you miss your shot with the
first ball, there's no way to be able to continue to play. Read the following section to learn how to
fix this behavior.

## Dead Balls

It's time to code some logic inside the near_callback function. Basically, this logic should state
that when the ball reaches the bottom of the table, the player can launch a new ball, until there are
no more balls left.

Inside the Blender model file, there is an object named "out_of_bound" at the bottom of the table.
You will now use the near callback functionality to determine if one of the ball's bounding boxes
gets near the bounding box of this object, which means that the current ball is dead and a new ball
should be sent on the table.

To implement this logic, go to the near_callback function and insert the following code on the line
before the btdispatcher.defaultNearCallback call:

```
char tmp[ MAX_CHAR ] = {""};
/* Dynamically create the name of the mesh for the current ball. */
sprintf( tmp, "ball%d", ball_index );

/* Check if the current collision involves the current ball and the
out of bound object. */
if( ball &&
    ( strstr( objmesh0->name, "out_of_bound" ) ||
      strstr( objmesh0->name, tmp ) )
    &&
    ( strstr( objmesh1->name, "out_of_bound" ) ||
      strstr( objmesh1->name, tmp ) ) ) {
        /* If yes, simply reset the current ball mesh pointer to NULL,
which will indicate inside the templateAppToucheBegan function that a new
ball has to be thrown. */
        ball = NULL;
    }
```

Build and run the app. Now you can get another ball on the table as soon as the current ball lands behind the flippers.

You almost have a full game here! All that's left is to deal with the game over and restart functionalities, which you'll be doing next.

## Game Over!

As things stand right now, when the last ball gets out of bounds, the player simply gets stuck. There is no way for him or her to restart the game. Follow these steps to implement the final logic code of the game and make it a bit more like a real pinball machine game:

**1.** Inside the `load_game` function, on the line right after the `load_physic_world` call, insert the following line to make the object name `"game_over"` invisible when the game starts:

```
OBJ_get_mesh( obj, "game_over", 0 )->visible = 0;
```

**2.** Move to the `near_callback` function and on the line above the `ball = NULL` call, insert the following code to evaluate if the player has run out of balls.

```
/* Simulate to get the next ball. */
get_next_ball();
/* Restore the ball index back to normal, since get_next_ball will increase
it +1.
 */
--ball_index;
/* If there is no ball pointer (ball == NULL), it means that the
player ran out of balls. In this case, display the game_over object. */
if( !ball ) OBJ_get_mesh( obj, "game_over", 0 )->visible = 1;
```

**3.** Inside the `templateAppToucheBegan` callback, add the following `if` clause at the beginning of the function to determine if the `"game_over"` object is visible, and if it is, the game should be restarted:

```
    /* Check if the game_over object is visible. if yes, toggle the
restart flag and exit the callback. */
    if( OBJ_get_mesh( obj, "game_over", 0 )->visible ) {
    restart_game = 1;
    return;
    }
```

**4.** Now paste the following code at the top of `templateAppDraw`, right after the function beginning bracket, to enable the game to restart:

```
    /* If you need to restart the game. */
    if( restart_game ) {
    /* Free everything from the memory. */
    templateAppExit();
    /* Reload the game. */
    load_game();
    /* Reset the ball index. */
    ball_index = 0;
```

```
/* Reset the restart flag. */
restart_game = 0;
}
```

**5.**   Build the game and run it. The player can now play this game in
its entirety and restart it as necessary.

You now have a fully working pinball machine running on your mobile
device, as displayed in Figure 6-8.

With just a bit more code and logic, you can add points based on which
object the ball collides with, add other flippers, or whatever you want
your game to do.

## SUMMARY

You have learned a lot in this chapter, from 2D physics to full-fledged
3D physics. You now have enough knowledge to be able to create
simple 2D and 3D games.

**FIGURE 6-8:** Your first
pinball machine in 3D
with real-time physics

In this chapter, you implemented logic based on physics collision
callbacks, which will enable you to track when objects are colliding.
You can also gain full control over contact points and receive triggers and callbacks when the
bounding volumes of two collision objects are overlapping.

On top of all that, you learned how to export rigid bodies and physics constraints, and load them
back into your physical world using the Bullet file format.

Your arsenal is now equipped with the all the necessary knowledge to implement the Bullet physics
library in your 2D or 3D apps, set linear and angular velocity to be able to move collision objects in
real time, gain access to rigid bodies properties, and a lot more!

Before moving on, make sure to review all the code and techniques demonstrated in this chapter.
As you dive deeper and deeper into hard-core game and graphics programming, all of these concepts
have to be assimilated.

In the next chapter, you will learn how to effectuate basic object clipping and will discover how to
handle different types of cameras and camera controls.

# 7

# Camera

## WHAT'S IN THIS CHAPTER?

- ➤ Building a touch-and-go camera

- ➤ Implementing frustum clipping based on the current model view and projection matrix

- ➤ Building and integrating a fly mode into your camera

- ➤ Creating a first-person shooter camera with collision detection

- ➤ Building a 3D camera tracking system

- ➤ Orbiting a camera around a specific object

- ➤ Using a Bullet collision ray

- ➤ Creating a third-person camera with collision detection

This chapter is all about cameras, the view matrix, and the frustum. You will learn how to create five different types of cameras through practical examples that will give you all the necessary knowledge to either integrate them inside your apps or build your own.

Another important aspect of this chapter is clipping (how to determine if an object is visible or not from the current camera view). This chapter will demonstrate how to use a universal method based on the model view and a projection matrix to build the six planes that form the view frustum.

Once the frustum is created, you will learn how to test the bounding box, bounding sphere, and points against the frustum to determine their visibility. You will also discover how to get the distance of a bound (perfect for geometry or shader LOD), and learn how to test if an object is inside, outside, or intersects the frustum.

## TOUCH AND GO!

In order to gently get started, let's first implement what I like to call a *touch-and-go* camera control. To quickly explain how this type of camera works, as the user touches the screen and drags their finger around, the camera will respond to the direction vector of the touch onscreen.

Moving up and down has a direct impact on the X and Y linear velocity of the camera, and left/right control of the rotation of the Z axis. This way, you can have a "semi first-person" camera as demonstrated in Figure 7-1.

**FIGURE 7-1:** Touch-and-go camera

**Available for download on Wrox.com**

To get started, duplicate the `template_chapter7` project located (as usual) at the root of the SDK, and rename the project directory **chapter7-1**. Then fire up the project in your favorite IDE, and study the code a bit before moving on with the necessary steps to implement this camera system.

As you can see, an important part of the code is missing. The model view matrix is not affected by any "look at" call, which means that if you execute the program, you won't see anything since there's no view matrix. To implement a view matrix that will respond to the touch and drag movements described at the beginning of this section, follow these steps:

1.  At the top of the `templateApp.cpp`, on the line right before the `program_bind_attrib_location` declaration, create the following variables:

    ```
    /* To contain the rotation on the Z axis of the camera. */
    float rotz = 0.0f;
    /* To remember the current touche location. */
    vec2 touche_location = { 0.0f, 0.0f },
        /* The touche delta (to use in the touche moved callback). */
        touche_delta    = { 0.0f, 0.0f };
    /* The current eye location of the camera in world coordinates. Give a
    little offset on the Z axis to simulate the position of a "human" eye
    looking at the scene. */
    vec3 eye_location  = { 0.0f, 0.0f, 1.84f };
    ```

2.  Before implementing the view matrix code, first implement how the movements of an onscreen touch will be interpreted. Jump to `templateAppToucheBegan`, and add the following code between the function brackets:

    ```
    /* Remember the touche location when the onscreen movement starts. */
    touche_location.x = x;
    touche_location.y = y;
    ```

3.  Inside the `templateAppToucheMoved`, add the following code to convert the direction of the touche into usable data:

```
/* Calculate the XY delta (that you will use as a direction vector)
for the current movement onscreen and clamp the range of both the movement
and the rotation since you don't want the movement to go wild because the
current delta unit is in pixels and the units inside your world are
in meters.
```

```
To insure a consistent movement on all platform, make sure you use
linear interpolation to smooth the values.
```

```
On iOS, the touche movements are already pretty smooth; however, on
Android, depending on the type of touch screen you are dealing with, you
might get some jaggy results. You will fix this problem by interpolating
the touche location. */
    touche_delta.x = touche_delta.x * 0.9f +
    CLAMP( touche_location.x - x, -0.1f, 0.1f ) * 0.1f;
    touche_delta.y = touche_delta.y * 0.9f +
    CLAMP( touche_location.y - y, -2.0f, 2.0f ) * 0.1f;
```

```
    /* Remember the current location for the next touche movement pass. */
    touche_location.x = x;
    touche_location.y = y;
```

```
/* Convert the touche delta Y into a rotation angle as you did previously
in your OBJ viewer. But this time, the rotation will not be affected on the
complex geometry but on the camera view matrix. */
    rotz += touche_delta.y;
```

**4.** To stop the movement, insert the following two lines of code inside the
`templateAppToucheEnded` event callback:

```
        touche_delta.x =
        touche_delta.y = 0.0f;
```

**5.** Inside the `templateAppDraw`, locate the `GFX_load_identity` call. On the next line, insert
the following block of code to convert the touche delta into a direction vector and affect the
linear motion of the camera:

```
        /* The touche delta Y only affects the rotation, so check if you got a
    value different than 0 to process the forward/backward movements. */
        if( touche_delta.x ) {
            /* Declare the forward vector. In this case, the forward direction is
    the position Y axis. */
            vec3 forward = { 0.0f, 1.0f, 0.0f },
                /* Declare the direction vector that you will use to affect the
    current eye location of the camera. */
                direction;
```

```
            /* Rotate the current forward vector based on the current Z rotation.
    By doing this, regardless of the rotation angle Z of the camera, up will
    always be forward and down will always be backward. */
            float r = rotz * DEG_TO_RAD,
                c = cosf( r ),
                s = sinf( r );
```

```
direction.x = c * forward.x - s * forward.y;
direction.y = s * forward.x + c * forward.y;
/* You now have a direction vector that is appropriately rotated to
the current coordinate system of the camera. Add the direction vector to
the eye_location to make the camera move. And use the touche_delta.x as the
speed factor. */
eye_location.x += direction.x * -touche_delta.x;
eye_location.y += direction.y * -touche_delta.x;
}
```

**6.** Now all you have to do is affect what you have calculated to the current model view matrix to create the camera view matrix, as follows:

```
/* First translate the model view matrix. */
GFX_translate( eye_location.x,
               eye_location.y,
               eye_location.z );

/* Then rotate it on the Z axis using the rotation controlled by the
movement of the onscreen touch. */
GFX_rotate( rotz, 0.0f, 0.0f, 1.0f );

/* Next, rotate the matrix of 90 degrees on the positive X axis to look
forward on the Y axis. */
GFX_rotate( 90.0f, 1.0f, 0.0f, 0.0f );

/* Invert the current model view matrix to create a camera view matrix. */
mat4_invert( GFX_get_modelview_matrix() );
```

**7.** Build and run the application. Once loaded, drag your finger up or down and hold it onscreen to continue the movement in the direction you specify. To rotate the camera on the Z axis, simply swipe your finger left or right depending on the direction you want to go.

## THE CAMERA FRUSTUM

Inside any 3D application, your main goal is to save as much processing as possible. Drawing only the objects that are visible onscreen is crucial to optimizing your application performance.

In this section, you will learn how to reconstruct the six frustum planes that your camera view is representing. Once you've created these planes, you'll be able to test the visibility of different virtual geometric bounds against them.

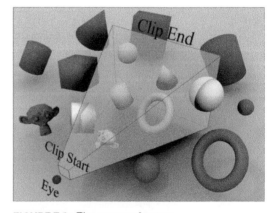

These planes can be reconstructed in real time using the current projection and model view matrix as well as the clip start and clip end data. The result of this reconstruction can basically be represented by a pyramidal shape similar to the one shown in Figure 7-2.

**FIGURE 7-2:** The camera frustum

The visibility test of an object can be executed on the frustum, which can be categorized in three distinct results (as demonstrated in Figure 7-2): inside the frustum, outside the frustum, and finally if it intersects the frustum. (If you have the colored version of the figure, green objects are inside the frustum, red objects are outside the frustum, and yellow objects intersect with the frustum.)

In game programming, most of the time only the first two types are relevant (inside or outside the frustum), since your main goal is to determine if a complex geometry is visible or not. However, you could always implement a more-sophisticated algorithm based on the fact that a geometry is intersecting the frustum, allowing you to clip part of the geometry.

## How to Build the Frustum

The technique that I'm about to show you will work with any type of camera. Without going into too much detail about the math behind this implementation (since you can just do a search on Google for that), I will strictly focus on its usage in the code. For more information, feel free to consult the function `build_frustum` in `utils.cpp` located in the `common` directory of the SDK for the full code implementation. The code of this function might look scary at first; however, you only have to call it once every time your camera view matrix or projection matrix changes.

Once the frustum planes are created, you can then use one of the following functions to test your geometry against the frustum (also located in `utils.cpp`):

➤ `sphere_distance_in_frustum`: By far my personal favorite, this function is fast (CPU-wise) and works for every type of geometry. It returns 0 if the object is not in the frustum; or if the object is in the frustum, it returns the current distance of the bounding sphere from the viewer. The distance returned by the function can then be used for clipping (if the distance is different than 0) and for geometry LOD and/or shader LOD (perfect!). However, since the shape used is a sphere (and uses the radius of the object), if your object is somewhat cube-shaped, the clipping will not be as tight as if you were using one of the following box functions.

➤ `point_in_frustum`: This function returns 1 or 0 to determine whether or not a point is inside the frustum. This function is not really powerful alone; it has to be implemented with an array of points to be powerful.

➤ `box_in_frustum`: This function tests an axis-aligned bounding box against the frustum based on the object's XYZ dimension and its pivot point. It returns 1 if the object is visible, or 0 if it is not.

➤ `sphere_intersect_frustum`: This is for your convenience only. I personally always implement it inside the 3D and game engines that I write, but never really make full use of it. This function returns 1 if the object is fully visible, 0 if it is not, or 2 if the sphere is partially inside the frustum.

➤ `box_intersect_frustum`: This function is basically the same as `sphere_intersect_frustum`, but it's for an axis-aligned bounding box.

# Frustum Clipping Implementation

Now that you have a good overview of the API and the related helper functions, it's time to implement them inside your own applications.

Begin by duplicating the `chapter7-1` directory and rename it **chapter7-2**. Then follow these steps:

**1.** At the top of the `templateApp.cpp`, on the next line after the `eye_location` declaration, insert the following variable to hold the frustum planes:

```
vec4 frustum[ 6 ];
```

**2.** Locate the call to `mat4_invert` (inside the `templateAppDraw` function). At this point in the execution, you have the latest projection and model view matrix, so on the next line after the `mat4_invert` call, you can now build the frustum by calling the following:

```
/* Build the frustum planes. Always make sure that you call this
function after the model view and project matrix have been fully updated;
otherwise, the frustum calculation will be wrong. */
build_frustum( frustum,
               GFX_get_modelview_matrix(),
               GFX_get_projection_matrix() );
```

**3.** Delete the whole `while` loop block (still inside the `templateAppDraw` function) to render the objects (including the counter variable `i` initialization), and replace it with the following code block, which includes the bounding sphere frustum check to determine if the object should be sent to the GPU for drawing or not:

```
unsigned int i = 0,
             n = 0; /* Visible objects counter. */

while( i != obj->n_objmesh ) {
    OBJMESH *objmesh = &obj->objmesh[ i ];

    /* Get the distance of the current mesh in the frustum. */
    objmesh->distance =
    sphere_distance_in_frustum( frustum,
                                &objmesh->location,
                                objmesh->radius );

    /* If the distance of the mesh is != than 0, it means that the object
is visible, so you should draw it onscreen. */
    if( objmesh->distance ) {
        GFX_push_matrix();
        GFX_translate( objmesh->location.x,
                       objmesh->location.y,
                       objmesh->location.z );
        glUniformMatrix4fv(
        program->uniform_array[ 0 ].location,
        1,
        GL_FALSE,
        ( float * )GFX_get_modelview_projection_matrix() );
```

```
            OBJ_draw_mesh( obj, i );
            GFX_pop_matrix();

            /* Increment the visible object counter. */
            ++n;
        }
        /* Increment the counter to test the next object. */
        ++i;
    }
    /* Report on the console the number of objects currently visible
in the frustum. */
    console_print( "Visible Objects: %d\n", n );
```

You have now implemented object clipping inside your application. All objects that are outside the frustum will not be sent to the video card for processing. Only the fully visible or partially visible objects will be drawn onscreen.

If you need more information about how to calculate the bounding sphere radius or the bounding box dimension of an arbitrary geometry, feel free to consult the OBJ_update_bound_mesh (SDK/common/obj.cpp) function source. It includes the full code implementation.

Ready to test the code? Compile and execute the application, and then move around the scene. Pay close attention to the Console (XCode) or LogCat (Eclipse) to check how many visible objects are currently sent to the GPU based on your current camera view.

## More Clipping Functions

As mentioned in the previous section, I personally prefer to use sphere_distance_in_frustum as the generic clipping method inside my engines. However, depending on the situation or on your requirements, other clipping methods may have to be used.

The following instructions are optional. This information is provided in case you want to test the different clipping methods offered within the SDK so you can find the best one to fit your needs.

If you want to test the various clipping methods, duplicate the chapter7-2 directory and rename it **chapter7-2a**. Then follow these steps:

1. On the line above the if( objmesh->distance ) call, insert the following code to declare a variable that will hold half of the extend of the object dimension. This is the bounding box size that you will have to use if you want to test the frustum clipping functions that are effectuated on the bounding box of an object.

    ```
    vec3 dim = { objmesh->dimension.x * 0.5f,
                 objmesh->dimension.y * 0.5f,
                 objmesh->dimension.z * 0.5f };
    ```

2. Replace the if( objmesh->distance ) line with one of the following if statements, depending on the method you want to test:

    ➤ To test a single point in the frustum:

    ```
    if( point_in_frustum( frustum, &objmesh->location ) )
    ```

➤ To test the visibility of an axis-aligned bounding box against the frustum:

```
if( box_in_frustum( frustum, &objmesh->location, &dim ) )
```

➤ To test the visibility of a bounding sphere that may intersect the frustum:

```
if( sphere_intersect_frustum( frustum,
                              &objmesh->location,
                              objmesh->radius ) )
```

➤ To check if an axis-aligned bounding box is visible or not or if it intersects at least one of the current frustum planes:

```
if( box_intersect_frustum( frustum, &objmesh->location, &dim ) )
```

This concludes the section on clipping! You now have a new and very powerful weapon to add to your arsenal. With this universal method, you can easily determine, and at a relatively low processing cost, the visibility of any geometric object inside your camera view.

For the sake of this example, you have used 3D geometries, but the same clipping methods can also be used for lamps, sounds, or anything else that can be represented by a virtual boundary in space. Enjoy!

## CAMERA FLY MODE

Since you have the necessary knowledge to create and use Euler-based cameras (as you did in the previous exercises), and are able to clip objects in space, it's time to crank it up a bit and implement a more-complex camera behavior.

The type of camera implementation that will be demonstrated in this section is similar to what's used in popular 3D software as well as in some first-person shooters. This type of camera allows you to manipulate the view and "fly" freely around a scene, just like in Figure 7-3.

In the following exercise, you will implement two virtual analog sticks that respond to touche movements on both sides of the screen. When the user smoothly touches the left side, it will allow them to move forward and backward and strafe left and right. Strong movement forward or backward will make the camera fly in that direction.

**FIGURE 7-3:** Camera fly mode

And if the touche is on the right side of the screen, it will allow the user to move the camera XZ rotation axis, just like in a first-person shooter.

Begin this exercise by duplicating the `template_chapter7-3` project directory and rename it **chapter7-3**. Once again, this is just for convenience in order to give you a base framework for this exercise.

The template already includes all the loading and rendering of the scene as well as the basic camera code to look at the scene (as you implemented previously) and frustum culling.

If you build and run the program, you'll see that everything is in place except for the camera movement. To implement the camera movement, follow these steps:

**1.** At the top of the `templateApp.cpp`, on the line right after the `vec4 frustum` initialization, create the following global variables:

```
/* Since you are basically going to split the screen in two in order to
have the left and right sides as an independent analog stick, declare the
following variable to be able to remember the screen width in
landscape mode. */
float screen_size = 0.0f;
/* Declare 2 two-dimensional vectors: one to remember the touche starting
location on the right side of the screen, and the other to calculate the
delta when the touche is moved. */
vec2 view_location,
    view_delta = { 0.0f, 0.0f };
/* Same as above for the view, but this time for the camera location.
In addition, create another variable for the movement delta. Note that you
declare it as a 3D vector because you will be using the Z as the force
factor to smooth the movement. */
vec3 move_location = { 0.0f, 0.0f, 0.0f },
    move_delta;
```

**2.** Now go to the `templateAppInit` function and add the following line at the top of the function code:

```
/* Remember the screen height (in landscape mode, the width of the
screen). */
screen_size = height;
```

**3.** Before implementing the movement and the view in the rendering loop, jump to the `templateAppToucheBegan` function and integrate the following user interaction:

```
/* Analyze on which side of the screen the touche is emitted. And
depending on whether it's on the left or the right, remember the starting
point of the touche for either the movement or the view. */
if( y < ( screen_size * 0.5f ) ) {
    move_location.x = x;
    move_location.y = y;
}
else {
    view_location.x = x;
    view_location.y = y;
}
```

**4.** Inside the `templateAppToucheMoved`, implement the following code to keep track of the movement and the view rotation:

```
/* First create a "dead zone" that occupies 10% of the screen size,
located at the center of the screen. This way, if the user is on one side
of the screen and swipes all the way to the other side, you can then stop
```

the movement. */
```
   if( y > ( ( screen_size * 0.5f ) -
            ( screen_size * 0.05f ) ) &&
      y < ( ( screen_size * 0.5f ) +
            ( screen_size * 0.05f ) ) ) {
      /* Stop the current movement for the view or if the camera is
on the move. */
      move_delta.z =
      view_delta.x =
      view_delta.y = 0.0f;
      /* In order to make things easier for the user, assign the current
location of the touche to be either the starting point of the view or the
movement, since you never know in which direction the user will move the
touche. */
      move_location.x = x;
      move_location.y = y;
      view_location.x = x;
      view_location.y = y;
   }
   /* If the touche start is on the left side of the screen, deal with it
as a camera movement. */
   else if( y < ( screen_size * 0.5f ) ) {
   /* Store the current touche as a 3D vector. */
   vec3 touche = { x,
                   y,
                   0.0f };
   /* Calculate the delta to determine which direction the touche is
going. */
   vec3_diff( &move_delta,
              &touche,
              &move_location );
   /* Normalize the delta to have a direction vector in the range of
-1 to 1. */
   vec3_normalize( &move_delta, &move_delta );
   /* Calculate the force (basically the distance from the starting
movement location to the current touche location) and divide it by a factor
in pixels. This way, the closer to the starting point, the slower the
movement will be, and as the touch distance increases, the movement speed
will increase up to its maximum. */
   move_delta.z = CLAMP(
                   vec3_dist( &move_location, &touche ) / 128.0f,
                   0.0f,
                   1.0f );
   }
   /* Since the touche is on the right side of the screen, simply calculate
the delta for the view so you can then use it to manipulate the X and Z
rotation of the camera. */
   else {
      /* Calculate the view delta and linearly interpolate the values to
smooth things out a bit. */
      view_delta.x = view_delta.x * 0.75f +
      ( x - view_location.x ) * 0.25f;
      view_delta.y = view_delta.y * 0.75f +
      ( y - view_location.y ) * 0.25f;

      /* Remember the current location as the starting point for the next
```

```
movement (if any). */
    view_location.x = x;
    view_location.y = y;
}
```

**5.** The view movements will be stopped directly inside the rendering loop, because you want the user to simply swipe once to rotate the camera in the desired angle. However, for the camera movements, you don't want the user to continuously swipe — you want them to simply drag in one direction and, as long as the finger is on the screen, continue in that direction. In order to stop the camera movements, add the following line inside the `templateAppTouchEnded` function to reset the force when the touche is released:

```
/* Stop the movement by setting the force to 0. */
move_delta.z = 0.0f;
```

**6.** You now have all the necessary data to be able to implement both the movement and the view interaction inside the rendering loop and animate the camera in real time. Jump to the `templateAppDraw` function and, on the line right after the `GFX_load_identity` call, add the following code to let the user control the camera view rotation:

```
/* First make sure that either the X or Y view_delta actually has a
value, in order to avoid processing movements for nothing. */
if( view_delta.x || view_delta.y ) {
    /* If the delta Y is active (!=0), affect it to the rotation Z of the
camera. */
    if( view_delta.y ) rotz -= view_delta.y;
    /* If the delta X is active, affect it to the X rotation. And since
you don't want the view to start flipping, clamp it in the range of 0 to
180. This way, the user will be restricted to look from straight up to
straight down (since forward is 90 degrees). */
    if( view_delta.x ) {
    rotx += view_delta.x;
    rotx = CLAMP( rotx, 0.0f, 180.0f );
    }
    /* Set the deltas back to 0. */
    view_delta.x =
    view_delta.y = 0.0f;
}
```

**7.** Before moving on with the camera movement code, build and run your application. Once it's loaded, use the right side of the screen as an analog stick to test how the camera rotation behaves with the code that you've just created.

**8.** Now you need to handle the camera movements, since what you are trying to achieve is something that behaves like the good old classic WASD control. To do this, implement the forward and backward movements as well as the strafe left and right movements by inserting the following code right after the one in step 6:

```
/* Check if you have a force (!=0). */
if( move_delta.z ) {
    /* Rotate the move_delta coordinate system by the current Z rotation
```

of the camera. This way, forward will always be up backward will always be down, left will always be left, and right will always be right. */

```
        vec3 forward;
        float r = rotz * DEG_TO_RAD, /* Convert the rotz to radiant. */
                c = cosf( r ), /* Get the cosine for the Z rotation. */
                s = sinf( r ); /* Get the sine for the Z rotation. */
        /* Calculate the movement direction rotated on the Z axis; in other
words, the forward vector based on the movement direction (delta) using the
camera rotation space. */
        forward.x = c * move_delta.y - s * move_delta.x;
        forward.y = s * move_delta.y + c * move_delta.x;
        /* Add the vector to the current camera location and multiply it by a
factor (basically the camera speed) to regulate the movements. */
        location.x += forward.x * move_delta.z * 0.1f;
        location.y += forward.y * move_delta.z * 0.1f;
    }
```

**9.** You have now implemented fully working, first-person camera movements. Build and run the app to get a feel of the movement control you've just coded.

**10.** And now for the finale of this exercise, you will implement the fly mode code. However, if you just simply integrate the fly mode code, when the user pushes forward or backward, the Z location will be increased or decreased along with the X axis, which is probably not what the user wants. To resolve this issue, you need to avoid dealing with the Z-axis incrementation until the movement delta on the X axis is at its maximum value. The following code interprets the method. You can append it right after where you left off in step 8, or more precisely, right before the end bracket of the code you inserted for the step.

```
        /* Get the sine for the rotx and offset it 90 degrees to make sure it
fits with the world positive Y axis (the forward vector). */
        forward.z = sinf( ( rotx - 90.0f ) * DEG_TO_RAD );
        /* If the movement delta on the X axis (either positive or negative) is
almost a fully straight movement (near -1 or 1), take in consideration the
Z elevation. */
        if( move_delta.x < -0.99f )
            location.z -= forward.z * move_delta.z * 0.1f;
        else if( move_delta.x > 0.99f )
            location.z += forward.z * move_delta.z * 0.1f;
```

**11.** Run the code one more time and change the camera rotation on the X axis. Then give a full straight movement on the left side of the screen to elevate the camera as you go forward.

Congratulations! You have now a fully functional camera that includes both first-person and fly mode capabilities. Enjoy the moment flying around your scene, and then move on to the next section where you will learn how to integrate a physics-based, first-person camera that collides with the scene.

## FIRST-PERSON CAMERA WITH COLLISION DETECTION

In this section, you will discover how to add collision detection on your camera by re-implementing the first person camera code of the previous exercise. But this time, you will add a physics bound to the camera and, using the Bullet API, control the linear velocity of the collision shape to move around the scene.

To get started quickly, duplicate the `template_chapter7-4` folder and rename it **chapter7-4**. The template already includes the same physics structure that you studied in the previous chapter, as well as the first-person camera control that you created in the previous section's exercise.

You also have access to a `.bullet` file, which has already been linked to the project (located inside the `SDK/data/chapter7-4`) and has been exported from the Blender scene used for this tutorial. So before starting to code, study the `untitled.blend` file located in `SDK/data/chapter7-4`, because it is slightly different than the one you have been using so far in this chapter.

More precisely, focus on the physics properties that have been set for each object. Basically, the interior is using a static triangle mesh shape, and the cylinder object called "camera" uses a capsule shape. You do not have stairs in this scene, but if you did, a capsule shape would be a lot smoother to move around or climb stairs on compared to a cylinder that has a rough edge at its base.

The way to implement collision detection for your camera is to use the physics bound of an arbitrary collision shape (in this case, a capsule) and then use its position (which is maintained by Bullet) as the camera location. The collision object of the camera should be a dynamic object (no rolling physics) in order for it to always stay straight in space.

Follow the next steps to convert your existing first-person camera code into a fully functional, first-person camera that collides with the boundaries of your scene:

1.  At the top of the `templateApp.cpp`, on the line after the `move_delta` variable declaration, add the following OBJMESH pointer variable to remember the camera collision object:

    ```
    OBJMESH *camera = NULL;
    ```

2.  Inside the `templateAppInit` function, on the line right after the call to `load_physic_world`, insert the following code to query and remember the camera mesh pointer, and then once queried, force the physical object to be dynamic and make it invisible for rendering (since you are strictly interested in the collision shape of the object and do not want to draw the mesh itself onscreen):

    ```
    /* Query the camera mesh pointer. */
    camera = OBJ_get_mesh( obj, "camera", 0 );
    /* Set the rigid body to be a dynamic body. */
    camera->btrigidbody->setAngularFactor( 0.0f );
    /* Make the object invisible at render time. */
    camera->visible = 0;
    ```

3.  Move to the `templateAppDraw` function and, on the line before the end bracket of the `if( move_delta.z )`, insert the following code to be able to affect the linear velocity of the camera physical object based on the movement delta using the associated Bullet API:

    ```
    /* Assign the linear velocity of the collision object and multiply
    the delta by 6.7m/s (the average distance that a human achieve while
    running). */
        camera->btrigidbody->setLinearVelocity(
        btVector3( forward.x * move_delta.z * 6.7f,
                   forward.y * move_delta.z * 6.7f,
                   0.0f ) );
    ```

```
        /* Make sure that the rigid body is activated; otherwise, the
    setLinearVelocity call above will have no effect, because the body
    might be deactivated. */
        camera->btrigidbody->setActivationState(
        ACTIVE_TAG );
```

4. Between the `else` statement brackets that are located right below the code you just appended in step 3, insert the following line to put the camera physical object to sleep if there is no movement. (If you don't add this code, the inertia will start kicking in, and the user will feel like they're skating on ice.)

```
        camera->btrigidbody->setActivationState( ISLAND_SLEEPING );
```

5. Right before the first call to `GFX_rotate`, add the following line to use the camera object location to position the eye of the viewer in space:

```
    GFX_translate( camera->location.x,
                   camera->location.y,
                   /* Give an offset on the Z axis since the location
    represents the position of the object pivot point. You need to simulate a
    real human eye looking at the scene, so add to the current Z value half of
    the Z dimension of the object bounding box, to simulate that the eye
    position is located at the top of the collision object. */
                   camera->location.z +
                   ( camera->dimension.z * 0.5f ) );
```

6. Inside the `while( i != obj->n_objmesh )`, on the next line after calling `GFX_push_matrix`, insert the following code to get the current transformation matrix associated with the collision object to place your geometries (which are now controlled by Bullet) into space:

```
    mat4 mat;
    /* Ask Bullet to return the OpenGL matrix for the current mesh and store
    it inside a 4x4 matrix. */
    objmesh->btrigidbody->getWorldTransform().getOpenGLMatrix(
    ( float * )&mat );
    /* Update the mesh location by copying the last row of the
    matrix, to make sure the latest location will be used by the
    clipping method (if any). */
    memcpy( &objmesh->location, ( vec3 * )&mat.m[ 3 ], sizeof( vec3 ) );
    /* Multiply the matrix by the current model view matrix. */
    GFX_multiply_matrix( &mat );
```

And that's it! In six easy steps, you now have a full-fledged, first-person camera with collision. To test it, simply compile and run the program. You should now end up with a scene like the one shown in Figure 7-4 and be able to collide with walls, which prevent you from going outside of the room.

**FIGURE 7-4:** First-person shooter camera with collision detection

# 3D CAMERA TRACKING

This section will teach you how to implement a static camera that is tracking an object in 3D space. You can find this type of camera implemented in some RPG and action games. Every time you move the character inside a scene, the camera takes a static position and follows the movement of the player. Based on the same approach, "on rail" cameras behave in a similar fashion while following a predefined path.

To get started, duplicate the `template_chapter7-5` project directory and rename it **chapter7-5**. The template provides you with a basic structure where the scene that you have been using in the previous section is automatically loaded.

Starting at a few meters from the ground, there is a ball called "player." This will be the entity that you will control inside the scene, as demonstrated in Figure 7-5.

Everything implemented in the template has been previously explained. All that's left to be done is to implement the camera tracking and the necessary code to move the ball inside the scene based on the user movement direction. The template provides you with all the basic scene

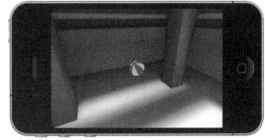

**FIGURE 7-5:** 3D camera tracking

initialization as well as the physical world, so you don't have to re-implement what you have already touched base with. The same thing goes for the touche callbacks, because they also re-implement the same movement mechanism that you coded earlier.

The only difference is that this time, the movement will have to be applied on the ball and not on the camera itself. Follow these steps to learn how to use physics and a camera-tracking method to control the ball entity in space:

1. At the top of the `templateApp.cpp`, where the global variables for this program are defined (on the next line right after the `move_delta` variable), insert the following set of variables (which you will need throughout the program):

   ```
   /* The variables that you are going to plug into the GFX_look_at function. */
   vec3 eye,
        center,
        up = { 0.0f, 0.0f, 1.0f };
   /* Global OBJMESH to remember the player object pointer. */
   OBJMESH *player = NULL;
   ```

2. On the line after the `load_physic_world` function call, insert the following code:

   ```
   /* Get the OBJMESH pointer for the player object. */
   player = OBJ_get_mesh( obj, "player", 0 );
   /* Set the friction of the rigid body to 10. With a high friction, the
   ball will not spin on itself before moving to the appropriate location, but
   will "stick" on the floor and execute the movement right away. */
   player->btrigidbody->setFriction( 10.0f );
   ```

```
/* Copy the initial location of the ball to the eye variable and to the
center variable. This way, you have an initial location where the camera is
going to start looking when the program starts. */
    memcpy( &eye, &player->location, sizeof( vec3 ) );
    memcpy( &center, &player->location, sizeof( vec3 ) );
    /* Give a little offset on the Y axis to make sure that the scene can be
covered by the camera eye position (well at least mostly). */
    eye.y -= 3.0f;
```

**3.** Move to the `templateAppDraw` callback and, right after you clean up the model view matrix (by calling `GFX_load_identity`), insert the following block of code to control the player object. Note that this time, you will be using `setAngularVelocity` to be able to roll the ball in the appropriate direction controlled by the user relative to the world coordinate system.

```
/* First check if you have a force. */
if( move_delta.z ) {
    /* Just like you did in the previous chapter for the capsule shape,
assign the movement delta (aka the direction vector) coming from the touch
screen to the ball collision shape. */
        player->btrigidbody->setAngularVelocity(
        /* Reverse the move_delta.x to fit the current coordinate system. */
        btVector3( -move_delta.x * move_delta.z * 6.7f,
                    move_delta.y * move_delta.z * 6.7f,
                    0.0f ) );
        /* Activate the rigid body; otherwise, the setAngularVelocity call
will have no affect if the ball is deactivated. */
        player->btrigidbody->setActivationState( ACTIVE_TAG ); }
```

**4.** The last step is to actually set the position of the player object to be the camera target (the `center` variable). However, you do not want to update it right away — the motion will look a lot better if the transition of the center location is done smoothly. Right after the block that you added in step 3, insert the following code to update and linearly interpolate the current camera center position before sending it to the `GFX_look_at` function:

```
/* Linearly interpolate the current center point of the camera with the
current location of the player object in space. */
    center.x = center.x * 0.975f + player->location.x * 0.025f;
    center.y = center.y * 0.975f + player->location.y * 0.025f;
    center.z = center.z * 0.975f + player->location.z * 0.025f;
    /* Feed the variables to the GFX_look_at function to create the view
matrix based on the current data. */
    GFX_look_at( &eye,
                 &center,
                 &up );
```

You did it again! In only a few steps, you have now implemented a completely different way of handling the camera inside a scene. Feel free to build and run the app to test the code you just created. Once the app is loaded, drag your finger on the touch screen to control the movement of the ball inside the 3D world.

Please take note that at times, depending on the current camera angle, the control might look inverted. This is because the movements are always in absolute world space coordinate. If you wish to compensate for this offset, simply rotate the control based on the camera Z rotation (as shown in the next section of this chapter).

# THIRD-PERSON CAMERA WITH COLLISION

As the title says, this section is about how to implement a third-person camera with collision. Once again, you will use the ball as the main character in your scene. In this section's tutorial, you will learn how to implement a camera that orbits around the player and that is aware of the environment around it. To do this, you will use a Bullet collision ray to detect if something stands between the camera and the ball.

With the knowledge that you will gather in this section on how to use collision ray, this will give you the opportunity to create more complex collision detection for your cameras. This will allow you to create more complex behaviors for your own applications. So, let's get started.

First, duplicate the project `template_chapter7-6` directory and rename it **chapter7-6**.

The template is using the same touche code that you used in `chapter7-4` (where half of the screen is used for moving the camera, and the other half is used to control the view), and the rest of the code is similar to `chapter7-5`.

In addition, for this tutorial, you will again use `GFX_look_at` instead of Euler angles, just to make things easier to understand. Before getting started, make sure that you review the code (inside `templateApp.cpp`).Once you've done that, follow these steps to implement a complete third-person camera tracking system with collision:

1.  At the beginning of the `templateApp.cpp`, right after the `OBJMESH *player` declaration code, insert the following global variables:

    ```
    /* Variable that you are going to use to interpolate the current eye
    position to the next. */
    vec3 next_eye;
        /* The camera rotation on the X axis, with a default value of -165. */
    float rotx = -165.0f,
        /* To interpolate the camera rotation X. At initialization, give it
    the same value as the initial X rotation. */
        next_rotx  = rotx,
        /* Similar to the rotx variable, but for the Z axis rotation. */
        rotz       = 180.0f,
        next_rotz  = rotz,
        /* The camera will orbit around the player (the 3D ball).
    This variable determines the default distance the eye should be from the
    object (assuming there is no collision with the walls). */
        distance   = -5.0f;
    ```

2.  On the line just above the `templateAppDraw` function callback, add the following code to create a modified version of the default `btCollisionWorld::ClosestRayResultCallback` class. This new version will allow you to pass in parameter a `btRigidBody` pointer on top of the two points that form the line of the collision ray. Then when the ray is executed, if the

object that the ray collides with is the same as the rigid body that you specify to the class, it will simply ignore it, and the ray will continue trying to collide with something else.

```
class ClosestNotMeRayResultCallback:public
btCollisionWorld::ClosestRayResultCallback {
    public:
        ClosestNotMeRayResultCallback(
        btRigidBody *rb,
        const btVector3 &p1,
        const btVector3 &p2 ) :
        btCollisionWorld::ClosestRayResultCallback( p1, p2 ) {
        m_btRigidBody = rb; }

    virtual btScalar addSingleResult(
        btCollisionWorld::
        LocalRayResult &localray,
        bool normalinworldspace ) {
            if( localray.m_collisionObject == m_btRigidBody )
            { return 1.0f; }
            return ClosestRayResultCallback::addSingleResult(
            localray, normalinworldspace );
        }

    protected:
        btRigidBody *m_btRigidBody;
};
```

In this implementation, you will be casting a ray from the player object to the eye position to be able to determine if a wall (or something else) is blocking the way. Of course, the first object that the ray is going to collide with is the player. For this specific case, you have no choice but to customize the default Bullet collision ray callback and re-implement your own version of it (the preceding code) to be able to omit a certain rigid body as explained in this step. Make sure that you fully understand this technique, because it can be used in many other ways and in different variations.

**3.** Inside the `templateAppDraw` function code, right after the `GFX_load_identity`, insert the following code block to handle the rotation of the X and Z axis based on the user movements:

```
/* First check if the direction vector on the X or Y axis was triggered
from the user touche on the right side of the screen. */
if( view_delta.x || view_delta.y ) {
    /* If the Y is active (!=0), then add the value to the next Z
rotation. Since you are going to interpolate the rotation, you have to
assign the value to the next camera Z rotation. */
    if( view_delta.y ) next_rotz -= view_delta.y;
    /* Same as above, but this time for the X rotation axis. In addition,
clamp the value in the range of -180 to -90 degrees to allow the camera to
only look from straight up to straight down. */
    if( view_delta.x ) {
        next_rotx -= view_delta.x;
        next_rotx = CLAMP( next_rotx, -180.0f, -90.0f );
    }
```

```
      /* Reset the view deltas to avoid triggering another pass inside this
block on the next rendering pass. */
      view_delta.x =
      view_delta.y = 0.0f;
   }
```

**4.** Now, add the following code right where you left off in step 3 to be able to handle the movement coming from the left side of the screen. This will also involve rotating the coordinate system to fit the current Z rotation of the camera, as you did previously.

```
   /* If you got a force coming from the left side of the screen. */
   if( move_delta.z ) {
      /* Temp. variable to calculate the direction (aka forward) vector. */
      vec3 direction;
      /* Rotate the coordinate system to fit the current Z rotation
of the camera. */
      float r = rotz * DEG_TO_RAD,
            c = cosf( r ),
            s = sinf( r );
      direction.x = c * move_delta.y - s * move_delta.x;
      direction.y = s * move_delta.y + c * move_delta.x;
      /* Assign the direction vector to the angular velocity of the ball. */
      player->btrigidbody->setAngularVelocity(
      btVector3( direction.y * ( move_delta.z * 6.7f ),
                -direction.x * ( move_delta.z * 6.7f ),
                 0.0f ) );
      /* Make sure the state of the rigid body is active in order to
trigger the rotation. */
      player->btrigidbody->setActivationState( ACTIVE_TAG );
   }
```

**5.** Integrate the following code where you left off in step 4 to calculate the next eye position and make the camera orbit around the ball based on the X (rotx) and Z (rotz) rotations and the distance parameter specified at the top of the file:

```
   next_eye.x = player->location.x +
                distance *
                cosf( rotx * DEG_TO_RAD ) *
                sinf( rotz * DEG_TO_RAD );

   next_eye.y = player->location.y -
                distance *
                cosf( rotx * DEG_TO_RAD ) *
                cosf( rotz * DEG_TO_RAD );

   next_eye.z = player->location.z +
                distance *
                sinf( rotx * DEG_TO_RAD );
```

**6.** At this point, you have calculated the next eye position where the camera is going to interpolate to. But before integrating the interpolation code, you have to first determine if the camera can really go there. It is time to use a collision ray to ensure that the `next_eye` position is not ending up behind a wall or one of the pillars:

```
/* Declare the starting point and end point of the collision ray.
Basically what you are trying to achieve is that the ray starts from the
ball and aims straight at the next_eye position. If anything collides with
the ray (with the exception of the ball), you need to re-adjust the
next_eye position to be located where there is a hit. This will prevent the
camera from seeing through the walls and insure that the ball is focused at
all times. */

    btVector3 p1( player->location.x,
                  player->location.y,
                  player->location.z ),

            p2( next_eye.x,
                next_eye.y,
                next_eye.z );
/* Initialize the collision ray, passing in as parameters the ball rigid
body pointer and the start and end points of the ray. */
    ClosestNotMeRayResultCallback back_ray( player->btrigidbody,
                                            p1,
                                            p2 );
/* Launch the ray in 3D space. */
dynamicsworld->rayTest( p1,
                        p2,
                        back_ray );
/* If the collision ray got a hit. */
if( back_ray.hasHit() ) {
    /* Normalize the hit point normal. */
    back_ray.m_hitNormalWorld.normalize();
    /* Adjust the next_eye position to be located where the collision ray
hits inside the world. In addition, to make sure that the camera stays
inside the scene and does not simply "stick" on the wall, add a slight
offset based on the hit point normal. This will ensure that the camera
next_position will always be located in front of where the collision ray
hits. */
    next_eye.x =    back_ray.m_hitPointWorld.x() +
                    ( back_ray.m_hitNormalWorld.x() * 0.1f );
    next_eye.y =    back_ray.m_hitPointWorld.y() +
                    ( back_ray.m_hitNormalWorld.y()* 0.1f );
    next_eye.z =    back_ray.m_hitPointWorld.z() +
                    ( back_ray.m_hitNormalWorld.z()* 0.1f );
}
```

**7.** Now add the following code to interpolate the rotation and the position of the camera:

```
/* Linearly interpolate the rotation between the current and the next. */
rotx = rotx * 0.9f + next_rotx * 0.1f;
rotz = rotz * 0.9f + next_rotz * 0.1f;

/* Same as for the rotation, but this time for the current eye position
and the next. */
```

```
eye.x = eye.x * 0.95f + next_eye.x * 0.05f;
eye.y = eye.y * 0.95f + next_eye.y * 0.05f;
eye.z = eye.z * 0.95f + next_eye.z * 0.05f;

/* Give an offset to the player Z location to make sure that the camera
is always looking at the top of the ball and not at its center. This way,
even in tight corners, the user will always be able to see in front of the
ball. */
player->location.z += player->dimension.z * 0.5f;

/* Feed the current eye position and player location to the GFX_look_at
function to be able to generate the view matrix. */
GFX_look_at( &eye,
             &player->location,
             &up );
```

Build and run the program. You should now have something similar to Figure 7-6 running on your screen.

To interact with the ball, simply use the left side of the screen as you would normally do with an analog stick to make the ball roll in the direction the camera is looking at. And to adjust the rotation of the camera around the sphere, simply swipe your finger in any direction on the right side of the screen.

**FIGURE 7-6:** Third-person 3D camera with collision

## SUMMARY

This chapter covered five different types of cameras. You now have the ability to integrate serious first- and third-person camera interactions inside your apps using the touch screen.

You can now orbit, rotate direction vectors, and cast 3D collision rays inside any type of scene. In addition, you learned about frustum clipping, and can now determine the visibility of your objects inside the camera view. This knowledge will also allow you to create more complex and/or customized clipping systems that fit your particular needs and requirements.

Once again, a lot of material was covered in this chapter, so make sure that you review and understand all of the code implemented in this chapter and its exercises. You will reuse most of this as you proceed through the rest of this book.

In the next chapter, you'll learn about pathfinding.

# 8

# Pathfinding

From first-person shooter to point-and-click, pathfinding plays an important role in navigating levels and for artificial intelligence. Pathfinding allows your characters to move to a specific location by themselves, while avoiding obstacles. You can also use it to enable an NPC (non-player character) to find the player inside a scene, and a lot more.

## RECAST AND DETOUR

In this chapter, you will be studying the Recast and Detour libraries. As a quick introduction, Recast is a state-of-the-art library that allows you to construct a navigation mesh from an arbitrary geometry, or a set of different geometries. And the Detour library supports dynamic navigation tiles, crow simulation, ray casting, and dynamic obstacles that can be generated at run time, as well as many other goodies, based on the navigation mesh created by Recast.

More information on Recast and Detour can be found at `http://code.google.com/p/`
`recastnavigation/`, where you can download the latest source code, SDK, and demo app
(as shown in Figure 8-1) from SVN.

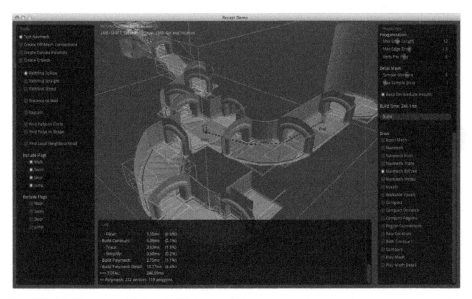

**FIGURE 8-1:** Recast and Detour SDK demo app

A navigation mesh is very similar to a collision map. It's a low-resolution model of the boundaries
where the player or NPC can and cannot go. Inside your games, you can either choose to create two
models (one for the collision map and one for the navigation mesh) or simply reuse the same model
if appropriate.

Once you have a navigation mesh created, you can use the Detour library, which offers pathfinding
and spatial reasoning functions. The library will then allow you to pass a start and end point, and it
will return all the way points to get there, or as close as possible to your destination.

Time to start coding and explore how to implement all of this within your apps!

## NAVIGATION

Duplicate the `template_chapter8`
project from the root of the SDK
and rename it **chapter8-1**. Take a
look at the source code inside the
`templateApp.cpp` and launch the
program to visualize what the result
looks like. Your screen should display
something similar to Figure 8-2.

**FIGURE 8-2:** The maze

As you can see, you have a maze with physics loaded. If you swipe your finger up, down, left, and right, you can control how the camera orbits around the maze. In addition, please take note that, as usual, all the assets for this chapter can be found in the SDK/data/ directory.

## CREATING THE NAVIGATION MESH

The goal of this first implementation is to build the navigation mesh. For this demo, you will be using the triangle mesh collision shape that forms the maze as the navigation mesh.

To create the navigation mesh, follow these steps:

**1.** Declare the following global variables at the top of the templateApp.cpp on the next line after the #include:

```
/* The player object (the blue arrow). */
OBJMESH *player = NULL;
/* The maze itself. */
OBJMESH *maze = NULL;
/* This is an easy-to-use structure that wraps up the Recast and Detour
low-level API into one object that can create a navigation mesh and that
you can use to query way points. The code is located inside the
navigation.cpp/.h file, which is inside the /common directory of the SDK.
The implementation is a bit too big to cover in detail in this chapter, so
the focus will just be on the code implementation and the usage of this
structure. */
NAVIGATION *navigation = NULL;
```

**2.** Inside the templateAppInit function callback, right after the start bracket of the first while loop, insert the following code to adjust parameters for the agent (the player that will be navigating the maze), and then build the navigation mesh for the maze:

```
/* If the current mesh is the maze. */
if( strstr( obj->objmesh[ i ].name, "maze" ) ) {
    /* Initialize the NAVIGATION structure. */
    navigation = NAVIGATION_init( ( char * )"maze" );

    /* Set up the height of the player, which is basically the same
as the Z dimension of the player. */
    navigation->navigationconfiguration.agent_height = 2.0f;

    /* Set up the radius of the player (the X dimension of the player
divided by 2). The configuration parameters are really important, because
the navigation mesh will be built according to these settings. More tweaks
can be made by accessing the navigation->navigationconfiguration parameters
to fit your needs. */
    navigation->navigationconfiguration.agent_radius = 0.4f;

    /* Build the navigation mesh. The function will return 1 if successful
or 0 if not. If the generation fails, it might be because the scene is too
small for the agent, or if there are no triangles that can be used. Always
make sure that you call this function before building or optimizing the
```

```
mesh. */
    if( NAVIGATION_build( navigation, obj, i ) )
    { console_print( "Navigation generated.\n"); }
    else
    { console_print( "Unable to create the navigation mesh." ); }
}
```

**3.** Still inside the `templateAppInit` function, right after the `load_physic_world` function call, insert the following code to be able to get the `OBJMESH` pointer for the maze and the player in order to set the player rigid body to be a dynamic object (no rolling physics):

```
/* Get the player mesh pointer. */
player = OBJ_get_mesh( obj, "player", 0 );
/* Set the player to be a dynamic rigid body. */
player->btrigidbody->setAngularFactor( 0.0f );
/* Get the maze object. */
maze = OBJ_get_mesh( obj, "maze", 0 );
/* Adjust the camera distance so it can frame the maze. */
distance = maze->radius * 2.0f;
```

**4.** Locate the `GFX_look_at` call inside the `templateAppDraw` function callback, and on the preceding line, add the following code to synchronize the camera eye to always look at the maze pivot point:

```
center.x = maze->location.x;
center.y = maze->location.y;
center.z = maze->location.z;
```

**5.** Inside the `templateAppExit`, right after the function start bracket, add the following line to free the navigation object from the memory when the program quits:

```
NAVIGATION_free( navigation );
```

**6.** Optionally (for debugging purposes), you can add the following command inside the `templateAppDraw` function on the line above the `dynamicsworld->stepSimulation` call. This will draw, using a semi-transparent blue, the resulting triangles of the navigation mesh generation:

```
NAVIGATION_draw( navigation );
```

Now build and run the application and monitor the console (or LogCat) to make sure that the navigation mesh has been generated properly.

To visualize what you have just created, you can load the `maze.obj` inside the RecastDemo app (available within the Recast/Detour SDK) and build the navigation mesh using the same agent parameters that you set in step 2. The result will look similar to Figure 8-3.

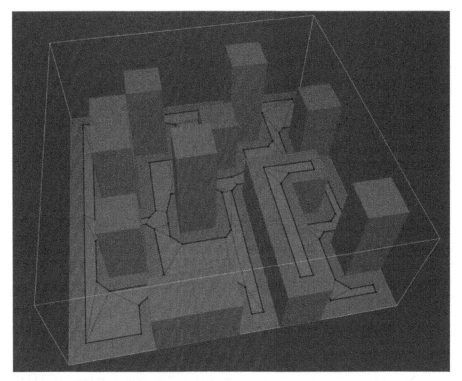

**FIGURE 8-3:** The maze navigation mesh

All areas delimited by the black contour on the ground are areas that the agent can walk on. You now have the collision mesh and the navigation mesh ready, so you can make the player walk on the surface. All you have to do is to query Detour about where the player is and where it should go, but in order to do this, you are going to need to be able to pick a position on the maze in 3D.

## 3D PHYSICS PICKING

In this section, you will learn how to pick a 3D point in space from your 2D screen. To do this, you will be implementing a collision ray, as you did in the previous chapter; however, this time you will be casting the ray from the current camera eye position to an arbitrary point on the far plane of the frustum.

To keep things clear, duplicate the chapter8-1 project and rename it **chapter8-2**. Then load the project inside your IDE and follow these steps:

**1.** At the top of templateApp.cpp on the next line after the #include, declare the following new global variable to be able to analyze when the user double-taps on the screen, which will give you the necessary trigger in order to cast the collision ray:

```
unsigned char double_tap = 0;
```

**2.** Also declare the following two variables that you will use for the pathfinding query and its resulting points (if any):

```
/* The navigation path query. This structure will be used to construct the
query to be processed by Detour. */
NAVIGATIONPATH navigationpath_player;
/* The result of the query. If this structure is successful, it will be
filled by the way points (along with other data) that form the path. */
NAVIGATIONPATHDATA navigationpathdata_player;
```

**3.** Now add the following line right after where you left off in step 2 to declare a 2 by 2 matrix of integers to store the current viewport matrix, as the picking code that you are about to implement needs to be aware of the screen dimension.

```
int viewport_matrix[ 4 ];
```

**4.** It's time to store the viewport matrix in the variable you created in the previous step with the current viewport position and dimension. On the line right after the glViewport call inside the templateAppInit function callback, insert the following code to query the viewport matrix directly from GLES:

```
/* Query OpenGLES to return the current viewport matrix (which is
basically set with the glViewport command). */
    glGetIntegerv( GL_VIEWPORT, viewport_matrix );
```

**5.** At the top of the templateAppToucheBegan, right after the function start bracket, add the following code to handle the double-tap trigger:

```
/* Check if the screen received a double-tap. */
if( tap_count == 2 ) double_tap = 1;
```

**6.** Now back to the render function. On the line after the GFX_look_at function call, insert the following code to effectuate 3D picking on the maze collision object. (This is a large chunk of code, so pay close attention to the code comments.)

```
if( double_tap ) {
    /* Variable to hold the 3D location on the far plane of the frustum. */
    vec3 location;
    /* This function converts a 2D point from the screen coordinates
to a 3D point in space. The return value is 1 or 0, depending on
whether or not the query is successful. It's a GFX helper, but built
basically the same way as the standard gluUnproject
(http://www.opengl.org/sdk/docs/man/xhtml/gluUnProject.xml) function. */
    if( GFX_unproject(
        /* The X coordinate on screen. */
        view_location.x,
        /* The origin of the OpenGLES color buffer is down left, but its
location for iOS and Android is up left. To handle this situation, simply
use the viewport matrix height data (viewport_matrix[ 3 ]) to readjust the
Y location of the picking point onscreen. */
        viewport_matrix[ 3 ] - view_location.y,
        /* This parameter represents the depth that you want to query, with
```

1 representing the far clipping plane and 0 representing the near clipping plane. In this case, you are only interested in the far clipping plane value, which explains the value 1. */

```
    1.0f,
    /* The current model view matrix of the camera. */
    GFX_get_modelview_matrix(),
    /* The current projection matrix of the camera. */
    GFX_get_projection_matrix(),
    /* The current viewport matrix. */
    viewport_matrix,
    /* If the query is successful, the result will be stored in
location.xyz, which will represent the point on the far plane. */
    &location.x,
    &location.y,
    &location.z  ) ) {
    /* Now that you have the XYZ location on the far plane, you can
create the collision ray. Begin by creating the starting point, which is
basically the current camera eye position. */
    btVector3 ray_from( eye.x,
                        eye.y,
                        eye.z ),
                /* Translate the resulting location of GFX_unproject based
on the current eye location to make sure that the coordinate system will
fit with what the player currently sees onscreen. */
                ray_to( location.x + eye.x,
                        location.y + eye.y,
                        location.z + eye.z );
    /* Create the collision ray. */
    btCollisionWorld::ClosestRayResultCallback
    collision_ray( ray_from,
                   ray_to );
    /* Launch the ray in space. */
    dynamicsworld->rayTest( ray_from,
                            ray_to,
                            collision_ray );
    /* Check if the collision ray gets a hit, and check if the collision
object involved is the maze btRigidBody. */
    if( collision_ray.hasHit() &&
        collision_ray.m_collisionObject ==
        maze->btrigidbody ) {
        /* Normalize the world normal. */
        collision_ray.m_hitNormalWorld.normalize();
        /* Check if the normal Z is pointing upward to make sure the hit
is on the floor of the maze. */
        if( collision_ray.m_hitNormalWorld.z() == 1.0f ) {
            /* Since you got a valid hit, it is time to create the
pathfinding query to send to Detour. First, assign the current player
location as the starting point of the query. */
            navigationpath_player.start_location.x =
            player->location.x;
            navigationpath_player.start_location.y =
            player->location.y;
            navigationpath_player.start_location.z =
            player->location.z;
```

```
                    /* Then simply use the collision ray hit position XYZ as the
        end point of the path query. */
                    navigationpath_player.end_location.x =
                    collision_ray.m_hitPointWorld.x();
                    navigationpath_player.end_location.y =
                    collision_ray.m_hitPointWorld.y();
                    navigationpath_player.end_location.z =
                    collision_ray.m_hitPointWorld.z();
                    /* The query is ready to be sent to Detour, so send it over.
        If Detour was able to find a path, the function will return 1 and will
        store the way points information inside the navigationpathdata_player
        variable; otherwise, the function will return 0. */
                    if( NAVIGATION_get_path(
                      navigation,
                      &navigationpath_player,
                      &navigationpathdata_player ) ) {
                    /* Simple counter to loop through the way points. */
                    unsigned int i = 0;
                    /* Loop while you've got some way points. Please note that
        by default, the function will assign the number of path_point_count to be
        the way points returned by Detour. However, the function implementation
        added another point which is the exact same end location that you specified
        in your query. The reason is that, most of the time, the ending point is
        not exactly on the navigation mesh, so the library will return the closest
        point. Depending on what you want to achieve, you may or may not want to
        use this extra way point. But for this tutorial, you are going to take it
        into consideration. */
                        while( i !=
                        navigationpathdata_player.path_point_count + 1 ) {
                          /* Print the way points' XYZ coordinates on the console. */
                          console_print(
                          "%d: %f %f %f\n",
                          i,
                          navigationpathdata_player.path_point_array[ i ].x,
                          navigationpathdata_player.path_point_array[ i ].y,
                          navigationpathdata_player.path_point_array[ i ].z );
                          /* Next way point please... */
                          ++i;
                        }
                        console_print( "\n" );
                    }
                }
            }
        }
        /* Disable the double-tap flag. */
        double_tap = 0;
    }
```

7. The final step before testing your app is to increase the value of the far plane. Since GFX_unproject requires you to pass a ratio from 0 to 1 for the far plane (the winz parameter from the function definition), the higher the clip_end value that is passed to the GFX_set_perspective function, the more precise the picking will be. For this step, all you have to do is simply find the GFX_set_perspective call inside the templateAppInit, and modify the clip end parameter from 100.0f to **1000.0f**.

Now build and run the app. Once the app is loaded onto your device or simulator, double-tap anywhere on the walkable area of the maze and monitor the console.

# PLAYER'S AUTO DRIVE

What you have been doing so far is all great, but it doesn't really have any visual impact. In this section, you will be using the Bullet physics API to implement the necessary code to be able to make the player follow the way points automatically (player's auto drive).

Start by duplicating the chapter8-2 project directory and rename it **chapter8-3**. Then follow these steps:

**1.** At the top of the templateApp.cpp source file, declare the following variable to be able to track the way point that the player is moving towards (if any):

```
int player_next_point = -1;
```

**2.** On the line before the templateAppDraw function declaration, insert the following function code to be able to move an arbitrary entity in space based on the current data held in a NAVIGATIONPATHDATA structure:

```
void move_entity( OBJMESH *objmesh,
                  NAVIGATIONPATHDATA *navigationpathdata,
                  int *next_point,
                  float speed ) {
    /* Set the Z location of the mesh to be 0. (You are only interested in
    the X and Y position to compute the forward direction vector.) */
    objmesh->location.z =
    navigationpathdata->path_point_array[ *next_point ].z = 0.0f;
    /* Calculate the distance between the mesh location and the way point. */
    float distance =
    vec3_dist( &objmesh->location,
               &navigationpathdata->path_point_array[ *next_point ] );
    /* If the distance is less than 10cm, it means that the mesh is close
    enough to its destination and the next index should be incremented to the
    next way point. */
    if( distance < 0.1f ) {
        ++*next_point;
        /* If the next_point is equal to the path point pointer +1
    (the end location), it means that the mesh has reached its
    destination. Set the next_point back to -1 to stop the movement. */
        if( *next_point ==
            ( navigationpathdata->path_point_count + 1 ) ) {
            *next_point = -1;
        }
    }
    /* If the next point is not -1, it means that the mesh is on the move. */
    if( *next_point != -1 ) {
        /* Variable to calculate the direction vector from the mesh to the
    way point. */
        vec3 direction;
        /* Calculate the forward direction vector. */
        vec3_diff( &direction,
```

```
                        &navigationpathdata->path_point_array[ *next_point ],
                        &objmesh->location );
            /* Normalize it. */
            vec3_normalize( &direction,
                        &direction );
            /* Assign the direction vector to the linear velocity of the rigid
    body pointer attached to the mesh multiplied by the speed passed in
    parameter to this function. */
            objmesh->btrigidbody->setLinearVelocity(
            btVector3( direction.x * speed,
                        direction.y * speed,
                        0.0f ) );
            /* Activate the rigid body so the linear velocity will be affected. */
            objmesh->btrigidbody->setActivationState( ACTIVE_TAG );
        }
        /* The next_point value is -1, which means that the mesh should stop
    moving. To do this, simply specify that the rigid body wants deactivation,
    and to keep things clean, reset the number of way points. */
        else {
            objmesh->btrigidbody->setActivationState( WANTS_DEACTIVATION );
            navigationpathdata->path_point_count = 0;
        }
    }
```

**3.** Right after the start bracket of the `if( NAVIGATION_get_path` clause, add the following line to specify that when a valid path is found, the player should move to the first way point (since point 0 is basically its current location):

```
player_next_point = 1;
```

**4.** On the line before the `PROGRAM_draw` call, add the following code block to call the `move_entity` function to make the player follow the way points (if any):

```
    if( navigationpathdata_player.path_point_count ) {
        move_entity(
        /* The player OBJMESH pointer. */
        player,
        /* The player navigation path data structure. */
        &navigationpathdata_player,
        /* The way point the player is moving towards. */
        &player_next_point,
        /* The speed to use as factor to the linear velocity of the
    btRigidBody. */
        3.0f );
    }
```

Now build and run the program. Once the program is loaded, tap anywhere on the screen over the "walkable" area of the maze to specify a destination where you want the player (the blue arrow) to move to. As soon as a valid path is found, the player starts moving towards it until the end location is reached, as demonstrated in Figure 8-4.

**FIGURE 8-4:** The player is on the move, following the way points.

# VISUALIZING THE WAY POINTS

At the moment, the navigation is not very complex, and everything is pretty straightforward. However, as soon as you start implementing more entities and want to add artificial intelligence to them, it becomes very hard to see where the entities are going and on which path they are moving along. In addition, if something goes wrong with your code, you will need to be able to visualize what is happening for debugging purposes.

To visualize what's going on, what I personally like to do is draw points and lines to show the current path that the entity is following, and print them onscreen using a texture-based bitmap font.

In this section, I will cover the drawing of the lines and points, and in the next section, I'll describe how to use a True Type Font (.ttf) file that is loaded at run time. However, printing debug information onscreen will be left to you as an extra exercise for this chapter.

In this exercise, you'll implement the debug drawing of the way points. To begin, duplicate the chapter8-3 project directory and rename it **chapter8-4**. Then follow these steps:

**1.** Declare the following new shader program variable at the top of the file:

```
PROGRAM *path_point = NULL;
```

**2.** Link to your project the point_frag.glsl and point_vert.glsl files located inside the SDK/data/chapter8-4 directory. Drawing points and lines is basically the same as drawing any other type of primitive. The only exception is that you will have to specify the size of the point inside the vertex shader like this:

```
gl_PointSize = 5.0;
```

**3.** Now back to templateApp.cpp. On the line before the move_entity function declaration, add the following code to create a new function to handle drawing the way points for a specific NAVIGATIONPATHDATA pointer:

```
void draw_navigation_points( NAVIGATIONPATHDATA *navigationpathdata,
                             vec3 *color ) {
   /* Adjust the Z location of all points to make it easier to see them on
the floor of the maze. */
   unsigned int i = 0;
   while( i != navigationpathdata->path_point_count + 1 ) {
      navigationpathdata->path_point_array[ i ].z = 1.0f;
      ++i;
   }
   /* Reset the VAO and VBO indexes since you are about to draw using
glDrawArrays. The data is always dynamic, so there's no need to create a
VBO and VAO for this. */
   glBindVertexArrayOES( 0 );
   glBindBuffer( GL_ARRAY_BUFFER, 0 );
   /* Enable alpha blending just to get fancy. */
   glEnable( GL_BLEND );
   glBlendFunc( GL_SRC_ALPHA, GL_ONE_MINUS_SRC_ALPHA );
   /* If the path_point shader program does not exist, simply create it
when it's the first time the execution pointer reaches this location. */
```

```
        if( !path_point ) {
            path_point = PROGRAM_create(
                         ( char * )"path_point",
                         ( char * )"point_vert.glsl",
                         ( char * )"point_frag.glsl",
                         1,
                         0,
                         program_bind_attrib_location,
                         NULL );
        }
        /* Set the shader program for drawing. */
        PROGRAM_draw( path_point );
        /* Send the current model view multiplied by the projection matrix to
    the shader. */
        glUniformMatrix4fv(
        PROGRAM_get_uniform_location(
        path_point,
        ( char * )"MODELVIEWPROJECTIONMATRIX" ),
        1,
        GL_FALSE,
        ( float * )GFX_get_modelview_projection_matrix() );
        /* Send the RGB colors that were sent to the function to the shader. */
        glUniform3fv(
        PROGRAM_get_uniform_location(
        path_point,
        ( char * )"COLOR" ),
        1,
        ( float * )color );
        /* Make sure that the first vertex attribute is ON, because you are
    going to use it to pass the way points data. */
        glEnableVertexAttribArray( 0 );

        glVertexAttribPointer( 0,
                               3,
                               GL_FLOAT,
                               GL_FALSE,
                               0,
                               navigationpathdata->path_point_array );
        /* Draw each point individually. */
        glDrawArrays( GL_POINTS,
                      0,
                      navigationpathdata->path_point_count + 1 );
        /* Draw a line that connects the points. */
        glDrawArrays( GL_LINE_STRIP,
                      0,
                      navigationpathdata->path_point_count + 1 );
        /* Disable blending. */
        glDisable( GL_BLEND );
    }
```

4. Inside the `templateAppDraw` function, just before you call `move_entity`, add the following code to draw the path while the player is moving (in other words, when the `path_point_count` is not 0):

```
vec3 color = { 0.0f, 0.0f, 1.0f };
draw_navigation_points( &navigationpathdata_player, &color );
```

**5.** Add the following lines inside the `templateAppExit` function to clean up the `path_point` shader:

```
if( path_point ) {
    SHADER_free( path_point->vertex_shader );
    SHADER_free( path_point->fragment_shader );
    PROGRAM_free( path_point );
    path_point = NULL;
}
```

**6.** Now compile and execute the program. Once the program is loaded, double-tap anywhere on the screen to trigger the computation of a navigation path.

You can now follow and visualize in real time the path of the player and the way points that it's following, just like in Figure 8-5.

**FIGURE 8-5:** Way points visualization

## CATCH ME IF YOU CAN!

In this section, you'll apply the navigation and pathfinding knowledge that you've gathered so far to implement a simple, yet quite addictive mini game. The goal of the game is to escape an NPC (a red arrow) that is running faster than the player (the blue arrow) inside the maze. The player needs to find the fastest way to escape and double-tap on the screen to set a new course.

The NPC will be driven automatically along a navigation path that will be regenerated at a regular pace at run time, always aiming at the player's current location.

If the NPC catches the player, the game is over (see Figure 8-6). To restart the game, the player just needs to double-tap the screen.

**FIGURE 8-6:** Catch Me If You Can mini game

In addition, while implementing the game, you will learn how to load a True Type Font file (.ttf) using the FONT structure that is included in the SDK. This structure will allow you to generate at run time a smooth bitmap character texture that can then be used by the structure to print dynamic text onscreen.

Start by duplicating the `template_chapter8-5` project from the SDK. This template is basically the same as the `chapter8-4` project file that you worked with in the last section, except the `foo.ttf` font file from the `SDK/data` directory has been linked to it, and the assets have been updated with the ones located inside the `SDK/data/chapter8-5` directory. Now rename the duplicated folder **chapter8-5**, and then load the project into your IDE.

Have an initial run at the program. As you can see, there is now another arrow located on the red square. This arrow will be the enemy that will be chasing the player inside the maze.

Now follow these steps to start implementing the game:

1. Before starting with the main core code, you need to declare the following variables for this exercise:

```
/* The font structure to load and use the TTF file inside your app. */
FONT *font = NULL;
/* Pointer to the OBJMESH structure for the "enemy" object. */
OBJMESH *enemy = NULL;
/* The navigation path query for the enemy. */
NAVIGATIONPATH navigationpath_enemy;
/* The navigation path data for the enemy, where the way points are going
to be stored after a successful navigation query to Detour. */
NAVIGATIONPATHDATA navigationpathdata_enemy;
/* Variable to handle the next navigation point of the enemy. */
int enemy_next_point = -1;
/* Flag to handle the game_over state. */
unsigned char game_over = 0;
```

2. On the line before the `templateAppInit` function callback declaration, insert the following near collision callback function:

```
void near_callback( btBroadphasePair &btbroadphasepair,
                    btCollisionDispatcher  &btdispatcher,
                    const btDispatcherInfo &btdispatcherinfo ) {
    /* Check if the near callback collision object involves the player and
the enemy. */
    if( ( player->btrigidbody ==
          btbroadphasepair.m_pProxy0->m_clientObject ||
          player->btrigidbody ==
          btbroadphasepair.m_pProxy1->m_clientObject )
        &&
        ( enemy->btrigidbody ==
          btbroadphasepair.m_pProxy0->m_clientObject ||
          enemy->btrigidbody ==
          btbroadphasepair.m_pProxy1->m_clientObject ) ) {
        /* If the previous is true, simply toggle the game over flag ON. */
        game_over = 1;
    }
    btdispatcher.defaultNearCallback( btbroadphasepair,
                                      btdispatcher,
                                      btdispatcherinfo );
}
```

3. On the line before the `templateAppInit` function callback declaration, create the following new function:

```
/* Function to load/reload the game. */
void load_game( void )
{

}
```

**4.** Select the code inside the `templateAppInit` function, starting from `obj = OBJ_load` all the way down before the end bracket of the function. Then cut it into your clipboard and paste it right after the start bracket of the `load_game` function that you just created.

**5.** It's time to do some tweaking inside the `load_game` function. On the line right after you call `load_physic_world`, insert the following code block to set the near callback, retrieve the enemy object pointer, set it as a dynamic object, and reset the paths and next point index of both the player and the enemy. With this code, the function can be called over and over, and it will always reset all of the game states.

```
/* Set the near callback. */
dispatcher->setNearCallback( near_callback );
/* Retrieve the enemy OBJMESH pointer. */
enemy = OBJ_get_mesh( obj, "enemy", 0 );
/* Set the rigid body to not respond to rolling physics. */
enemy->btrigidbody->setAngularFactor( 0.0f );
/* Set both the player and enemy path_point_count to 0. */
navigationpathdata_player.path_point_count =
navigationpathdata_enemy.path_point_count  = 0;
/* Reset the next point index back to -1. */
player_next_point =
enemy_next_point  = -1;
```

**6.** To make sure the game starts right away, add the following line before the end bracket of the `templateAppInit` function:

```
load_game();
```

You now have the base structure of the game. In the following sections, you will adjust, tweak, and add code to this current structure to turn it into a playable game.

## KNOW YOUR ENEMY

It's time to integrate some bits of intelligence inside the game. This section will teach you how to integrate the necessary code to have the NPC chase the player inside the maze. To keep things simple, you'll just generate a new path where the end location is the current player's location, so the NPC can start chasing it.

The first thing you have to do is trigger a new navigation path at a regular interval. Then, you use the same mechanism that you learned in previous sections to control the player to follow the way points, and use the structures associated with the enemy to execute the same routine to follow the way points to chase the player. The following steps will show you how to implement these actions:

**1.** Move to the `templateAppDraw` function, and on the line just before you call the `PROGRAM_draw` function, insert the following code to generate a new path for the enemy every second:

```
/* Declare a static variable to remember the time. */
static unsigned int start_time = get_milli_time();

/* If 1 second elapses, regenerate a new navigation path for the enemy.
Note that the function is dealing with milliseconds, so 1000 is equal to
```

```
1 second. */
   if( get_milli_time() - start_time > 1000 ) {

      /* Use the current enemy location as the starting point. */
      navigationpath_enemy.start_location.x = enemy->location.x;
      navigationpath_enemy.start_location.y = enemy->location.y;
      navigationpath_enemy.start_location.z = enemy->location.z;

      /* Use the current player location as the end point. */
      navigationpath_enemy.end_location.x = player->location.x;
      navigationpath_enemy.end_location.y = player->location.y;
      navigationpath_enemy.end_location.z = player->location.z;

      /* Send the query to Detour. */
      NAVIGATION_get_path( navigation,
                           &navigationpath_enemy,
                           &navigationpathdata_enemy );

      /* Specify that the next way point the enemy should follow is the first
   one inside the way points array. */
      enemy_next_point = 1;

      /* Remember the current time so you can trigger a new navigation path a
   second after. */
      start_time = get_milli_time();
   }
```

2.  Next comes the tricky part of the game: the enemy auto navigation. In order to be able to trigger the game_over state, the enemy obviously needs to go faster than the player (but not so much that the game won't be fun). Right after the code block you implemented in the previous step, add the following code to auto drive the enemy throughout the maze:

```
/* Make sure that the enemy has some way points generated. */
if( navigationpathdata_enemy.path_point_count ) {
/* Specify the color to use to draw the points and lines for the
enemy navigation path. */
   vec3 color = { 1.0f, 0.0f, 0.0f };
   /* Use the same function to drive the player, but this time, send over
the enemy data. */
   move_entity( enemy,
                &navigationpathdata_enemy,
                &enemy_next_point,
                /* Make the enemy go faster than the player. */
                4.0f );
/* Draw the navigation points of the enemy. */
draw_navigation_points( &navigationpathdata_enemy, &color );
}
```

To test what you have created, you can build and run the game. You will notice right from the start (or more specifically, one second after the game starts) that the enemy is going straight after the player. You can double-tap on any walkable area at any time after the game starts to set a new course to escape from the enemy. As you can see, the game play is accurate; however, if you get caught by the enemy, you will find that the game logic is incorrect. The way things stand now, when the enemy catches up with the player, the enemy will keep pushing the player away to a new location and regenerate a new path to continue the purchase, and this pattern will never end. In the next section, you'll learn how to integrate the "Game Over" logic, which will solve this problem.

## GAME STATE LOGIC

To fix the issue mentioned at the end of the previous section, you need to handle the necessary game logic states in code to tell the player that the game is over, and then, based on the player's input, restart the game.

Follow these steps to fix the game:

**1.** In `templateAppDraw`, on the line after the `glClear` function call, insert the following code block. This block will restart the game if the `game_over` state is equal to 2.

```
if( game_over == 2 ) {
/* Clean up the memory. */
templateAppExit();
/* Reload the game. */
load_game();
/* Reset the game_over state back to normal. */
game_over = 0;
}
```

**2.** In the `templateAppInit` function, select and cut this block:

```
GFX_set_matrix_mode( PROJECTION_MATRIX );
GFX_load_identity();
GFX_set_perspective( 80.0f,
                     ( float )width / ( float )height,
                     1.0f,
                     1000.0f,
                     -90.0f );
```

and paste it inside the `templateAppDraw` function just after the `glClear` call.

**3.** Since you are going to use the FONT structure to draw text onscreen, you need to have a projection matrix that fits the screen pixel ratio. So before drawing the 3D part of the scene, you need to make sure that the matrix is properly set to a 3D perspective view. To do this, in the code you just pasted in step 2, change the `width` to **viewport_matrix[ 2 ]** and height to **viewport_matrix[ 3 ]**.

**4.** Almost everything is in place to have the full game logic code implemented. This step will show you how to handle the `game_over` state when the player and the enemy collide, as well as how to use the FONT structure to print "Game Over!" on the screen. Still inside the `templateAppDraw`, delete the line where you call `dynamicsworld->stepSimulation` and replace it with the following code block:

```
/* If the game is NOT over, update the physics simulation. */
if( !game_over ) dynamicsworld->stepSimulation( 1.0f / 60.0f );

else {
    /* Select the projection matrix to set a perspective that fits the
```

screen pixel ratio (as you did in Chapter 2). You are about to draw text onscreen, which requires you to draw in pixels. */

```
GFX_set_matrix_mode( PROJECTION_MATRIX );
GFX_load_identity();
float half_width  =
        ( float )viewport_matrix[ 2 ] * 0.5f,
        half_height =
        ( float )viewport_matrix[ 3 ] * 0.5f;
GFX_set_orthographic_2d( -half_width,
                          half_width,
                          -half_height,
                          half_height );

/* Adjust the projection to fit the current device orientation. */
GFX_rotate( -90.0f, 0.0f, 0.0f, 1.0f );
GFX_translate( -half_height, -half_width, 0.0f );

/* Select the model view matrix. */
GFX_set_matrix_mode( MODELVIEW_MATRIX );
GFX_load_identity();
/* Start with a black color for the font. */
vec4 color = { 0.0f, 0.0f, 0.0f, 1.0f };
/* The message that you want to display on screen. */
char msg[ MAX_CHAR ] = {"GAME OVER!"};

/* If the font has not been initialized. */
if( !font ) {
    /* Initialize the FONT structure and give it the name foo.ttf, so
```
you can use the font name to load the font from disk on the next line. */
```
    font = FONT_init( ( char * )"foo.ttf" );
    /* Load the TTF file, re-using the font name as the file to load. */
    FONT_load( font,
               font->name,
               /* Specify that the path of the file is relative. */
               1,
               /* The font size in pixels. */
               64.0f,
               /* The width and height of the texture to use to
```
auto-generate the bitmap for the font. */
```
               512,
               512,
               /* The starting character ASCII. */
               32,
               /* Generate 96 characters from the starting ASCII.
```
By specifying 96, you have all the numbers as well as all lowercase and uppercase characters. */
```
               96 );
}
```

/* Pre-calculate the middle position of the screen on the X axis based on the current viewport matrix. In addition, use the FONT_length function to get the length in pixels of the text you are about to draw in order to be able to center it onscreen. */
```
float posx = ( viewport_matrix[ 3 ] * 0.5f ) -
```

```
                              ( FONT_length( font, msg ) * 0.5f ),
                      /* Offset the Y position down the top height of the screen. */
                      posy = viewport_matrix[ 2 ] - font->font_size;

              /* The font is now ready to be used for printing text onscreen.
        First draw the "Game Over" text in black, giving it a little offset of
        4 pixels on the X and Y axis. */
              FONT_print( font,
                          posx + 4.0f,
                          posy - 4.0f,
                          msg,
                          &color );
              /* Change the color to green, and draw the "Game Over" text again,
        right on top of the black text, but this time without an offset. This will
        make the text onscreen look like it has a shadow under it. */
              color.y = 1.0f;
              FONT_print( font,
                      posx,
                      posy,
                      msg,
                      &color );
        }
```

5. To free the font memory when the game exits, add the following code inside the `templateAppExit`:

```
        /* If the font pointer is initialized. */
        if( font ) {
        FONT_free( font );
        font = NULL;
        }
```

6. The final step is to restart the game based on the player's input. Inside the `templateAppToucheBegan` function, replace this line:

```
        if( tap_count == 2 ) double_tap = 1;
```

with the following code block to restart the game if the `game_over` state is ON:

```
        /* If you got a double-tap. */
        if( tap_count == 2 ) {
              /* Is the game_over flag ON? If yes, set the game_over state to 2
        so the render loop can trigger to reload the level. */
              if( game_over == 1 ) game_over = 2;
              /* Else, if the player wants to select a path on the maze,
        proceed as usual. */
              else double_tap = 1;
        }
```

Your mini game is ready to be played! Build and execute it on your device or simulator to get a feel for the player experience. In a few steps, you have successfully implemented a CPU-driven NPC character that responds to some very basic intelligence, but good enough to have the game up-and-running. This was the last tutorial for this chapter. I do have *a lot* more to say on the subject, but I'm unfortunately limited (page count–wise) to write more about it. You now have all the basics in hand to start implementing some *real* artificial intelligence using Bullet physics, Recast, and Detour.

## SUMMARY

In this chapter, you learned quite a lot of useful stuff that will make your games a lot more fun. You have received a quick overview of what Recast and Detour can do for you, and how to make them interact with GLES2 and the Bullet physics library.

You have also gathered enough knowledge to start implementing your own navigation system for your games. You also learned how to use a physical collision object for picking, so you can easily integrate and implement this behavior inside your apps.

As a bonus in this chapter, you've also discovered that you can mix different projection matrices to overlay 2D True Type Font–based text on top of your 3D scenes. This will allow you to print dynamically at run time any type of text and font that you want.

Make sure that you review each and every exercise of this section to fully grasp all the pathfinding and navigation possibilities that you have now. Also, make sure that you visit the Recast/Detour website and download the source code of the library demo so you can fully explore what these two libraries can offer you.

Now move on to the next chapter, where you will learn how to playback audio in real time as well as other miscellaneous rendering techniques.

# Audio and Other Cool Game Programming Stuff

## WHAT'S IN THIS CHAPTER?

➤   Learning how to use the low-level OpenAL APIs and the high-level audio APIs of this book's SDK

➤   Learning how to use the OGG Vorbis file format

➤   Handling ambient and positional sounds

➤   Decompressing an audio stream into another thread for real-time playback

➤   Handling an OpenAL listener and linking it to your camera

➤   Implementing and using color picking

➤   Linking shaders and dynamically loading a GFX shader file directly from an .mtl file

➤   Creating an accelerometer camera and player controls

➤   Animating textures and adding mist to hide the far clipping plane

This chapter mainly covers the audio aspect of your games. Since implementing audio is relatively short and easy, this chapter will walk the extra mile and introduce you to other useful techniques for your "daily game programming needs."

You will first discover how to initialize and use the low-level APIs of OpenAL. You will learn about the different types of sound sources and sound buffers, and will implement two basic, practical programs that will give you a good overview of the capabilities of OpenAL, using at first a raw sound file.

This chapter will also teach you how to create other thread(s) and use this separate process(es) to decompress in real time, sync, and queue multiple sound buffer chunks attached to a single sound source.

Moving on through this chapter, you will then crank it up by implementing a simple sound-based memory game using compressed audio sound buffers. This will give you the opportunity to learn how to work with the OGG Vorbis file format, as well as the audio APIs available in this book's SDK.

For this first game, you will also discover how to implement a new and universal picking method based directly on the color buffer. You can use this method in 2D, 2.5D, and 3D.

As you progress through the chapter, you will implement a second game, a rolling ball game. This tutorial will allow you to master using the accelerometer of your device to create new types of camera systems and player controls, and to gain full control over 3D positional sound sources.

This second game will also teach you how to link the OpenAL listener to your camera. This will allow you to provide real-time 3D positional sound feedback in stereo, and will allow you to create cooler and more realistic sound effects.

# OPENAL

OpenAL is a cross-platform 3D audio API built to be used in games and 3D applications.

On iOS, OpenAL is supported by default, so no extra work is required (with the exception of linking the framework to your project, of course).

For Android, you will have to compile OpenAL from source in order to be able to use the API functionalities. The version used on Android is slightly different in terms of licensing than the one on iOS. It is basically LGPL and has to be compiled as a shared object library if you plan to use it for commercial purposes. Make sure you read the OpenAL end user license agreement (SDK/eula/openal.txt) to make sure your app complies.

The way the OpenAL framework works is very simple and effective. It is built around a buffer and source approach: The buffer represents the audio data, and the source is the emitter. To be able to play a source, you'll have to link it to a buffer. Using this effective approach, one buffer can then be used by multiple sound sources.

Sound sources in games can be divided into two distinct groups: ambient and positional. The term *ambient* can be applied for sound sources that are always relative to the listener (which is most likely the camera in your scene), like background music.

The second type is called *positional*, and represents a source that has a 3D position in space and a relative distance (how far the sound can be heard). In other words, this type of sound source will get louder as the listener comes closer to it, and will progressively fade as the listener is moving away.

Once you've analyzed the first category of your sound source, you'll have to determine another subcategory to which it belongs. This subcategory is directly affected by the size in bytes of the raw (after decompression, if any) sound buffer, which will classify it as *in-memory* or *streamed.*

In-memory applies only if the raw sound buffer size is small enough. If it is only a few kilobytes (KB), the whole raw sound file can be stored in audio memory at initialization time, and reused throughout the application.

If the raw sound buffer size is larger than a few KB (as it typically is for background music, for example), the buffer will have to be streamed. In this case, you will have to decompress chunks of the buffer at run time (either in the main thread or in another thread) and then queue them for playback.

Once the source has played a chunk, you will need to refill it with data and send it back to the queue. This queuing process will have to continue until the end of the file is reached.

## OGG VORBIS

Raw (uncompressed) sound files are huge! As a result, it is recommended that you use some form of audio compression for your games and 3D apps.

Despite the popularity of the MP3 format, I personally don't recommend it. What most people don't know about this format is that it is patented, and if you are using it, you might have some legal issues.

For this book, you will work with the OGG Vorbis format (`http://www.vorbis.com`), which is very similar to MP3 in terms of compression ratio and quality. What is great about OGG is that it is fully open, nonproprietary, and patent- and royalty-free!

To edit and convert your existing sound files to the OGG Vorbis audio format, I recommend Audacity. Audacity is free, open source software for recording and editing sounds. Figure 9-1 shows the interface of this software. You can grab a copy of the software for your specific platform at `http://audacity.sourceforge.net`.

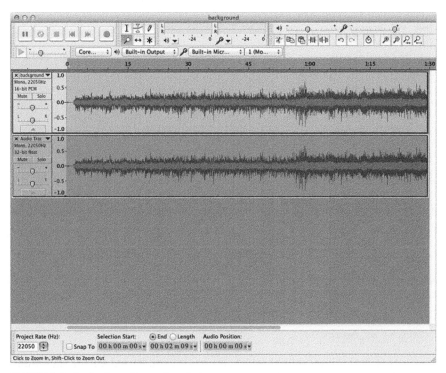

**FIGURE 9-1:** Audacity software interface

In Audacity, you can load almost all types of popular sound files and export them to the OGG Vorbis file format. You can then simply link your OGG files to your project as you normally do with any other type of asset.

## HELLO WORLD OPENAL STYLE

Now that you have a good overview of how OpenAL works, it's time to get your hands dirty and create a simple program using the low-level APIs of OpenAL.

## INITIALIZING OPENAL

Duplicate the `template` project from the SDK root directory, rename it **chapter9-1**, and then open the project in your IDE. Clean up all the source code comments and unnecessary functions in order to have a clean project to start working with (but keep `templateAppInit`, `templateAppDraw`, and `templateAppExit`). Then follow these steps:

**1.** At the top of the `templateApp.cpp`, declare the following global variables:

```
/* The hardware device to use with OpenAL. */
ALCdevice *al_device;
/* The OpenAL context. This context contains the global OpenAL
states and variables. This is also where the IDs for the sound
buffers and sound sources are maintained. */
ALCcontext *al_context;
```

**2.** At the end of the `templateAppInit`, right before the end bracket of the function, add the following code to initialize OpenAL:

```
/* Open the first valid device OpenAL finds and use it for playback. */
al_device = alcOpenDevice( NULL );
/* Create a vanilla OpenAL context (linking the device initialized above). */
al_context = alcCreateContext( al_device, NULL );
/* Activate the context you've just created and make it the current
context. */
alcMakeContextCurrent( al_context );
```

**3.** Insert the following code inside the `templateAppExit` function to uninitialize OpenAL properly:

```
/* Set a null context so the one you created in the previous step
can be destroyed. */
alcMakeContextCurrent( NULL );
/* Destroy the OpenAL context. */
alcDestroyContext( al_context );
/* Close the device. */
alcCloseDevice( al_device );
```

Build and run the application. If the application builds successfully, you have done the right thing. At the moment, OpenAL is fully initialized and ready for implementation.

# STATIC IN-MEMORY SOUND PLAYBACK

Time to make some noise! You will first load a raw uncompressed sound buffer, and then you'll attach it to a sound source for playback. This basic workflow has to be repeated for every sound that you want to play back inside you apps.

To test this approach, follow these steps:

**1.** Link to your project the `test.raw` file which is located inside the SDK/data/chapter9-1 directory. As the extension specifies, this is a raw sound file that has been saved from an uncompressed OGG. The file is a mono sound of 16 PCM (pulse-code modulation) that has a playback rate of 22050 Hz.

**2.** At the top of the `templateApp.cpp`, right after the `#include`, declare the following global variables to hold the sound buffer and sound source IDs:

```
ALuint soundbuffer;
ALuint soundsource;
```

**3.** At the end of the `templateAppInit` callback, on the line right before the end bracket of the function, add the following code block to create and load the sound buffer from disk:

```
/* Ask OpenAL to give you a valid ID for a new sound buffer. */
alGenBuffers( 1, &soundbuffer );
/* Load the raw sound file in memory. */
MEMORY *memory = mopen( ( char * )"test.raw", 1 );
/* Send over the content of the file to the audio memory. */
alBufferData( soundbuffer, /* The sound buffer ID. */
              /* Tell OpenAL that the sound file is mono and 16 PCM. */
              AL_FORMAT_MONO16,
              /* The complete sound file memory buffer. */
              memory->buffer,
              /* The total size of the sound buffer in bytes. */
              memory->size,
              /* The playback rate of the sound in Hz. */
              22050 );
/* Close and free the memory. At this point, the sound buffer data is
maintained by OpenAL and is stored in audio memory, so there's no need to
keep the buffer alive in local memory. */
memory = mclose( memory );
```

**4.** Right after the code that you added in step 3, add the following to generate a new sound source, link the buffer, and request OpenAL to start the playback:

```
/* Ask OpenAL to generate a new source ID. */
alGenSources( 1, &soundsource );
/* Attach the sound buffer ID to the sound source. This operation will tell
OpenAL that when the source is played, the data associated with the sound
buffer ID will be used. */
alSourcei( soundsource,
           AL_BUFFER,
           soundbuffer );
/* Play the sound buffer for the current sound source. */
alSourcePlay( soundsource );
```

**5.** Move to the `templateAppDraw` function callback and insert the following code block on the line before the end bracket to get visual feedback as long as the sound is playing:

```
/* Temp. variable to hold the state of the sound source. */
int state = 0;
/* Request OpenAL to give you the current state of the source. The result
will indicate if the source is currently playing, paused, or simply
stopped. */
alGetSourcei( soundsource, AL_SOURCE_STATE, &state );
/* If the sound is playing. */
if( state == AL_PLAYING ) {
   /* Set the clear color of the screen to green. */
   glClearColor( 0.0f, 1.0f, 0.0f, 1.0f );
   /* Declare a temporary variable to hold the current playback time. */
   float playback_time = 0.0f;
   /* Request the current offset in seconds for the current sound source. */
   alGetSourcef( soundsource,
                 AL_SEC_OFFSET,
                 &playback_time );
   /* Print the current playback time on the console. */
   console_print( "%f\n", playback_time ); }
else
   /* The sound stops playing; set the clear color to red. */
   glClearColor( 1.0f, 0.0f, 0.0f, 1.0 );
```

**6.** Right after the start bracket of the `templateAppExit` function, add the following two lines to delete the sound buffer and the sound source ID that you created earlier:

```
/* Delete the sound buffer and invalidate the ID. */
alDeleteBuffers( 1, &soundbuffer );
/* Delete the sound source and invalidate the ID. */
alDeleteSources( 1, &soundsource );
```

**7.** Before running the program on your device or simulator, make sure that the volume is at the top. Then simply build and run the program.

When the program starts, you can see right away that the screen stays green as long as the sound is playing. When the sound stops, the screen turns to red. You can also monitor in real time the current offset of the sound buffer in seconds from the console (Xcode) or LogCat (Eclipse).

Et voila! You've successfully initialized OpenAL, loaded a sound buffer and created a relative sound source that is playing sound in real time.

## POSITIONAL SOUND SOURCE

Duplicate the `chapter9-1` project directory and rename it **chapter9-2**. Then modify the code so that instead of creating a relative sound source, it creates a positional sound source in which the sound intensity is affected by distance and the listener's orientation. To do this, follow these steps:

1. To create a positional sound, you will first have to set the relative property of the sound source to false. To do this, simply add the following line just before the `alSourcePlay` function call:

   ```
   alSourcei( soundsource, AL_SOURCE_RELATIVE, AL_FALSE );
   ```

2. Because the source is not relative, you also have to specify the location and orientation of the listener. To do this, insert the following block of code inside your rendering loop, just before the end bracket of the `templateAppDraw` function callback:

   ```
   float orientation[ 6 ] =
     /* The direction vector the listener is looking at. */
   { 0.0f, 1.0f, 0.0f,
     /* The world up vector. */
     0.0f, 0.0f, 1.0f };
     /* Send the direction and up vector of the listener. In OpenAL terms,
   this is called the "listener orientation". */
     alListenerfv( AL_ORIENTATION, &orientation[ 0 ] );
     /* Specify the position of the listener in world space coordinates. */
     alListener3f( AL_POSITION,
                   0.0f,
                   0.0f,
                   0.0f );
   ```

3. By default, a sound source position is located at 0, 0, 0 in world coordinates. In order to hear the difference compared to the previous program, add the following code (right after the code you added in step 2) to dynamically move the sound source location in space:

   ```
   /* Static variable to make the sound source position go forward on the
   Y axis, away from the listener. */
   static float y = 0.0f;
   /* Assign the new position to the sound source. */
   alSource3f( soundsource, AL_POSITION, 0.0f, y, 0.0f );
   /* Increase the sound Y position. */
   y += 0.5f;
   ```

4. Compile and run the program.

   Once the program is loaded, you can clearly feel that the sound is moving away from you. Because the source is directly in front of the listener, both of the speakers (or the two head-phones) are playing the sound equally as it goes away.

5. Because the sound is positional and OpenAL fully supports sound interpolation from one direction to another, depending on the location of the source, you can also get a feel of direction in stereo. To test this behavior, simply modify the `alSource3f` line as follows:

   ```
   alSource3f( soundsource, AL_POSITION, 2.0f, y, 0.0f );
   ```

6. Build and run the program again. As the sound starts playing, you can clearly hear that the sound source is coming from the right.

7. Now modify the `2.0f` for `-2.0f`. Build and run the program again to feel the changes.

# PIANO GAME

In order to apply what you have learned so far about ambient sound to a real-game scenario, and to discover how to use the audio APIs bundled within this book's SDK, you will be building a simple game that is purely driven by sounds.

The player's goal in this mini-game is to remember the sound sequence that is randomly generated and then use a virtual piano to replay that sequence. If the replay matches the original sequence, the player jumps to the next level, and a new note is added to the sequence. Otherwise, the player has to restart from level 1.

By the end of this section, you will have a fully working game that will look like the one demonstrated in Figure 9-2.

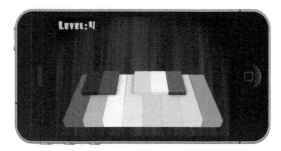

**FIGURE 9-2:** Piano game

For this game, you will also learn how to implement a new picking method based on color. Contrary to the previous picking that you have worked with, which requires physics data, this new method relies directly on the color buffer and can be used in conjunction with any type of projection (2D, 2.5D, and 3D).

Start by duplicating the template_chapter9-3 project directory and rename it **chapter9-3**. Open the templateApp.cpp source file and review the code structure so you are familiar with it before you actually begin using it in the next exercise. Next, build and run the application to visualize the scene. When you're ready, move on to the next section and start coding.

## Loading a Static and Streamed Sound

Working directly with the low-level APIs of OpenAL is not very practical on a large scale. This book's SDK gives you access to higher-level audio APIs that are wrapped around the pure OpenAL calls. To learn how to use this high-level API and corresponding OpenAL calls, follow these steps:

**1.** At the top of the templateApp.cpp source file, define the following variable, which represents the maximum number of keys on the piano:

```
#define MAX_PIANO_KEY 13
```

**2.** Declare the following variables to hold the piano keys' in-memory ambient sound data as well as the sound when the player fails to reproduce the sound sequence (which you will be generating in a moment):

```
/* To handle the sounds for each piano key. */
SOUNDBUFFER *soundbuffer[ MAX_PIANO_KEY ];
SOUND *soundsource[ MAX_PIANO_KEY ];
/* The sound buffer and the sound source for playing the "wrong" sound when
the player misses a key in the sequence. */
SOUNDBUFFER *wrongbuffer;
SOUND *wrong;
```

As you might have guessed, the SOUNDBUFFER and SOUND structures are part of this book's SDK. They wrap multiple low-level OpenAL calls into easy-to-use structures. For more information about the APIs implemented by these structures and their related functions, take a look at the sound.cpp and .h files inside the SDK/common directory.

3. Now declare the following variables, which you will use to create and stream the background music, as well as a THREAD structure to create another process to offload the decompression from the main thread (since decompression is somewhat CPU-intensive):

```
SOUNDBUFFER *ambientbuffer;
SOUND *ambient;
THREAD *thread = NULL;
```

For more information on the threading implementation, review the thread.cpp/h source file (also located inside the SDK/common directory).

4. Right after the GFX_start call, add the following line to initialize OpenAL:

```
/* Helper function to initialize the device and context as you did at the
beginning of this chapter. */
AUDIO_start();
```

5. It's time to load the static sound buffers and link them to their respective sound sources. Insert the following code block on the line right after the end bracket of the while( i != obj->n_objmesh ) loop (inside the templateAppInit function):

```
/* Declare an empty memory pointer to store the sound buffers. */
MEMORY *memory = NULL;
/* Reset the counter. */
i = 0;
/* Loop until the maximum number of piano keys is reached. Basically,
all piano keys have an object name that corresponds to an OGG file. In this
example, the 00.ogg sound file will be associated to the mesh name 00 and
so on. */
while( i != MAX_PIANO_KEY ) {
/* Generate a sound filename based on the current loop counter. */
char soundfile[ MAX_CHAR ] = {""};
sprintf( soundfile, "%02d.ogg", i );
/* Load the sound file into memory. */
memory = mopen( soundfile, 1 );
/* Create a new sound buffer pointer and associate the content loaded
from disk to it. Note that the OGG decompression is automatically handled
inside the SOUNDBUFFER_load function. */
soundbuffer[ i ] =
SOUNDBUFFER_load( soundfile, memory );
/* Free the memory. At this stage, the sound buffer has been sent to the
audio memory, so there is no need to keep the sound file alive in local
memory. The buffer is ready to be used. */
mclose( memory );
/* Create a new sound source and link the sound buffer you just created
to it. */
soundsource[ i ] =
SOUND_add( obj->objmesh[ i ].name, soundbuffer[ i ] );
```

```
++i;
}
/* Next, load the sound to play if the user makes a mistake. */
memory = mopen( ( char * )"wrong.ogg", 1 );
wrongbuffer =
SOUNDBUFFER_load( ( char * )"wrong", memory );
mclose( memory );
wrong =
SOUND_add( ( char * )"wrong", wrongbuffer );
```

**6.** Now that all ambient in-memory sounds have been loaded and stored, you can deal with the background music. Because the sounds have to be streamed, the initialization will be slightly different than for static sounds. To perform this initialization, add the following immediately after the preceding code block:

```
memory = mopen( ( char * )"lounge.ogg", 1 );
/* Create the sound buffer using the SOUNDBUFFER_load_stream API, this
function will initialize multiple sound buffer ID internally and will fill
them with uncompressed chunks of the OGG stream. The function will also
automatically queue them in sequence for real-time playback. */
ambientbuffer =
SOUNDBUFFER_load_stream( ( char * )"lounge", memory );
ambient = SOUND_add( ( char * )"lounge", ambientbuffer );
/* The sound buffer has to be continuously streamed from memory, so you
will have to decompress small pieces of the OGG file and queue these
chunks. To make sure that this operation will not affect the performance of
the main thread (the one that is drawing), create a new thread that will be
used strictly for decompression and queuing. */
thread = THREAD_create(
decompress_stream, /* The thread callback function (which you will
declare in the next step. */
NULL, /* User data pointer used to pass whatever information you want to
make available inside the new process created by the thread. */
THREAD_PRIORITY_NORMAL, /* The thread priority. */
1 ); /* The thread timeout, or sleep time if you prefer, in
milliseconds. By setting this parameter, you can control the update
frequency of the thread on top of its priority. */
/* Start the thread. */
THREAD_play( thread );
/* Set the volume. */
SOUND_set_volume( ambient, 0.5f );
/* Start playing the ambient sound in a loop (by specifying 1 as the
last function parameter). */
SOUND_play( ambient, 1 );
/* Contrary to what you did previously, do not free the sound buffer
from the local memory. The buffer needs to be available for real-time
decompression. */
```

As you may have already noticed, the whole streaming structure from this book's SDK is dynamic. And if you want, you can tweak the maximum number of buffers (MAX_BUFFER, which is 4 by default) to suit your needs, as well as the size of the chunks in bytes (MAX_CHUNK_SIZE, which is 8 KB by default). These two parameters are defined inside the sound .h header file — feel free to modify them as you see fit.

**7.** In order to have the new thread that you created in step 6 respond to its associated callback, add the following new function on the line above the `templateAppInit` function declaration:

```
/* The thread function callback. Note that the void *ptr parameter is the
userdata pointer that might have been set when you called the THREAD_create
function. It is up to you to cast it back to its original type before being
able to use the variable. */
void decompress_stream( void *ptr ) {
    /* Update the sound source queue for the ambient sound. By calling
this function, the buffer chunks that have been processed will be
un-queued and filled with fresh new data decompressed directly from
the OGG sound buffer
in memory. */
    SOUND_update_queue( ambient ); }
```

**8.** To keep things neat and clean, insert the following code block at the beginning of the `templateAppExit` function. This will get rid of all the memory that has been assigned by the sound sources, sound buffers, thread, and the OpenAL context.

```
/* Stop and free the decompression thread. */
THREAD_free( thread );
/* Loop while until the maximum number of piano key is reached. */
unsigned int i = 0;
while( i != MAX_PIANO_KEY ) {
/* Stop and free the sound sources for each piano key as well as
their associated buffer. */
SOUND_free( soundsource[ i ] );
SOUNDBUFFER_free( soundbuffer[ i ] );
++i;
}
/* Same as above but for the "wrong" sound. */
SOUND_free( wrong );
SOUNDBUFFER_free( wrongbuffer );
/* Free the ambient source. */
SOUND_free( ambient );
/* Now it is time to free the ambient buffer memory. Since no more
streaming will take place, you can now freely dispose of it. As you can
see, the memory pointer has been stored within the SOUNDBUFFER structure,
so you can free it when the application exits. */
mclose( ambientbuffer->memory );
/* Free the sound buffer structure for the ambient music. */
SOUNDBUFFER_free( ambientbuffer );
/* Stop OpenAL, and free the device and its associated context. */
AUDIO_stop();
```

**9.** Build and run the project. Right from the start, the background music begins and continues playing smoothly as the chunks are decompressed and queued in real time.

At this point, on top of having full control over static sound sources, you now have the ability to stream very long sound files at a fraction of the memory that it would cost if you were to use a raw sound buffer.

## Color Picking

Before jumping into the logic part of the game, you first need to add the necessary code to enable the piano to play music. Since no collision shape is associated with the geometry that you have loaded, it is impossible to use the physics-based picking technique that you learned earlier. However, there is a way to do this *without* Bullet.

The method that you're about to learn is called *color picking*. The concept is quite simple. First, you render each of your objects with a unique RGB color. Once that's done, all you have to do in order to determine which object has been picked is to retrieve the RGB color value under the touch onscreen.

To keep things simple and save you from having to convert and approximate 16-bit RGB values to 32-bit values and vice versa, you will work with pure 32-bit RGBA values. However, in order to do this, you will have to change the default drawable properties of your color buffer to RGBA 32 bits instead of the default RGB 16 bits (565).

To change this for iOS, open the `EAGLview.mm` Objective-C++ source file (under the `Classes` folder in XCode) and replace the default drawable property `kEAGLColorFormatRGB565` in the `initWithCoder` function to `kEAGLColorFormatRGBA8`.

For Android, in Eclipse open the `GL2view.java` file (under the `com.android.templateApp` folder) and inside the `GL2view` class definition, replace the `ConfigChooser` values from `ConfigChooser( 5, 6, 5, 0, 1, 1 )` to `ConfigChooser( 8, 8, 8, 8, 1, 1 )`.

You are now ready to add color picking to your app and enable your piano to play some sounds. Open `templateApp.cpp` and follow these steps:

**1.** Add the following variables to the current globals of your program that are already defined:

```
/* Flag to determine if the player tries to pick something onscreen. */
unsigned char pick = 0;
/* Temporary variable to store the color used for picking. */
vec4 color;
/* Index of the sound associated with the object that has been picked. */
unsigned int sound_index = 0;
```

**2.** Inside the `templateAppToucheBegan`, at the beginning of the function code, add the following line to raise the flag when the user touches the screen:

```
pick = 1;
```

**3.** Open the `fragment.glsl` shader file attached to your app and add the following uniform variable:

```
uniform lowp vec4 COLOR;
```

You will use this `vec4` to pass to the shader the unique color for the current object you want to draw.

**4.** Modify the `gl_FragColor` affectation as follows, adding the color uniform to the current texture color:

```
/* Add the COLOR uniform variable to the current texture color. */
gl_FragColor = texture2D( DIFFUSE, texcoord0 ) + COLOR;
```

**5.** Go back inside the templateApp.cpp, locate the PROGRAM_draw function call inside the templateAppDraw, and insert the following picking code on the line that precedes the call:

```
/* If you receive a signal that the user wants to pick something. */
if( pick ) {
    /* Change the DIFFUSE texture channel to be a channel that you do not
use, so the texture color will be black. With the modifications you've made
to the fragment shader, you will be able to simply affect the fragment
color with a uniform color pass to the shader, and because black + color =
color, your object will be drawn using this unique color.*/
    glUniform1i( PROGRAM_get_uniform_location( program,
                ( char * )"DIFFUSE" ), 7 );
    /* Loop for the maximum amount of piano key avoiding to draw the curtain
(which is the last object recorded in the OBJ file).*/
    unsigned int i = 0;
    while( i != MAX_PIANO_KEY ) {
    /* Get the current OBJMESH structure pointer, and adjust the current
model view matrix to render the object onscreen. */
    OBJMESH *objmesh = &obj->objmesh[ i ];
    GFX_push_matrix();
    GFX_translate( objmesh->location.x,
                   objmesh->location.y,
                   objmesh->location.z );
    glUniformMatrix4fv(
    PROGRAM_get_uniform_location( program,
    ( char * )"MODELVIEWPROJECTIONMATRIX" ),
    1,
    GL_FALSE,
    ( float * )GFX_get_modelview_projection_matrix() );

    /* Use the following helper function to generate a unique RGBA value for
the current loop index. */
    generate_color_from_index( i, &color );
    /* Send the color to the fragment shader. */
    glUniform4fv(
    PROGRAM_get_uniform_location( program,
    ( char * )"COLOR" ),
    1,
    ( float * )&color );
    /* Draw the object using the unique color that you have generated
above. */
    OBJ_draw_mesh( obj, i );
    GFX_pop_matrix();
    ++i;
    }

    /* Now that you've fully rendered the current scene so that each object
has its own unique color, it's time to ask GLES to identify the color under
the user touche onscreen. The RGBA result that you will be requesting will
be returned in an unsigned byte form. You can then easily extract the
numbers in their pure form and associate them with a piano key number. */
    ucol4 ucolor;
    /* Be careful with this function, because it requires OpenGLES to fully
process all the commands sent down the pipeline and will cause the server
```

```
(in other words, the driver) to stall until the final color is calculated
for the pixels you will be requesting. */
   glReadPixels(
   /* The X coordinate of the touche. */
   touche.x,
   /* Invert the Y position of the touche, because the OpenGLES color
buffer origin is located at the bottom left of the screen. */
   viewport_matrix[ 3 ] - touche.y,
   /* Request 1 pixel width by 1 pixel height. */
   1,
   1,
   /* The requested pixel format. */
   GL_RGBA,
   /* The requested pixel type. */
   GL_UNSIGNED_BYTE,
   /* Store the result in the unsigned char RGBA structure. */
   &ucolor );

   /* By default, you have 13 objects that have been rendered onscreen
(each piano key). And because the colors generated have been incremented
depending on the current index of the loop counter, the result (if a piano
key is picked) shown never exceeds the maximum number of the key index (0
to 12). This means that the value of the blue (b) component contains the
corresponding index of the piano key. */
   if( ucolor.b < MAX_PIANO_KEY ) {
       /* Convert the name of the OBJMESH indexed by the b color component
to an unsigned int value, which will correspond to the index of the piano
key sound source in the array. */
       sscanf( obj->objmesh[ ucolor.b ].name,
               "%d",
               &sound_index );
       /* Set the volume for the key at the top. */
       SOUND_set_volume( soundsource[ sound_index ], 1.0f );
       /* Play the piano key sound. */
       SOUND_play( soundsource[ sound_index ], 0 );
       }
   /* Clear the depth buffer and color buffer, because you are about to
draw the scene again. */
   glClear( GL_DEPTH_BUFFER_BIT | GL_COLOR_BUFFER_BIT );
   }
   pick = 0; /* Reset the picking state. */
```

**6.** To provide visual feedback on which key of the piano is currently playing, add the following code on the line right before the last OBJ_draw_mesh call inside the templateAppDraw function:

```
/* Convert the current mesh name to an index that corresponds to the sound
source index of the piano key sound source array. */
sscanf( objmesh->name, "%d", &sound_index );
/* Check if the sound source is currently playing. */
if( !strstr( objmesh->name, "curtain" ) &&
    SOUND_get_state( soundsource[ sound_index ] )
    == AL_PLAYING ) {
    /* Set full brightness as the color to use for the piano key that is
```

about to be drawn onscreen (since your fragment shader now supports color additions on the final gl_FragColor value. */

```
    color.x = 1.0f;
    color.y = 1.0f;
    color.z = 1.0f;
    color.w = 1.0f;
    }
    else {
    /* Set the color to be fully black so the color won't affect the texture
color of the piano key (because black + color = color). */
    color.x =
    color.y =
    color.z = 0.0f;
    color.w = 1.0f;
}
/* Send over the current color. */
glUniform4fv(
PROGRAM_get_uniform_location( program,
( char * )"COLOR" ),
1,
( float * )&color );
```

**7.** You can now build and run the application and start jamming on the piano!

Mastering this new picking method will give you a great deal of flexibility over the picking functionalities of your apps. And because this method is strictly color-based, you can use it for 2D, 2.5D, or 3D!

However, keep in mind that `glReadPixels` is probably one of the slowest GLES commands (due to the reasons explained earlier).

## Piano Game Logic

Your scene interaction is now fully functional. Now it's time to integrate the final touch that will allow the user to play the game.

Basically, all you have to do at this point is generate a sequence of numbers that is associated to a sound attached to a piano key. If the player replays the right sequence, the level will increase and more piano notes will be added. If the player plays a "wrong" sound in the sequence, the game is over, and they will have to restart from level 1.

To implement the logical workflow for this game, follow these steps:

**1.** Start by declaring the following global variables at the top of the `templateApp.cpp` file:

```
/* The maximum amount of levels. */
#define MAX_LEVEL 50
/* Flag to control the game_over state. */
unsigned char game_over = 0;
/* The current level index. */
unsigned int cur_level = 0,
/* The current sound of the level that has to be played automatically when
a new sequence is generated. */
```

```
                    cur_level_sound,
     /* Array to contain the auto-generated piano key index for the levels. */
                    level[ MAX_LEVEL ],
     /* The current sound played by the user. This value will increment as the
     player tries to reproduce the current sequence used in the level. */
                    cur_player_sound;
```

2. Before the `templateAppInit` function declaration, create the following new function to automatically fill the `level` array with a new piano key index for the next level:

```c
void next_level( void ) {
   unsigned int i = 0;
   /* Increase the current level number. */
   ++cur_level;
   /* Randomly generate a piano keys index based on the current
level number. */
   while( i != cur_level ) {
   level[ i ] = rand() % MAX_PIANO_KEY;
   ++i;
   }
   /* Reset the current sound level so the player can see and hear the
sequence to reproduce for the current level. */
   cur_level_sound = 0;
}
```

3. Before the end bracket of the `templateAppInit` function, add the following code to generate the random seed and the key for the first level:

```c
srandom( get_milli_time() );
next_level();
```

4. On the line right before the `if( pick )` statement of the `templateAppDraw` function, insert the following code block to automatically play the piano key for the current level (to provide the player with a preview):

```c
/* If the current preview sound is different than the current level, it
means that the whole generated sequence has not been played back to the
user yet. */
   if( cur_level_sound != cur_level ) {
   /* Static variable to remember the time. */
   static unsigned int start = get_milli_time();
   /* Wait 1 second between each sound preview, because playing all of the
sounds one after another without any pause between each sound would be too
hard for the player to remember.*/
   if( get_milli_time() - start >= 1000 ) {
      if( SOUND_get_state(
      soundsource[ level[ cur_level_sound ] ] ) != AL_PLAYING ) {
      SOUND_set_volume(
      soundsource[ level[ cur_level_sound ] ], 1.0f );
      SOUND_play(
      soundsource[ level[ cur_level_sound ] ], 0 );
      /* Increase the current preview sound counter. */
      ++cur_level_sound;
```

```
            /* Remember the start time you last played the note. */
            start = get_milli_time();
            }
            /* Reset the current piano note index that the player inputs. */
            cur_player_sound = 0;
        }
    }
    /* Transform the previous if into an else-if so the player won't be able to
    play with the piano while the preview is running. */
    else
```

5.  Delete the `if( ucolor.b < MAX_PIANO_KEY )` block completely and replace it with
    the following code block. This code checks if the key that the player taps on the piano is the
    right one (the key that corresponds to the one in the sequence). If not, the code simply plays
    the "wrong" sound and raises the game_over flag. If the player input is right, this code
    increases the `cur_player_sound` counter so the next piano key that the player taps will
    correspond to the next entry in the level sound index array.

```
    if( ucolor.b < MAX_PIANO_KEY ) {
        sscanf( obj->objmesh[ ucolor.b ].name, "%d", &sound_index );
        if( level[ cur_player_sound ] != sound_index ) {
            SOUND_set_volume( wrong, 1.0f );
            SOUND_play( wrong, 0 );
            game_over = 1;
        }
        else {
            SOUND_set_volume( soundsource[ sound_index ], 1.0f );
            SOUND_play( soundsource[ sound_index ], 0 );
            ++cur_player_sound;
        }
    }
```

6.  The following instructions will allow you to determine if the player should go to the next level.
    At this point, all you have to do is a simple logic check to see if there is no sound currently
    playing and if the `cur_player_sound` is equal to the `cur_level`. In the `templateAppDraw`,
    on the line after you assign `pick = 0`, declare the following variable:

```
    unsigned char source_playing = 0;
```

    Then on the line after the start bracket of the `if( SOUND_get_state( soundsource
    [ sound_index ] ) == AL_PLAYING )` statement, add the following line to raise a flag to
    indicate that there is still at least one sound playing:

```
    source_playing = 1;
```

    Then insert the following statement before the end bracket of the `templateAppDraw`
    function:

```
    /* If the current player sound index is equal to the current level number,
    it means that the player has cleared the level and entered all the piano
    keys in the right order. Time to move on to the next level! */
    if( cur_player_sound == cur_level && !source_playing ) next_level();
```

**7.** In order for the player to be able to restart the game if the `game_over` state is on, delete the `pick = 1;` affectation inside the `templateAppToucheBegan` callback and replace it with the following block to restart the game if the player double-taps the screen:

```
/* If the game is not over, allow the player pick a piano key. */
if( !game_over ) pick = 1;
/* If the game is over and the player double-taps the screen. */
else if( game_over && tap_count >= 2 ) {
    /* Reset the game_over state and set the current level back to 0. */
    game_over =
    cur_level = 0;
    /* Restart the game at level 1. */
    next_level();
}
```

**8.** Build and run the game.

The logic is now fully implemented, and you can play and replay the game as much as you want. However, something is missing — the player is not given any real feedback as the game progresses or when the game is over. In the next section, you'll make some adjustments to provide this feedback and finalize this mini-game.

## Final Adjustments

Basically, all you have to do to make the game friendlier is print some text on the screen. In the following steps, you'll first indicate the current level and provide the player with direct feedback on the current progression of the game to the player. And second, you'll display a message when the game is over, so the player can then double-tap the screen to restart.

**1.** At the top of the `templateApp.cpp`, where your other globals are declared, declare the following two global FONT structure pointers (one for a small font and one for a big font):

```
FONT *font_small = NULL,
     *font_big = NULL;
```

**2.** Just before the end bracket of the `templateAppInit` function, insert the following block of code to initialize and generate the two font textures for the `foo.ttf` TrueType font file:

```
font_small = FONT_init( ( char * )"foo.ttf" );
FONT_load( font_small, /* Font structure pointer. */
           font_small->name, /* Font file. */
           1, /* Use a relative path to load the TTF. */
           32.0f, /* The font size. */
           512, /* Texture width. */
           512, /* Texture height. */
           32, /* First character offset in ASCII. */
           96 ); /* How many characters to generate. */

font_big = FONT_init( ( char * )"foo.ttf" );
FONT_load( font_big,
           font_big->name,
           1,
```

```
                              64.0f,
                              512,
                              512,
                              32,
                              96 );
```

**3.** Before the end bracket of the `templateAppDraw`, insert the following block to show the current level onscreen and display "Game Over" when the appropriate game state is on:

```
GFX_set_matrix_mode( PROJECTION_MATRIX );
GFX_load_identity();
float half_width  = ( float )viewport_matrix[ 2 ] * 0.5f,
      half_height = ( float )viewport_matrix[ 3 ] * 0.5f;
GFX_set_orthographic_2d( -half_width,
                          half_width,
                         -half_height,
                          half_height );
GFX_rotate( -90.0f, 0.0f, 0.0f, 1.0f );
GFX_translate( -half_height, -half_width, 0.0f );
GFX_set_matrix_mode( MODELVIEW_MATRIX );
GFX_load_identity();
char str[ MAX_CHAR ] = {""};
if( game_over ) {
   strcpy( str, "GAME OVER" );
   /* Yellow. */
   color.x = 1.0f;
   color.y = 1.0f;
   color.z = 0.0f;
   color.w = 1.0f;
   FONT_print( font_big,
               viewport_matrix[ 3 ] * 0.5f -
               FONT_length( font_big, str ) * 0.5f,
               viewport_matrix[ 2 ] -
               font_big->font_size * 1.5f,
               str,
               &color );
}
sprintf( str, "Level:%d", cur_level );
/* Green. */
color.x = 0.0f;
color.y = 1.0f;
color.z = 0.0f;
color.w = 1.0f;
FONT_print( font_small,
5.0f,
viewport_matrix[ 2 ] - font_small->font_size,
str,
&color );
```

**4.** Make sure to clean up the font structures before quitting the application. To do this, insert the following lines right after the start bracket of the `templateAppExit` function:

```
FONT_free( font_small );
FONT_free( font_big );
```

**5.** Build and run this "slightly improved" version of the game. The player will now see the level that they're currently on, or a "Game Over" message if they miss a key.

This mini-game tutorial demonstrated how you can use the SOUND and SOUNDBUFFER structures, and a lot more. You learned how to stream a large OGG file in another thread and how to use color-picking. You also now have a good overview of how to use the AUDIO API and integrate it inside your own apps.

In the next section, you're going to implement a practical example that focuses on positional sound sources.

## ROLLING BALL GAME

In Chapter 7, you learned about different ways to handle cameras, and at the beginning of this chapter, you learned the basic theory behind positional sound sources. In this section, you'll apply all this to a rolling ball game scenario. When you're done, you'll know how to connect the camera location and direction to the listener, as well as how to get real 3D stereo sound feedback for each positional source.

**FIGURE 9-3:** Rolling ball game template

Before you begin coding the actual game, duplicate the template_chapter9-4 project and rename it **chapter9-4**. Open it in your IDE and do an initial build of it. The template of your upcoming rolling ball game is demonstrated in Figure 9-3.

Right away, the goal of the game is quite clear: Pick up as many gems as possible in the shortest period of time before reaching the end goal of the scene.

Now take a look at the template source code for this chapter. You are already very familiar with most of the framework. However, notice that this time, the shaders are not loaded manually; instead, they are directly linked within the 3D editor and are available through the scene's .mtl file.

## GFX Shaders

There are just a few more things that you need to do and understand before you begin the tutorial. First, open the .blend file that is located in the SDK/data/chapter9-4 folder.

Then select an object and open the Texture panel within Blender. Browse the channel attached to the material, and you should instantly notice that a .gfx file is associated to the translucency. The reason I did this is because you are not using a translucency channel for this project; however, it can be any other available channel that is supported by the OBJ Wavefront format.

A .gfx file is a shader program file that contains the code for both vertex and fragment shaders. All you have to do to auto generate a shader program at loading time from within your application is to link a GFX file to one of the texture channels supported (and of course, use the OBJ and PROGRAM API from this book's SDK).

To create your own .gfx, all you have to do is add markers inside the source code contained in the file. The markers will tell the loader where the appropriate shader code starts; these tags are GL_VERTEX_SHADER and GL_FRAGMENT_SHADER.

It is a very simple approach, but it enables you to use your favorite 3D editor to attach shader files directly to your material(s) instead of loading each and every one of them manually. You can then treat these shaders more like regular assets (similar to the way you treat textures), which can be very convenient.

To see an example of how this approach works, simply open SDK/data/chapter9-4/diffuse.gfx with your favorite text editor, to learn how a GFX file is built, and how to add basic fog to your scene.

If you are using a GFX file with your material(s), you can use (most likely at loading time) the following pseudo code to extract and load the shaders and automatically attach them to your materials when the OBJ_build_material function is called (just like for textures):

```
/* Counter for the loop. */
unsigned i = 0;
/* Loop for the number of programs in the obj resource. */
while( i != obj->n_program ) {
   /* Build the program. */
   OBJ_build_program(
   /* The OBJ structure. */
   obj,
   /* The program index. */
   i,
   /* The callback to bind the attribute location(s). */
   program_bind_attrib_location,
   /* Callback to use when the program is about to be use for drawing. */
   program_draw,
   /* Use a relative path for the .gfx file. */
   1,
   /* The path where the shader programs are located. */
   obj->program_path );
   ++i; /* Next shader program. */
}
```

As you can see, this method is very similar to the way you have been handling textures inside an .mtl so far. This code has already been put in place for you in the templateApp.cpp for the chapter9-4 exercise. You can find it inside the load_level function.

This approach is widely used in game engine design, because it allows artists to link and test shaders with their 3D models and textures without the need of a programmer.

## Linking the Positional Sound Sources

In addition to the usual background music, there are quite a few positional sound sources to place inside the scene. Each gem will require a different sound to be emitted when the player picks it up, and each "substance" under the bridges (the water, lava, and toxic material) will also need to emit a sound. To link these sound sources, follow these steps:

1. At the top of the `templateApp.cpp`, right after the `#include` statement, declare the following global variables to handle the different sound sources and buffers used in the scene:

```
/* The background music. */
SOUNDBUFFER *background_soundbuffer = NULL;
SOUND *background_sound = NULL;
/* To use with the four gem colors: red, green, blue, and yellow, in this
specific order. */
SOUNDBUFFER *gems_soundbuffer[ 4 ];
SOUND *gems_sound[ 4 ];
/* To handle the water sound under the first bridge. */
SOUNDBUFFER *water_soundbuffer = NULL;
SOUND *water_sound = NULL;
/* To handle the lava sound under the second bridge. */
SOUNDBUFFER *lava_soundbuffer = NULL;
SOUND *lava_sound = NULL;
/* To handle the toxic sound under the last bridge. */
SOUNDBUFFER *toxic_soundbuffer = NULL;
SOUND *toxic_sound = NULL;
```

2. In the `load_level` function, right before the end bracket, insert the following code to load and generate the gem sounds:

```
/* Declare a memory structure that you will use (and reuse) to load
each sound buffer. */
MEMORY *memory = NULL;
/* Reset the counter. */
i = 0;
/* Loop for each gem color. */
while( i != 4 ) {
  switch( i ) {
    case 0: { /* Load the red.ogg file. */
      memory = mopen( ( char * )"red.ogg", 1 );
      break;
    }
    case 1: { /* Load the green.ogg file. */
      memory = mopen( ( char * )"green.ogg", 1 );
      break;
    }
    case 2: { /* Load the blue.ogg file. */
      memory = mopen( ( char * )"blue.ogg", 1 );
      break;
    }
    case 3: { /* Load the yellow.ogg file. */
      memory = mopen( ( char * )"yellow.ogg", 1 );
      break;
    }
  }
  /* For the current gem buffer index, create a sound buffer using the
```

```
content of the memory structure that you have loaded. */
     gems_soundbuffer[ i ] =
     SOUNDBUFFER_load( ( char * )"gem", memory );
     mclose( memory );
     /* Create a new sound source for the current index and link the
current sound buffer. */
     gems_sound[ i ] =
     SOUND_add( ( char * )"gem", gems_soundbuffer[ i ] );
     /* Set the volume for the source, but do not start playing it yet.
You will handle the playback code inside the contact_added_callback only
when the player collides with a gem. */
     SOUND_set_volume( gems_sound[ i ], 1.0f );
     ++i;
   }
```

At first glance, you might think that theses gems will simply be handled like regular ambient sounds, but in fact, they won't. Later, you will dynamically assign the sound source position and "reference distance" at run time.

3. In this step, you'll use a different method to position the sound sources for the "substances" under the bridges. Because there are only three substances and they have very large reference distances and are static in memory, you can directly create and assign their locations and then reference their distances at loading time. To create and assign these sound sources, insert the following code block right below the code you added in step 2:

```
     /* Temporary variable to contain the mesh pointer of the object that
will be emitting the sound. */
     OBJMESH *objmesh = NULL;
     /* Load the water.ogg file in memory. */
     memory = mopen( ( char * )"water.ogg", 1 );
     /* Create the sound buffer for the OGG. */
     water_soundbuffer =
     SOUNDBUFFER_load( ( char * )"water", memory );
     /* Free the memory, because the sound buffer is loaded as a
static sound and the raw audio buffer has been transferred to the
audio memory by the previous function call. */
     mclose( memory );
     /* Create the water sound source. */
     water_sound = SOUND_add( ( char * )"water", water_soundbuffer );
     /* Here comes the part of code where you are going to associate the
sound source to the object. First, get the objmesh pointer for the water
object. */
     objmesh = OBJ_get_mesh( obj, "water", 0 );
     /* Assign to the sound source the location of the mesh in 3D space and
use the radius as the reference distance (how far the sound can be heard). */
     SOUND_set_location( water_sound,
                         &objmesh->location,
                         objmesh->radius );
     /* Set the volume of the water at 50%. */
     SOUND_set_volume( water_sound, 0.5f );
     /* Start playing the water sound. */
     SOUND_play( water_sound, 1 );

     /* Same as above, but this time for the lava sound. */
     memory = mopen( ( char * )"lava.ogg", 1 );
```

```
lava_soundbuffer =
SOUNDBUFFER_load( ( char * )"lava", memory );
mclose( memory );
lava_sound =
SOUND_add( ( char * )"lava", lava_soundbuffer );
objmesh = OBJ_get_mesh( obj, "lava", 0 );
SOUND_set_location( lava_sound,
                    &objmesh->location,
                    objmesh->radius );
SOUND_set_volume( lava_sound, 0.5f );
SOUND_play( lava_sound, 1 );

/* And finally for the toxic waste sound under the last bridge. */
memory = mopen( ( char * )"toxic.ogg", 1 );
toxic_soundbuffer =
SOUNDBUFFER_load( ( char * )"toxic", memory );
mclose( memory );
toxic_sound =
SOUND_add( ( char * )"toxic", toxic_soundbuffer );
objmesh = OBJ_get_mesh( obj, "toxic", 0 );
SOUND_set_location( toxic_sound,
                    &objmesh->location,
                    objmesh->radius );
SOUND_set_volume( toxic_sound, 0.5f );
SOUND_play( toxic_sound, 1 );
```

4.  Now load the background music as a streamed buffer the same way you did in the Piano Game. Append the following block right below the code you added in step 3:

```
/* Load the background sound as a streamed buffer. */
memory = mopen( ( char * )"background.ogg", 1 );
background_soundbuffer =
SOUNDBUFFER_load_stream( ( char * )"background", memory );
background_sound =
SOUND_add( ( char * )"background", background_soundbuffer );
SOUND_set_volume( background_sound, 0.5f );
/* Play the background sound in a loop. */
SOUND_play( background_sound, 1 );
/* Start the decompression thread. */
THREAD_play( thread );
/* Don't free the memory, because you need to keep it alive in local
memory for streaming. */
```

5.  Add the following line of code in the `decompress_stream` thread callback function to handle the chunks decompression and to update the queue for the `background_sound` source:

```
SOUND_update_queue( background_sound );
```

6.  As usual, you now have to clean up whatever you have initialized when the app exits or when the level is freed. To do this, add the following block at the top of the `free_level` function, right after the function start bracket:

```
unsigned int i = 0;
/* Pause the thread, because you don't want the process to
```

```
continue to decompress while you are trying to free the background
music. That would make your app crash for sure. */
   THREAD_pause( thread );
   /* Free the background sound source. */
   background_sound = SOUND_free( background_sound );
   /* Because the background music was streamed, free the sound buffer from
the local memory structure. */
   background_soundbuffer->memory = mclose( background_soundbuffer->memory );
   /* It is now okay to free the sound buffer. */
   background_soundbuffer = SOUNDBUFFER_free( background_soundbuffer );

   /* Loop while you've got a gem colors. */
   while( i != 4 ) {
      /* Free the sound source and the associated buffer. */
      gems_sound[ i ] = SOUND_free( gems_sound[ i ] );
      gems_soundbuffer[ i ] = SOUNDBUFFER_free( gems_soundbuffer[ i ] );
      ++i;
   }

   /* Now deal with the water, lava, and toxic stuff sound sources
and buffers. */
   water_sound = SOUND_free( water_sound );
   water_soundbuffer = SOUNDBUFFER_free( water_soundbuffer );

   lava_sound = SOUND_free( lava_sound );
   lava_soundbuffer = SOUNDBUFFER_free( lava_soundbuffer );

   toxic_sound = SOUND_free( toxic_sound );
   toxic_soundbuffer = SOUNDBUFFER_free( toxic_soundbuffer );
```

**7.** Build and run the application. As expected, the background music starts playing, and in the background, you can hear the water sound (since it's the closest positional source near the starting point of the level).

In the next section, you are going to learn how to implement the player control based on the device accelerometer and adjust the listener position and direction.

## Accelerometer-Driven Camera

In Chapter 7, you learned about multiple types of camera implementations. However, for certain types of games (such as the rolling ball game that you're currently coding), the easiest and the most user-friendly way to handle the player and camera controls is to use the accelerometer.

The accelerometer may sound scary at first, but I can assure you that it is as easy as dealing with the touch screen. Once again, you'll be strictly dealing with a direction vector.

By default, the accelerometer is turned off in this book's template, because it is not needed for most of the exercises. To enable the accelerometer on iOS, open the `templateAppDelegate.mm` (under the `Classes` folder of your Xcode project) and uncomment the following lines inside the `didFinishLaunchingWithOptions` function:

```
[[UIAccelerometer sharedAccelerometer ]
setUpdateInterval:( 1.0f / 24.0f )];
[[UIAccelerometer sharedAccelerometer] setDelegate:self];
```

For Android, open the `templateApp.java` file and uncomment the following lines inside the `onCreate` method of the `templateApp` class:

```
mSensorManager =
( SensorManager ) getSystemService( SENSOR_SERVICE );
mSensorManager.registerListener(
this,
mSensorManager.getDefaultSensor(
SensorManager.SENSOR_ACCELEROMETER ),
41000 );
```

With this code in place, every time the accelerometer is refreshed internally by your device, you will receive a live feedback with the latest values recorded by the hardware (sent by default using the template to the `templateAppAccelerometer` function).

Once these values are collected, all you have to do is to pass them back to your application.

However, please note that the accelerometer can only be used on a real device. If you are using the iOS Simulator, for example, the accelerometer won't work.

To learn how to handle the player (or in this case, the ball) and camera controls using the accelerometer, follow these steps:

**1.** At the top of the `templateApp.cpp` file, declare the following global variables to control the player angular velocity and camera position:

```
/* The current accelerometer X and Y values. Because the application runs
in landscape mode, X is used to go forward and backward, and Y is used to
control the Z rotation of the camera. */
vec2 accelerometer = { 0.0f, 0.0f },
     /* The next accelerometer values to linearly interpolate to. Similar
to the touch screen on some devices, the accelerometer values can be quite
jumpy. In order to have a smooth motion, you will have to use linear
interpolation. */
     next_accelerometer = { 0.0f, 0.0f };
/* The maximum speed of the ball. */
float ball_speed  = 6.7f,
/* The sensitivity of the accelerometer. */
      sensitivity = 3.0f;
/* The current game state. 0 indicates that the game is running, 1 indicates
that the level is cleared, and 2 indicates that the level has to be
reloaded. You will be implementing the logic code later, but for now,
you'll declare the game state to be able to determine if the player is able
to control the ball or not based on the current game state. */
unsigned char game_state = 0;
```

**2.** Move to the `templateAppAccelerometer` callback and add the following code inside the function brackets:

```
/* Store and normalize the XYZ value of the accelerometer. These values
differ from iOS to Android, so working with a normalized vector will keep
things easier. */
    vec3 tmp = { x, y, z };
```

```
    vec3_normalize( &tmp, &tmp );
    /* Add a little offset to the X axis of the accelerometer. The 0
position typically means that the device is fully flat, but because this
game is in landscape mode and the player is holding the device in their
hands, the 0 position should be slightly inclined. */
    accelerometer.x = tmp.x + 0.35f;
    The 0 value on the Y axis differs from iOs to Android on some devices
(such as the iPod Touch 4G and Nexus S, which I use). To compensate for
this difference on the Y axis of the accelerometer, check which platform
you are dealing with and adjust it accordingly. */
    #ifndef __IPHONE_4_0 /* Valid for every iOS version greater or
equal to 4.0 */
        accelerometer.y = tmp.y + 0.35f;
    #else
        accelerometer.y = tmp.y;
    #endif
```

3.  Jump to the `templateAppDraw` function and insert the following block of code right
    after the `GFX_load_identity` of the `MODELVIEW` matrix. This code will control the player
    movement and camera rotation based on the accelerometer normalized data.

```
    /* Linearly interpolate the accelerometer values to get a smooth
transition. */
    next_accelerometer.x =
    accelerometer.x * 0.1f + next_accelerometer.x * 0.9f;
    next_accelerometer.y =
    accelerometer.y * 0.1f + next_accelerometer.y * 0.9f;

    /* Assign the current Y rotation of the accelerometer to the Z rotation
of the camera, multiplied by the accelerometer sensitivity factor. */
    rotz += next_accelerometer.y * sensitivity;

    /* The forward vector of the ball. */
    vec3 forward = { 0.0f, 1.0f, 0.0f },
    /* The current direction vector of the ball. Basically, this is the
forward vector rotated by the camera's Z rotation. */
        direction;
    /* If the game is running, let the user move the ball. */
    if( !game_state ) {
    /* Pre-calculate a few variables before rotating the forward vector
by the camera's Z rotation. */
        float r = rotz * DEG_TO_RAD,
            c = cosf( r ),
            s = sinf( r );
    /* Rotate the forward vector and store the result into the
direction variable. Because both vectors are already normalized,
there's no need to re-normalize them again. */
        direction.x = c * forward.y - s * forward.x;
        direction.y = s * forward.y + c * forward.x;
    /* Calculate the current angular velocity (the speed) that should be
applied on the ball based on the value of the accelerometer that you will
be using as the force factor. Then clamp the result to make sure that the
speed is between the maximum and minimum ball_speed thresholds. */
        float speed =
```

```
            CLAMP( ( -next_accelerometer.x * sensitivity ) * ball_speed,
                    -ball_speed,
                    ball_speed );
        /* Assign the direction vector multiplied by the current speed to the
    angular velocity of the ball. */
        player->btrigidbody->setAngularVelocity(
        btVector3( direction.x * speed,
                    direction.y * speed,
                    0.0f ) );
        /* Activate the rigid body to make sure that the angular velocity
    will be applied. */
        player->btrigidbody->setActivationState( ACTIVE_TAG );
    }
```

4.  Now that your camera and player controls are all set up, you have to adjust the listener position and orientation to fit the current camera location and viewing direction relative to the player. Insert the following code right before the GFX_look_at call:

```
    /* Calculate the direction vector from the player to the current eye
    location. (If you did this the other way around, the listener orientation
    would be inverted.) */
    vec3_diff( &direction, &player->location, &eye );
    /* Normalize the direction vector. */
    vec3_normalize( &direction, &direction );
    /* Use this book's audio API to set the listener location, direction,
    and up vector. (As you might have noticed, this function is very similar to
    the GFX_look_at that you have already used quite a bit.) */
    AUDIO_set_listener( &eye, &direction, &up );
```

5.  Build and run the program for your device (since the accelerometer does not work in the simulator). You can now use the accelerometer to make the ball roll, allowing you to "roll" your way into the 3D world. Notice as you move around that you get real-time feedback about the location and intensity of the positional sound sources you created earlier.

As you navigate through the level and observe the environment, you'll notice that there are a few things that are not quite right. The textures of the substances below the bridges are just plain-colored, and the gems basically block your way. In the next section, you will learn how to implement some simple yet visually appealing effects to improve the quality of your game.

# Cheap FX

There are several visual effects that you can easily implement to enhance how your apps appear onscreen. Two of these effects, texture scroll and basic fog, are already implemented in the rolling ball game code. In this section, you'll learn how to adjust these two effects to make your game look better.

## Texture Scroll

Animating or dynamically generating textures in real time can be quite expensive, both for the CPU and GPU. Whether it is water flowing or clouds moving in the sky, a cheap (in terms of computation) alternative is to use the texture matrix to translate, rotate, and scale your UVs in real time.

In the current scene, the code to do texture scrolling is already implemented in the scroll_texture .gfx shader like this:

```
texcoord0 =
vec2( TEXTUREMATRIX *
        vec4( TEXCOORD0.x, TEXCOORD0.y, 1.0, 1.0 ) );
```

Now all you have to do to animate the water, lava, and toxic liquid under the bridges is to translate the TEXTURE matrix and send it over to the scroll_texture shader.

To send over the texture matrix, locate the program_draw function callback (inside templateApp.cpp), and insert the following lines of code before the incrementation of the i variable (++i):

```
/* Check if you are dealing with the TEXTUREMATRIX uniform. */
else if( !strcmp( program->uniform_array[ i ].name,
        "TEXTUREMATRIX" ) ) {
  /* Declare a static vec2 variable to keep track of the scroll value. */
  static vec2 scroll = { 0.0f, 0.0f };
  /* Set the focus on the texture matrix. */
  GFX_set_matrix_mode( TEXTURE_MATRIX );
  /* Push it down. */
  GFX_push_matrix();
  /* Increment the UV scroll value. */
  scroll.x += 0.0025f;
  scroll.y += 0.0025f;
  /* Translate the matrix as you would normally do with any other type
of matrix. */
  GFX_translate( scroll.x, scroll.y, 0.0f );
  /* Send the matrix over to the vertex shader. */
  glUniformMatrix4fv( program->uniform_array[ i ].location,
                      1,
                      GL_FALSE,
                      /* Another GFX helper, this one is to retrieve the
current texture matrix on top of the stack. */
                      ( float * )GFX_get_texture_matrix() );
  /* Pop back the matrix. */
  GFX_pop_matrix();
  /* Restore the current matrix mode back to the model view matrix. */
  GFX_set_matrix_mode( MODELVIEW_MATRIX );
}
```

Now build and run the program and head right to the first bridge. You should see the water texture scrolling based on the code you just added.

## Basic Fog

You must have already noticed while running the scene that at the clip end, there is a light fog that basically blends in with the glClearColor.

Fog is widely used in games, because it is a great way to make it look like a scene is actually larger than it is. However, as the complexity of a scene increases, it is crucial that you keep the clip end values as tight as possible in order to avoid having too many objects to be rendered for each frame.

Fog calculations can be expensive. This is because they are typically done on a fragment basis to provide the best visual results.

As a quick fix, here's a cheap one-line fog calculation method that you can add to your shaders to integrate a misty effect at the end of the far plane of your scenes:

```
/* Use the mix instructions to blend the texture color with an arbitrary
fog color based on the distance of the fragment onscreen. */
gl_FragColor = mix( texture2D( DIFFUSE, texcoord0 ),
                    /* The fog color. */
                    vec4( 1.0, 1.0, 1.0, 0.0 ),
                    /* The distance of the fragment divided by the far
clipping plane distance, the clip end parameter. */
                    ( gl_FragCoord.z / gl_FragCoord.w ) /
                    50.0 );
```

Note that this code has to be implemented in every shader program containing the objects that you want to use the fog effect on. You can find examples of this implementation in the `diffuse.gfx` and `scroll_texture.gfx` files.

## Game Logic and Tweaks

All that's left for you to do is integrate the necessary logic code to pick up gems, calculate points, and restart the level when the player reaches the end target. Follow these steps to turn your rolling ball game into a fully playable, addictive game:

**1.** Declare the following global variables at the top of the `templateApp.cpp` source file:

```
/* The current time spent inside the level. */
float game_time    = 0.0f,
/* Boost the reference distance of the positional sound sources of the gems
(since the gem radius is pretty small). */
      gem_factor   = 20.0f;
/* Total points gathered in the level so far. */
unsigned int gem_points = 0;
```

**2.** In the `contact_added_callback` function, before the `return` statement, add the following code to allow the player to pick up the gems and trigger the "Level Clear" game state if the ball touches the target object named `level_clear`:

```
/* If one of the mesh object names is like "level_clear" it means that the
ball has reached the end target. Set the game state to 1 to indicate that
the level has to be restarted. */
if( ( strstr( objmesh0->name, "level_clear" ) ||
      strstr( objmesh1->name, "level_clear" ) ) )
      game_state = 1;
/* If the two mesh objects that are involved in the collision are a gem and
the player. */
else if( ( strstr( objmesh0->name, "player" ) ||
           strstr( objmesh1->name, "player" ) )
         &&
         ( strstr( objmesh0->name, "gem" ) ||
```

```
                     strstr( objmesh1->name, "gem" ) ) ) {
     /* To store the gem mesh pointer and its collision object. */
     OBJMESH *objmesh = NULL;
     btCollisionObject *btcollisionobject = NULL;

     /* Depending on which mesh (either 0 or 1) is the gem, store the
 appropriate pointers. */
       if( strstr( objmesh0->name, "gem" ) ) {
          objmesh = objmesh0;
          btcollisionobject = ( btCollisionObject * )btcollisionobject0;
       }
       else {
          objmesh = objmesh1;
          btcollisionobject = ( btCollisionObject * )btcollisionobject1;
       }


     /* Temporary variable to store the gem index for the sound source based
 on the name of the current gem that gets picked up by the player. */
       unsigned char index = 0;
     /* If it's a red gem, add one gem point and store the index number 0. */
       if( strstr( objmesh->name, "red" ) ) {
          gem_points += 1;
          index = 0;
       }
     /* Same as above for the rest of the gem colors. */
       else if( strstr( objmesh->name, "green" ) ) {
          gem_points += 2;
          index = 1;
       }
       else if( strstr( objmesh->name, "blue" ) ) {
          gem_points += 3;
          index = 2;
       }
       else if( strstr( objmesh->name, "yellow" ) ) {
          gem_points += 4;
          index = 3;
       }

     /* Set the location of the sound source for the appropriate gem picked
 up and use the current location and radius of the mesh to modify the sound
 source location and reference distance. */
       SOUND_set_location( gems_sound[ index ],
                           &objmesh->location,
                           /* Gems have a small radius. Give it a boost so the
 player will hear the sound more clearly. */
                           objmesh->radius * gem_factor );
     /* Play the sound source. */
       SOUND_play( gems_sound[ index ], 0 );
     /* Set the current gem mesh to be invisible. It has been picked up, so
 you don't want to draw it again. */
       objmesh->visible = 0;
     /* Remove the rigid body and associated data from the physical
 world. When a gem is picked, it cannot be part of the physics
```

```
simulation any more. */
   delete objmesh->btrigidbody->getCollisionShape();
   delete objmesh->btrigidbody->getMotionState();
   dynamicsworld->removeRigidBody( objmesh->btrigidbody );
   dynamicsworld->removeCollisionObject( btcollisionobject );
   delete objmesh->btrigidbody;
   objmesh->btrigidbody = NULL;
}
```

**3.** The code that you added in the previous step will not have any effect until you enable the material collision callback on the rigid body of the objects. Move to the `load_level` function and append the following code block on the line after the `gContactAddedCallback` affection code:

```
/* Get the mesh object name level_clear, which is the cylinder located
in the middle of the level end target. */
   OBJMESH *level_clear = OBJ_get_mesh( obj, "level_clear", 0 );

/* On top of the usual CF_CUSTOM_MATERIAL_CALLBACK collision flag,
add CF_NO_CONTACT_RESPONSE. This collision flag makes your rigid
body object
act like a ghost, meaning that it will not respond to collision. This can
be used to turn off the collision response of any rigid body, which is
great for this typical scenario, where you only want the object to trigger
the callback. */
   level_clear->btrigidbody->setCollisionFlags(
   level_clear->btrigidbody->getCollisionFlags()   |
   btCollisionObject::CF_CUSTOM_MATERIAL_CALLBACK |
   btCollisionObject::CF_NO_CONTACT_RESPONSE );

/* Make the level_clear mesh invisible for rendering. */
   level_clear->visible = 0;

/* In the following block, you are going to loop through all the objects
and turn on the material collision callback for all of the gems. And while
you are there, you'll give the gems a random rotation so you can animate
them inside the rendering loop later on. */
   i = 0;
   while( i != obj->n_objmesh ) {
      /* Get the current mesh pointer. */
      OBJMESH *objmesh = &obj->objmesh[ i ];
      /* Check if the name is like "gem." */
      if( strstr( objmesh->name, "gem" ) ) {
         /* Generate a random rotation angle on the Z axis. */
         objmesh->rotation.z = ( float )( random() % 360 );
         /* Set the material collision callback for the current rigid body
attached to the mesh object. */
         objmesh->btrigidbody->setCollisionFlags(
         objmesh->btrigidbody->getCollisionFlags() |
         btCollisionObject::CF_CUSTOM_MATERIAL_CALLBACK );
      }
      ++i; /* Next object please. */
   }
```

**4.** At the top of the `free_level` function, right after the function start bracket, add the following affectations to reset the game state and other level-related variables:

```
gem_points =
game_state = 0;
game_time = 0.0f;
```

**5.** To load the next level (or in this case, simply reload the current one since there is no other level) if the game state is currently set to "reset" (2), add the following code after the start bracket of the `templateAppDraw` function:

```
if( game_state == 2 ) {
    free_level();
    load_level();
}
```

**6.** Inside the `templateAppDraw` function, on the line right before the `if( objmesh->btrigidbody )` call, add the following code to position and rotate the gem objects:

```
/* Check if the current objmesh name contains "gem." If yes, don't ask
Bullet for the transformation matrix and handle the position and rotation
manually. */
if( strstr( objmesh->name, "gem" ) ) {
    GFX_translate( objmesh->location.x,
                   objmesh->location.y,
                   objmesh->location.z );
    objmesh->rotation.z += 1.0f;
    GFX_rotate( objmesh->rotation.z, 0.0f, 0.0f, 1.0f );
}
/* Turn the current if( objmesh->btrigidbody ) into an else-if. */
else
```

**7.** Before the end bracket of the `templateAppDraw`, integrate the following code block to print onscreen the current gem points the player has collected, the game time, or if the level is cleared:

```
/* Color to use for the font, starting with black. */
vec4 font_color = { 0.0f, 0.0f, 0.0f, 1.0f };
/* Some temporary strings. */
char gem_str  [ MAX_CHAR ] = {""},
     time_str [ MAX_CHAR ] = {""},
     level_str[ MAX_CHAR ] = {""};
/* If the game state is different than 0. */
if( game_state ) {
    /* Build the string for level_clear. */
    sprintf( level_str, "Level Clear!" );
    /* Print on the screen (a bit up the center) that the level is
cleared, first in black with an offset down right, and then in yellow
without an offset. */
    FONT_print( font_big,
                viewport_matrix[ 3 ] * 0.5f -
                FONT_length( font_big, level_str ) * 0.5f + 4.0f,
```

```
                             viewport_matrix[ 2 ] -
                             font_big->font_size * 1.5f - 4.0f,
                             level_str,
                             &font_color );
          /* Yellow. */
          font_color.x = 1.0f;
          font_color.y = 1.0f;
          font_color.z = 0.0f;
          FONT_print( font_big,
                             viewport_matrix[ 3 ] * 0.5f -
                             FONT_length( font_big, level_str ) * 0.5f,
                             viewport_matrix[ 2 ] -
                             font_big->font_size * 1.5f,
                             level_str,
                             &font_color );
      }

    /* Make sure the color is black (since you might have change it in the
condition above). */
    font_color.x = 0.0f;
    font_color.y = 0.0f;
    font_color.z = 0.0f;

    /* Create the strings and print the gem points and the game time. */
    sprintf( gem_str, "Gem Points:%02d", gem_points );
    sprintf( time_str, "Game Time:%02.2f", game_time * 0.1f );

    FONT_print( font_small,
                       viewport_matrix[ 3 ] -
                       FONT_length( font_small, gem_str ) - 6.0f,
                       ( font_small->font_size * 0.5f ),
                       gem_str,
                       &font_color );

    FONT_print( font_small,
                       8.0f,
                       ( font_small->font_size * 0.5f ),
                       time_str,
                       &font_color );

    /* Yellow. */
    font_color.x = 1.0f;
    font_color.y = 1.0f;
    font_color.z = 0.0f;

    FONT_print( font_small,
                       viewport_matrix[ 3 ] -
                       FONT_length( font_small, gem_str ) - 8.0f,
                       ( font_small->font_size * 0.5f ),
                       gem_str,
                       &font_color );

    FONT_print( font_small,
                       6.0f,
```

```
                             ( font_small->font_size * 0.5f ),
                             time_str,
                             &font_color );
            /* Use the background sound source time to increase the total game time
      by requesting from OpenAL the current sound source playback time. */
            if( !game_state ) game_time += SOUND_get_time( background_sound );
```

**8.** Move to the `templateAppToucheBegan` callback and add the following code between the function brackets to let the user restart the level if the level is clear:

```
      if( game_state == 1 && tap_count >= 2 ) game_state = 2;
```

**9.** Compile and execute the program.

At the end of the game, your screen should look exactly like Figure 9-4.

A few more levels and lines of code, a bit of 3D modeling and texturing here and there, and the game is ready to hit the stores!

**FIGURE 9-4:** Finished rolling ball game

## SUMMARY

This chapter covered a lot of ground. You can now make full use of OpenAL, either manually or with this book's audio API. You can create static and positional sound sources as well as stream a large, compressed OGG audio file into another thread.

You learned how to select something onscreen using the color buffer, and you now have the knowledge to apply this technique in 2D, 2.5D, and 3D.

With the information that you've gathered about the accelerometer, you can now create other types of controls for your camera and characters. And you now have the ability to link an OpenAL listener to your camera to increase the level-immersive experience of the player.

In addition, you can now easily prepare a framework to let external artist(s) build scenes and link GFX shader files, as well as test their models directly inside your game engine.

Finally, with what you have learned about texture animation, you can simulate water, clouds, lava, and a wide range of other effects. With fog added to your scene, you can now keep a shorter far-clipping plane, which will allow you to render more objects.

Before jumping to the next chapter, make sure you review all of the tutorials and techniques that were covered in this chapter. Then when you are ready, move on to the next chapter, which is about advanced lighting.

# 10

# Advanced Lighting

**WHAT'S IN THIS CHAPTER?**

➤ Learning the different lamp types

➤ Implementing global per-pixel lighting using normal maps

➤ Implementing a directional lamp

➤ Implementing a point light

➤ Learning how to handle light attenuation

➤ Implementing a spherical point light

➤ Implementing a spot light with soft edges

➤ Learning the basics to implement a dynamic lighting system

In this chapter, I will strictly focus on teaching you how to create multiple types of per-pixel lamps using normal mapping (since I personally don't see the point of per-pixel lighting without normal maps). You will revisit what you learned about lighting earlier in this book and push the implementation to the next level.

You will first start learning about the main categories of lamps that exist in the real world. Then you will gradually implement different types of lamps in conjunction with other lighting-related effects to finally end up creating a somewhat complex and dynamic lighting system that you can then easily reuse inside your games and 3D apps.

# TYPES OF LAMPS

In the real world, there are basically three categories of lamps that you see in your everyday life. In order to create realistic 3D worlds, you will have to be able to identify them and handle them in code. That said, here are the three basic types of lamps that you will have to deal with:

➤ **Directional:** This type is determined when a light source has constant direction parallel light rays which do not diminish with distance. The best example of this type of light is the sun. Wherever you go, the direction of the sun will determine the lighting condition of the world around you based on the direction of its light ray. In 3D, directional lights can also be used to fake a kind of overall ambient illumination using more than one sun to reproduce lifelike lighting conditions.

➤ **Point:** Point light can be defined when a lamp provides an omnidirectional lighting source. This type of light illuminates the objects around it based on their current location relative to the point light position in space.

➤ **Spot:** This is basically a directional cone of light, like a street lamp or a projector. Spot lights illuminate only the objects that are contained within the light cone that they project.

Lamps are expensive and quite a burden for the GPU, because they require a lot of calculations in order to be realistic. However, there is a middle ground that provides you with good-looking lamps at a relatively cheap computation cost. And this is the middle ground that you will touch base with inside this chapter.

Before diving deeper into the different lamp implementations covered in this chapter, please note that the number of calculations required has a direct impact on how many pixels have to be lighted onscreen. The more lamps and the more pixels you have to dynamically handle onscreen, the slower your application will get. Always try to minimize the number of objects and pixels that have to be dynamically lighted in order to maintain good performance.

Only use dynamic lamps for objects that are dynamic or animated. For static objects, bake some light maps! You can easily create light maps using any decent 3D modeling software.

Baking light maps will allow you to pre-calculate and write to a texture the current lighting and/or shadowing conditions of your scene (but only for static objects). Then at run time, all you have to do is load these textures as you normally do, and modulate (multiply or mix) them with the diffuse channel to apply the pre-computed lighting and/or shadowing calculations to your objects.

# LET THERE BE LIGHT

As you already know, for each lamp that you have in your scene, a specific entry for it will have to be present in your vertex and fragment shaders. For large and dynamic scenes, hard-coding each light one-by-one or having multiple shader programs that handle a specific amount or type of lamp can be quite difficult to maintain.

In this section's exercise (and throughout this chapter), you will learn how to implement different dynamic lighting methods that you can then scale up for your specific needs.

For the sake of this exercise, you will fully illuminate each object of a scene. However, in a real game scenario, you should only tag objects that require dynamic lighting to make sure that only these objects are affected by the lamps.

On mobile devices, globally illuminating a scene in real time is almost impossible due to the limited processing power. In your own applications I suggest that you mark the object(s) that should be affected by dynamic lamps. For example, you can add a specific tag in the object names or use any other method that is convenient for you.

To start off the exercise, duplicate the `template_chapter10-1` project directory and rename it **chapter10-1**. Load the project, and then build and run it to get a feel for the environment that you are going to illuminate dynamically as illustrated in Figure 10-1.

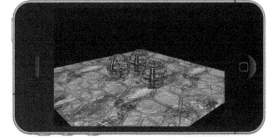

Most of the work in this chapter will focus mainly on the `lighting.gfx` file (already linked to the template project for this chapter). In this file, you will implement multiple lighting functions that will receive in parameter a lamp structure. By creating this system, you will then be able to handle multiple lights of different types using the same shader program. You'll learn how to do that later in this chapter.

**FIGURE 10-1:** Scene with only a diffuse texture

Before getting into complex lighting, you're going to learn how to implement the lamp types individually, beginning with a directional lamp. Open the `templateApp.cpp` and follow these steps:

1. At the top of the file (right above the `program_bind_attrib_location` function), create the following LAMP structure and a pointer variable of that same type to handle a directional lamp:

```
typedef struct {
    char name[ MAX_CHAR ];
    vec4 color;
    vec3 direction;
    unsigned char type;
} LAMP;

LAMP *lamp = NULL;
```

2. Add the following function to initialize the structure for a new directional lamp:

```
LAMP *LAMP_create_directional( char *name,
                               vec4 *color,
                               float rotx,
                               float roty,
                               float rotz ) {
    /* Declare the up axis vector to be static, because it won't change. */
    static vec3 up_axis = { 0.0f, 0.0f, 1.0f };
```

```
    /* Allocate memory for a new LAMP structure. */
    LAMP *lamp = ( LAMP * ) calloc( 1, sizeof( LAMP ) );
    /* Assign the name received in parameter to the structure, because it is
always nice to have an internal name for each structure. */
    strcpy( lamp->name, name );
    /* Assign the color to the lamp. */
    memcpy( &lamp->color, color, sizeof( vec4 ) );
    /* Use the following helper function (which can be found in utils.cpp)
to rotate the up axis by the XYZ rotation angle received as parameters.
I think it's a lot easier to deal with angles when it comes to direction
vectors. */
    create_direction_vector( &lamp->direction,
                             &up_axis,
                             rotx,
                             roty,
                             rotz );
    /* Set the type of the lamp as 0 for directional. */
    lamp->type = 0;
    /* Return the new lamp pointer. */
    return lamp;
}
```

3. Because you initialized the structure in memory, you need to add the following function to free it:

```
LAMP *LAMP_free( LAMP *lamp ) {
    free( lamp );
    return NULL;
}
```

4. In the `templateAppInit` function (before the end bracket), create a new directional lamp using the structure and function that you created previously:

```
vec4 color = { 1.0f, 1.0f, 1.0f, 1.0f };
lamp = LAMP_create_directional( /* The internal name of the lamp. */
                                ( char * )"sun",
                                /* The lamp color. */
                                &color,
                                /* The XYZ rotation angle in degree that
will be used to create the lamp direction vector. */
                                -25.0f,
                                0.0f,
                                -45.0f );
```

You might be asking yourself, "How come there is no position?" For a directional lamp, the position is irrelevant. As mentioned earlier, directional lamps cast a constant parallel ray light source, which explains why an XYZ position is not required. Wherever your geometry is located, the light will affect it the same way.

5. Inside the `templateAppExit` function, add the following line to free the directional lamp from the memory when the app exits:

```
lamp = LAMP_free( lamp );
```

Before going deeper into the C/C++ implementation of this exercise (such as sending uniforms to the shader), open the `lighting.gfx` file and follow the instructions in the next section in order to implement the directional lamp function and start building the shaders to handle the different types of lamps that you will be creating in this chapter.

## Directional Lamp Shader

Since your goal is to create something that you can reuse inside you own apps, you will start by creating structures inside the shader that are similar to the ones you are handling inside your C/C++ code.

GLSL fully supports structures in a way that is similar to how C handles them. Structures can make your shader code a lot cleaner, and you can use them to create dynamic functions that can receive a `struct` in parameter.

To start implementing the necessary code for your directional lamp, complete the following steps. (You will only focus on per-pixel lighting with normal mapping, because per-vertex lighting is so GLES v1 and uncool.)

**1.** Create the following `struct` in GLSL on the line below the `GL_VERTEX_SHADER` tag definition:

```
/* Create a lamp structure that has a direction property (because that is
the only one that you need right now for the vertex processing phase).*/
struct lamp {
   lowp vec3 direction;
};
```

**2.** Replace the following line in the `GL_VERTEX_SHADER` section of the GFX file:

```
uniform highp mat4 MODELVIEWPROJECTIONMATRIX;
```

with the following code block to handle the different matrices required by the vertex processing phase:

```
uniform highp mat4 MODELVIEWMATRIX;
uniform highp mat4 PROJECTIONMATRIX;
uniform lowp mat3 NORMALMATRIX;
/* Declare a uniform variable using the struct that you've created as the
type of the variable. */
uniform lamp LAMP_VS;
```

**3.** Add the following two `varying` variables right after the ones that are already declared in the vertex shader section:

```
/* The position of the vertex, is originally calculated in eye space and
then converted to tangent space (because you are going to use normal
mapping, and the normal map is in tangent space). */
varying highp vec3 position;
/* The light direction vector, sent over by the C/C++ application in
eye space and then converted to tangent space. */
varying highp vec3 lightdir;
```

**4.** Find the line starting with `gl_Position` and replace it with the following code block to calculate the TBN (tangent, binormal, normal) matrix, the position, and the lamp direction:

```
/* Declare a 3x3 matrix to handle the TBN matrix to be able to convert
the necessary lighting vectors to tangent space. */
   lowp mat3 tbn;
   /* Rotate the vertex normal by the current normal matrix. */
   tbn[ 2 ] = normalize( NORMALMATRIX * NORMAL );
   /* Rotate the tangent vector, which was created based on the direction
of the normal and the UV coordinate (see obj.cpp for more information). */
   tbn[ 0 ] = normalize( NORMALMATRIX * TANGENT0 );
   /* Here the binormal is simply computed by using the cross product of
the normal and the tangent, but you could also calculate it on the CPU to
save some GPU calculations if the object is static. */
   tbn[ 1 ] = cross( tbn[ 2 ], tbn[ 0 ] );
   /* Calculate the position of the vertex in eye space. */
   position = vec3( MODELVIEWMATRIX * vec4( POSITION, 1.0 ) );
   /* Multiply the eye space position of the vertex by the current
projection matrix to be able to place it onscreen. */
   gl_Position = PROJECTIONMATRIX * vec4( position, 1.0 );
   /* Convert the lamp direction vector from eye space to tangent space. */
   lightdir = LAMP_VS.direction * tbn;
   /* Convert the eye position of the vertex to tangent space and invert it
(because the direction in eye space is simply the invert of the vertex
eye space position). */
   position = -normalize( position * tbn );
```

**5.** Move to the `GL_FRAGMENT_SHADER` section of the GFX file and add the following `struct` declaration on the line after the fragment shader tag definition:

```
/* Declare a material structure (similar to the way you created the lamp
structure in GLSL). As you can see, this material structure uses similar
properties as an OBJMATERIAL structure that you have been using since the
beginning of the book. By doing this, it will be really easy for you to
bridge the material data held in client memory to the video memory. */
struct material {
   lowp vec4 ambient;
   lowp vec4 diffuse;
   lowp vec4 specular;
   mediump float shininess; /* Aka specular exponent. */
};
/* Declare another lamp structure, but this time for the fragment
processing phase. Even if the name is the same as the one in the vertex
shader GLSL, it will still be treated as a different entity, because vertex
and fragment shaders do not share variables (except for varyings). */
struct lamp {
   lowp vec4 color;
};
```

**6.** On the line after the `BUMP` uniform definition, add the following uniforms and varyings:

```
/* To be able to receive the lamp data for the fragment processing phase. */
uniform lamp LAMP_FS;
/* The current material data used by the geometry you are drawing
```

```
onscreen. */
uniform material MATERIAL;
/* The vertex position (in tangent space). */
varying highp vec3 position;
/* The light direction (in tangent space). */
varying highp vec3 lightdir;
```

**7.**  Now create a new function in GLSL on the line just before the `main` function to be able to effectuate the necessary calculation for a directional lamp. This function will receive variables in parameters and use other global variables that have been sent to the shader:

```
void directional_lamp( in lamp _lamp,
                       in lowp vec3 _lightdir,
                       inout lowp vec4 _final_color ) {
   /* Extract the current normal for the fragment from the normal map
(which is already in tangent space) and convert it to a valid range so you
can deal with it as a regular normal vector. */
   lowp vec3 normal =
   texture2D( BUMP, texcoord0 ).rgb * 2.0 - 1.0;
   /* Calculate the lambert term (light intensity) for the current
fragment. */
   lowp float ndotl =
   max( dot( normal, _lightdir ), 0.0 );
   /* If the result is greater than 0, it means that the fragment
received light. */
   if( ndotl > 0.0 ) {
       /* Calculate the intensity of the specular color by calculating the
dot product of the normal with the half vector (light direction +
position). */
       lowp float ndoth =
       max( dot( normal,
               normalize( _lightdir + position ) ), 0.0 );
       /* Calculate the diffuse color for the current fragment based on the
material diffuse color, the lamp color, and the light intensity. */
       _final_color += MATERIAL.diffuse *
                       _lamp.color *
                       ndotl;
   /* Do the same for the specular color, except this time calculate the
specular exponent based on the dot product of the specular intensity and
the material specular exponent (shininess or material hardness if you
prefer). */
       _final_color += MATERIAL.specular *
                       _lamp.color *
                       pow( ndoth, MATERIAL.shininess );
   }
}
```

**8.**  Now replace the `gl_FragColor` line with the following block to call the `directional_lamp` function with the current `LAMP` uniform and `lightdir` data that the fragment shader receives:

```
/* Declare a new variable to handle the final color of the
fragment and initialize it with the current material ambient color. */
```

```
    lowp vec4 final_color = MATERIAL.ambient;
    /* Call the directional_lamp function to send in parameter the current
LAMP_FS variable,light direction and the final color to use for the current
fragment. */
    directional_lamp( LAMP_FS, lightdir, final_color );
    /* Execute a simple texture lookup on the diffuse texture channel
and multiply it by the final color accumulated in the
directional_lamp function. */
    gl_FragColor = texture2D( DIFFUSE, texcoord0 ) * final_color;
```

Lighting in GLSL can be quite tricky, because it can be done in different spaces, such as in world space, eye space, or tangent space. Most beginners have issues with lighting due to the fact that their data are calculated in different spaces.

As a general trick, always keep in mind that it does not really matter in which space you calculate lighting as long as your data are all converted to that same space. Once your data is unified into the specific space of your choice, you can calculate lighting the same way.

At this point, your shader program is basically ready to run, but as you probably already know, one last piece is missing inside your C/C++ implementation. You have to pass the uniform variables to the shader. Read the following section to send over the necessary data to run your application.

## Struct as Uniforms

The beauty of using struct in GLSL is that you can handle variables as a whole object (or container if you prefer). They can also be used as they are in C — within arrays or as function parameters — which makes them extremely flexible. With this approach, you can maintain in C/C++ a struct that is similar to the one in GLSL and assign variables for both the vertex and fragment processing phase, as you see fit, using a single reference (very practical!).

Follow these steps to finalize your app and integrate the necessary code to send over the uniforms required by your shader:

1.  Go back to the templateApp.cpp, and inside the program_draw function callback, append the following code block after the BUMP uniform else if to send over the necessary matrices to the shader used by the current objmesh pointer:

```
// Matrix Data
else if( !strcmp( program->uniform_array[ i ].name,
        "MODELVIEWMATRIX" ) ) {
    glUniformMatrix4fv(
    program->uniform_array[ i ].location,
    1,
    GL_FALSE,
    ( float * )GFX_get_modelview_matrix() );
}

else if( !strcmp( program->uniform_array[ i ].name,
        "PROJECTIONMATRIX" ) ) {
    glUniformMatrix4fv(
    program->uniform_array[ i ].location,
    1,
```

```
                GL_FALSE,
                ( float * )GFX_get_projection_matrix() );
                /* Set the projection matrix to be constant. (You won't change it
    in real time, so you simply need to make sure that the matrix is sent once
    to the shader.) */
                program->uniform_array[ i ].constant = 1;
        }

        else if( !strcmp( program->uniform_array[ i ].name,
                "NORMALMATRIX" ) ) {
            glUniformMatrix3fv(
            program->uniform_array[ i ].location,
            1,
            GL_FALSE,
            ( float * )GFX_get_normal_matrix() );
        }
```

2.  Now send over the material data. Append the following code block on the line right below the code block of step 1 (and pay attention to the way the MATERIAL uniform property names are accessed):

```
        // Material Data
        else if( !strcmp( program->uniform_array[ i ].name,
                "MATERIAL.ambient" ) ) {
            glUniform4fv(
            program->uniform_array[ i ].location,
            1,
            ( float * )&objmesh->current_material->ambient );
            /* In this scene, all the materials (in this case, there are only
    two ) have the exact same properties, so simply tag the uniforms for the
    current material to be constant. This will also allow you to get better
    performance at runtime, because the data will not be sent over and over for
    nothing. */
            program->uniform_array[ i ].constant = 1;
        }

        else if( !strcmp( program->uniform_array[ i ].name,
                "MATERIAL.diffuse" ) ) {
            glUniform4fv(
            program->uniform_array[ i ].location,
            1,
            ( float * )&objmesh->current_material->diffuse );
            program->uniform_array[ i ].constant = 1;
        }

        else if( !strcmp( program->uniform_array[ i ].name,
                "MATERIAL.specular" ) ) {
            glUniform4fv(
            program->uniform_array[ i ].location,
            1,
            ( float * )&objmesh->current_material->specular );
            program->uniform_array[ i ].constant = 1;
        }

        else if( !strcmp( program->uniform_array[ i ].name,
```

```
                      "MATERIAL.shininess" ) ) {
            glUniform1f(
            program->uniform_array[ i ].location,
            objmesh->current_material->specular_exponent *
            0.128f );
            program->uniform_array[ i ].constant = 1;
        }
```

3. Before dealing with the uniform variables for the LAMP, on the line right before the LAMP_ free function declaration, create the following new function to be able to get the current light direction in eye space in order to send it over to the shader:

```
void LAMP_get_direction_in_eye_space( LAMP *lamp,
                                      mat4 *m,
                                      vec3 *direction ) {
    /* Multiply the current lamp direction by the view matrix received in
parameter to be able to calculate the lamp direction in eye space. */
    vec3_multiply_mat4( direction,
                        &lamp->direction,
                        m );
    /* Invert the vector, because in eye space, the direction is simply the
inverted vector.*/
    vec3_invert( direction, direction );
}
```

4. Go back to the program_draw callback, and on the line right before the end bracket of the function, add the following code block to deal with the LAMP uniform data. (Note that you are not including the code to send uniforms inside the while loop of the callback. You will see why in a later exercise.)

```
    /* A temp string to dynamically create the LAMP property names. */
    char tmp[ MAX_CHAR ] = {""};
    /* Create the uniform name for the color of the lamp. */
    sprintf( tmp, "LAMP_FS.color" );
    /* Get the uniform location and send over the current lamp color. */
    glUniform4fv(
    PROGRAM_get_uniform_location( program, tmp ),
    1,
    ( float * )&lamp->color );
    /* Check if the lamp type is directional. If yes, you need to send over
the normalized light direction vector in eye space. */
    if( lamp->type == 0 ) {
        /* Temp variable to hold the direction in eye space. */
        vec3 direction;
        /* Create the lamp direction property name. */
        sprintf( tmp, "LAMP_VS.direction" );
        /* Call the function that you created in the previous step to convert
the current world space direction vector of the lamp to eye space. Note
that at this point, the current model view matrix stack is pushed because
you are currently drawing the object. In order to calculate the right
direction vector of the lamp, what you are interested in is gaining access
to the camera model view matrix. To do this, all you have to do is request
the previous model view matrix, because you push it once in the
templateAppDraw function. */
```

```
LAMP_get_direction_in_eye_space(
lamp,
&gfx.modelview_matrix[ gfx.modelview_matrix_index - 1 ],
&direction );
/* Send over the direction in eye space. */
glUniform3fv(
PROGRAM_get_uniform_location( program, tmp ),
1,
( float * )&direction );
}
```

**5.** Build and run your app. Your screen should look exactly the same as in Figure 10-2.

It's looking good already, don't you think? And this is all running at full speed! The trick with per-fragment lighting is to run as many operations as you can on CPU or inside the vertex processing phase, and use as few instructions (and branching) as possible inside the fragment processing phase.

**FIGURE 10-2:** Directional lamp with normal mapping and specularity

In the next section, you will learn how to implement a point light.

## POINT LIGHT

Now that you have the main structure in place for this chapter's exercises, it's going to be a lot faster and easier to implement the other types of lamps.

For adding point light functionalities to your app, start by duplicating the chapter10-1 project and rename it **chapter10-2**.

Then, follow these instructions to learn how to modify your existing code to be able to support point light:

**1.** In templateApp.cpp, add the following property inside the LAMP structure definition (typedef struct):

```
/* The position of the lamp in world coordinates. */
vec4 position;
```

Contrary to directional lamps, point lights are all about where in space they are located. Point lamps will illuminate the fragment based on the direction of the vertex and the lamp position.

**2.** Now create a new helper function to create a point light. Insert the following function on the line after the end bracket of the LAMP_create_directional declaration (in order to keep all the creation functions together):

```
LAMP *LAMP_create_point( char *name,
                         vec4 *color,
                         vec3 *position ) {
```

```
        LAMP *lamp = ( LAMP * ) calloc( 1, sizeof( LAMP ) );
        strcpy( lamp->name, name );
        memcpy( &lamp->color, color, sizeof( vec4 ) );
        /* Assign the position received in parameter to the current lamp
    pointer. In addition, make sure that you specify 1 as the W component of
    the position, because you are going to need to multiply it by the model
    view matrix the same way as if you were dealing with a vertex position in
    eye space. */
        memcpy( &lamp->position, position, sizeof( vec3 ) );
        lamp->position.w = 1.0f;
        /* Specify that 1 represents a basic point light that emits a
    constant omnidirectional light. */
        lamp->type = 1;
        return lamp;
    }
```

**3.** Locate the call where you created your sun earlier (lamp = LAMP_create_directional), and comment it. Then on the next line, add the following code to create a point light that calls the helper function you just created:

```
    /* The 3D position in world space of the point light. */
    vec3 position = { 3.5f, 3.0f, 6.0f };
    /* Create a new LAMP pointer and declare it as a simple point light. */
    lamp = LAMP_create_point( ( char * )"point", &color, &position );
```

**4.** You are now ready to add to your current existing shader program the necessary code to handle this type of lamp. So open the lighting.gfx file and proceed to the next section.

## Point Light Shader Code

Right now, not much has to be changed inside your existing shader code to be able to handle point lights. Just follow these steps to make the necessary changes to handle the new type of lamp you just created:

**1.** Add the following position property to the lamp struct of the GL_VERTEX_SHADER section:

```
    /* The XYZ position of the lamp that will be received in eye space (in
    other words, already multiplied by the camera model view matrix). Note that
    this operation will be handled in C/C++ at runtime. */
    highp vec3 position;
```

**2.** Inside the main function of the shader, comment the following line:

```
    lightdir = LAMP_VS.direction * tbn;
```

And on the next line, add the following code to be able to handle the light direction:

```
    lightdir = ( LAMP_VS.position - position ) * tbn;
```

As you can see, this time the light direction for point lights is calculated on a per-vertex basis relative to the position of the vertex and the position of the lamp. These are both in eye space at first and are then converted to tangent space so that normal mapping will work correctly.

**3.** Move to the GL_FRAGMENT_SHADER section to implement the point lamp function. On the line after the end bracket of the directional_lamp function, insert the following code block for your point lamp:

```
/* As you can see, this is very similar to the function you created
for the directional lamp; however there are a few differences. */
void point_lamp( in lamp _lamp,
                 in highp vec3 _lightdir,
                 inout lowp vec4 _final_color ) {
    lowp vec3 normal = texture2D( BUMP, texcoord0 ).rgb * 2.0 - 1.0;
    /* Normalize the light direction vector in the fragment processing
phase. You will see why in a later exercise. */
    lowp vec3 nlightdir = normalize( _lightdir );
    /* Compare the normal with the normalized light direction based on the
position of the lamp and the vertex. */
    lowp float ndotl = max( dot( normal, nlightdir ), 0.0 );
    if( ndotl > 0.0 ) {
        /* Use the normalized version of the light direction vector to
calculate the half vector. */
        lowp float ndoth =
        max( dot( normal, normalize( nlightdir + position ) ), 0.0 );
        _final_color += MATERIAL.diffuse *
                        _lamp.color *
                        ndotl;
        _final_color += MATERIAL.specular *
                        _lamp.color *
                        pow( ndoth, MATERIAL.shininess );
    }
}
```

**4.** Finally, comment the following line:

```
directional_lamp( LAMP_FS, lightdir, final_color );
```

And on the next line, add the following code to let the shader call your new function:

```
point_lamp( LAMP_FS, lightdir, final_color );
```

You now have everything in place to be able to handle both directional and point lamps. All you have to do is call the appropriate function for the type of lamp you are dealing with.

In order to keep things simple right now, you should only handle one lamp type at a time. However, you could always use an if statement and send over the current lamp type as a uniform to redirect the execution pointer to the appropriate lighting function.

The last piece that is missing before you can run the program consists of sending the lamp position to the shader program. To do that, simply get back to the templateApp.cpp and follow these last few steps.

**1.** To keep things clear and consistent, add the following function on the line after the LAMP_ get_direction_in_eye_space function end bracket to convert an arbitrary lamp position in eye space based on a model view matrix (in this case, the model view matrix of the current camera):

```
/* This function is basically very easy. In the same way that you convert
the position in your vertex shader, handle the conversion to eye space here
so you do not have to pass the model view matrix of the camera to the
shader, and offload a bit of work from the CPU. */
void LAMP_get_position_in_eye_space( LAMP *lamp,
                                     mat4 *m,
                                     vec4 *position ) {
    /* Multiply the position by the matrix received in parameters and
assign the result to the position vector. */
    vec4_multiply_mat4( position,
                        &lamp->position,
                        m );
}
```

2. Add the following condition to the current `if( lamp->type` statement in order to send the `position` of the lamp in eye space to the program if the current lamp is a point light:

```
else if( lamp->type == 1 ) {
    vec4 position;
    sprintf( tmp, "LAMP_VS.position" );
    LAMP_get_position_in_eye_space(
    lamp,
    &gfx.modelview_matrix[ gfx.modelview_matrix_index - 1 ],
    &position );
    glUniform3fv( PROGRAM_get_uniform_location( program, tmp ),
                  1,
                  ( float * )&position );
}
```

3. You are done with the point light implementation. Now just compile and execute the program to achieve the same lighting effect as demonstrated in Figure 10-3.

As you can see, the lighting effect achieved from a point light is drastically different from the effect of a directional lamp. (Compare Figure 10-3 with Figure 10-2.)

**FIGURE 10-3:** Constant point light with normal mapping and specularity

At the moment, the light attenuation is constant; thus the distance between the light source and your object will not cause the property of the light to diminish in intensity.

In the next section, you are going to learn how to add attenuation based on the distance of the fragment with the lamp, and learn how to set the falloff distance of the point light.

# Light Attenuation

Point lights are great; however, you probably won't want to illuminate a whole scene with one point light. In the real world, point lights generally illuminate only a specific area based on the falloff distance of the lamp, where the light rays simply fade and lose their intensity.

Implementing this behavior in GLSL couldn't be easier, and you already have everything in place to do so. To implement a new version of the point light that supports attenuation, duplicate the chapter10-2 project and rename it **chapter10-3**.

Load the project into your IDE and follow these steps:

**1.** Inside the templateApp.cpp, once again you will have to add more properties to the LAMP structure. Here are the properties you need to add:

```
/* Affect the attenuation of the light based on its distance from
the fragment. */
float linear_attenuation;
/* Affect the attenuation of the light based on the square of the distance
of the fragment with the light. */
float quadratic_attenuation;
/* The falloff distance of the light. The light will be at half of its
original intensity at this distance. */
float distance;
```

**2.** Right after the end bracket of the LAMP_create_point function, add the following code block to create a new helper function to generate a new point light with attenuation:

```
LAMP *LAMP_create_point_with_attenuation(
        char *name,
        vec4 *color,
        vec3 *position,
        float distance,
        float linear_attenuation,
        float quadratic_attenuation ) {
    LAMP *lamp = ( LAMP * ) calloc( 1, sizeof( LAMP ) );
    strcpy( lamp->name, name );
    memcpy( &lamp->color, color, sizeof( vec4 ) );
    memcpy( &lamp->position, position, sizeof( vec3 ) );
    lamp->position.w = 1.0f;
    /* Store the linear attenuation. */
    lamp->linear_attenuation = linear_attenuation;
    /* Store the quadratic attenuation. */
    lamp->quadratic_attenuation = quadratic_attenuation;
    /* Store the double distance, because the falloff distance parameter
represents the half distance where the light starts to be attenuated. */
    lamp->distance = distance * 2.0f;
    /* Create a new lamp type. */
    lamp->type = 2;
    return lamp;
}
```

**3.** Comment the following lamp creation line:

```
lamp = LAMP_create_point( ( char * )"point", &color, &position );
```

and on the next line, add this code:

```
/* The linear and quadratic attenuation are a values that range from 0 to
1, which will be directly affected by the falloff distance of the lamp. 1
means fully attenuated, and 0 represents constant (same as in the regular
point light calculations in the previous section). */
lamp = LAMP_create_point_with_attenuation( ( char * )"point1",
                                           &color,
                                           &position,
                                           10.0f,
                                           0.5f,
                                           1.0f );
```

## Point Light with Attenuation Code

Open the `lighting.gfx` file in order to create a new lamp function that supports attenuation for your new point light. In order for the attenuation to look good, you will have to integrate the necessary calculations in the fragment processing phase, because calculating it inside the vertex processing phase will not have much impact, especially if your geometry is not highly detailed. To integrate the per-fragment attenuation code, follow these steps:

**1.** Add the following variables to the `lamp` structure inside the `GL_FRAGMENT_SHADER` section:

```
mediump float distance;
lowp float linear_attenuation;
lowp float quadratic_attenuation;
```

**2.** Copy the whole `point_lamp` block, starting from the function definition line to the end bracket of the function and paste it on the line below, in order to end up with two `point_lamp` functions. Then rename the second function from `point_lamp` to **point_lamp_with_attenuation.**

**3.** Inside the `point_lamp_with_attenuation` function, insert the following code to calculate the attenuation on the line after the `if( ndotl` start bracket so the calculation will be effectuated only on lighted fragments:

```
    /* Get the distance of the fragment from the light position by
requesting the length of the light direction vector. */
    highp float dist = length( _lightdir );
    /* Calculate the square falloff distance. */
    highp float lampdistsqr = _lamp.distance * _lamp.distance;
    /* Use the linear value in conjunction with the distance to calculate
how much the linear attenuation will impact the fragment. */
    lowp float att =
    _lamp.distance /
    ( _lamp.distance + _lamp.linear_attenuation * dist );
    /* Take the current attenuation factor and process how much the
quadratic attenuation will affect the fragment. */
    att *= lampdistsqr /
    ( lampdistsqr + _lamp.quadratic_attenuation * dist * dist );
```

**4.** Still inside the `point_lamp_with_attenuation` function, multiply the attenuation (the `att` variable) calculated in step 3 as the final factor of the `diffuse` and `specular` color, like this:

```
_final_color += MATERIAL.diffuse *
                _lamp.color *
                ndotl *
                att; /* Multiplied by the attenuation. */

_final_color += MATERIAL.specular *
                _lamp.color *
                pow( ndoth, MATERIAL.shininess ) *
                att; /* Multiplied by the attenuation. */
```

**5.** Comment the line where you call `point_lamp( LAMP, lightdir, final_color );` and add the following line to be able to use the new function you create:

```
point_lamp_with_attenuation( LAMP_FS, lightdir, final_color );
```

The shader has been successfully modified to use your new point lamp with an attenuation function. In the next section, you'll learn how to send the uniforms to finish setting up point light attenuation.

## The Attenuation Uniforms

In order to visualize your newly created point light with attenuation, you need to send over the necessary uniforms to your shader program.

To send the attenuation calculation uniforms variable, simply open your `templateApp.cpp`, copy the following block, and paste it before the end bracket of the `program_draw` function:

```
else if( lamp->type == 2 ) {
    vec4 position;
    sprintf( tmp, "LAMP_VS.position" );

    LAMP_get_position_in_eye_space(
    lamp,
    &gfx.modelview_matrix[ gfx.modelview_matrix_index - 1 ],
    &position );

    glUniform3fv(
    PROGRAM_get_uniform_location( program, tmp ),
    1,
    ( float * )&position );

    sprintf( tmp, "LAMP_FS.distance" );
    glUniform1f(
    PROGRAM_get_uniform_location( program, tmp ),
    lamp->distance );

    sprintf( tmp, "LAMP_FS.linear_attenuation" );
    glUniform1f(
    PROGRAM_get_uniform_location( program, tmp ),
```

```
        lamp->linear_attenuation );

        sprintf( tmp, "LAMP_FS.quadratic_attenuation" );
        glUniform1f(
        PROGRAM_get_uniform_location( program, tmp ),
        lamp->quadratic_attenuation );
    }
```

Now build and run the program. Your screen should look like Figure 10-4.

As you can see from the illustration, the light is fading quite rapidly due to the values that you have set for the quadratic and linear attenuation.

**FIGURE 10-4:** Point light attenuation (distance 10, linear attenuation 0.5, quadratic attenuation 1.0)

By manipulating the distance and the attenuation parameters, you can really gain control over what is illuminated by a point light and what is not. Before moving on to the next section, I suggest that you test different point light attenuation values to see what impact they have on the lighting conditions. For example, Figure 10-5 shows the result of reducing the distance and quadratic attenuation to be half.

## Spherical Point Light

Even after you apply attenuation to a point light, it's still hard to have full control on which objects will be affected by this light source in the scene. For example, an object can be so

**FIGURE 10-5:** Point light attenuation (distance 5, linear attenuation 0.5, quadratic attenuation 0.5)

far from a specific point light source that the effect is hardly detectable by human eyes, but its lighting condition from this point light source is still calculated. And as you know, in OpenGL ES v2, it's all about minimizing the calculations to get the best effect at the minimal cost. Therefore, modifications for optimizing the computing process have to be considered to deliver the best result.

The point light modifications that you're going to make in this section consist of setting the light intensity to 0 for every fragment that is outside the point light radius controlled by the distance parameter (in the same way as you implemented the clipping in Chapter 7). This will allow you to easily calculate on the CPU which objects are inside the radius of a specific point light (using the vec3_dist function). Then, your implementation can determine which point light should be ON or OFF when drawing specific objects. This will drastically decrease the number of calculations on the GPU that would finally end up calculating a 0, giving you more GPU power to draw other effects.

To implement this new variant of the point light, duplicate the chapter10-3 project directory and rename it **chapter10-4**. Then load the project and follow these steps:

**1.** On the line after the LAMP_create_point_with_attenuation function end bracket, add the following function:

```
/* Basically create a point light, but with a distance parameter. */
LAMP *LAMP_create_point_sphere( char *name,
                                vec4 *color,
                                vec3 *position,
                                float distance ) {
    /* Redirect the execution pointer to create a simple point light, and
then adjust and tweak the other parameters to fit a new lamp type. */
    LAMP *lamp = LAMP_create_point( name, color, position );
    lamp->distance = distance;
    lamp->type = 3;
    return lamp;
}
```

**2.** Move to the `templateAppInit` function, and comment the following code:

```
lamp =
LAMP_create_point_with_attenuation( ( char * )"point1",
                                    &color,
                                    &position,
                                    10.0f,
                                    0.5f,
                                    1.0f );
```

and on the next line, add the following line to create a new "point sphere" lamp:

```
lamp =
LAMP_create_point_sphere( ( char * )"point2",
                          &color,
                          &position,
                          10.0f );
```

## Tweaking the Point Light Code

Next, you need to modify the shader code to allow your new point sphere lamp to set the light intensity to 0 if it's beyond the lamp distance. To do this, open the `lighting.gfx` file and follow these steps:

**1.** Copy the whole `point_lamp` function in the GL_FRAGMENT_SHADER section onto your clipboard and paste it after the end bracket of `point_lamp_with_attenuation`. Because you now have two `point_lamp` functions, rename the second one to be **point_sphere_lamp**.

**2.** Inside the `point_sphere_lamp` function, on the line after the start bracket of the `if( ndotl` statement, add the following line:

```
/* Calculate if the current fragment is inside the lamp sphere. */
lowp float sphere =
max( _lamp.distance - length( _lightdir ),
     0.0 ) / _lamp.distance;
```

**3.** Multiply the point lamp spherical intensity factor to the `diffuse` and the `specular` color computation, as the final factor of the `diffuse` and `specular` color (similar to what you did with the attenuation).

```
_final_color += MATERIAL.diffuse *
                _lamp.color *
                ndotl *
                sphere;

_final_color += MATERIAL.specular *
                _lamp.color *
                pow( ndoth, MATERIAL.shininess ) *
                sphere;
```

**4.** Comment the line where you call `point_lamp_with_attenuation` in the `main` function, and on the next line, insert the following call to trigger your new `point_sphere_lamp` function instead:

```
point_sphere_lamp( LAMP_FS, lightdir, final_color );
```

**5.** Back to the `templateApp.cpp`, append a new `else if` by inserting the following code before the end bracket of the `program_draw` callback:

```
/* This is basically the same as for type #1 (basic point light), except
that the distance is sent over to the shader. */
    else if( lamp->type == 3 ) {
        vec4 position;
        sprintf( tmp, "LAMP_VS.position" );
        LAMP_get_position_in_eye_space(
        lamp,
        &gfx.modelview_matrix[ gfx.modelview_matrix_index - 1 ],
        &position );
        glUniform3fv( PROGRAM_get_uniform_location( program, tmp ),
                1,
                ( float * )&position );

        sprintf( tmp, "LAMP_FS.distance" );
        glUniform1f( PROGRAM_get_uniform_location( program, tmp ),
                lamp->distance );
    }
```

**6.** Run the program. You should now see what's shown in Figure 10-6 on your screen. All the pixels whose distance values are greater than the sphere radius specified will not be affected by the light emitted by the point lamp and will simply use the ambient color as the final color for the fragment.

**FIGURE 10-6:** Spherical point light

The method demonstrated in this section is very useful on mobile devices. It is relatively fast, and it can really minimize the number of calculations on a fragment basis when combined with a higher-level lamp clipping system.

Before moving on to the next section, try different distance values as well as different lamp positions to make sure you fully grasp the potential of this implementation.

## Spot Light

This is probably the coolest of all lamps, and having a per-pixel spot projected on your scene is very effective. To start building your own spot light implementation, duplicate the chapter10-4 project and rename it **chapter10-5**.

Load the project into your IDE, open the templateApp.cpp source file, and then follow these steps:

**1.**  Add the following two properties to the LAMP structure:

```
/* The cosine of half the field of view of the spot (in radiant). */
float spot_cos_cutoff;
/* Factor ranging from 0 to 1 to smooth the edge of the spot circle. */
float spot_blend;
/* The spot direction is calculated by multiplying the direction vector by
the invert of the model view matrix of the camera. */
vec3 spot_direction;
```

**2.**  On the line after the end bracket of the LAMP_create_point_sphere function, add the following code to create a new function that is able to create a spot light:

```
LAMP *LAMP_create_spot( char *name,
                        vec4 *color,
                        vec3 *position,
/* The XYZ rotation angle of the spot direction vector in degrees. */
                        float rotx,
                        float roty,
                        float rotz,
/* The field of view of the spot, also in degrees. */
                        float fov,
/* The spot blend to smooth the edge of the spot. This value is between the
range of 0 and 1, where 0 represents no smoothing. */
                        float spot_blend ) {
    static vec3 up_axis = { 0.0f, 0.0f, 1.0f };
    LAMP *lamp = ( LAMP * ) calloc( 1, sizeof( LAMP ) );
    strcpy( lamp->name, name );
    memcpy( &lamp->color, color, sizeof( vec4 ) );
    /* Calculate the spot cost cut off. */
    lamp->spot_cos_cutoff = cosf( ( fov * 0.5f ) * DEG_TO_RAD );
    /* Clamp the spot blend to make sure that there won't be a division by 0
inside the shader program. */
    lamp->spot_blend = CLAMP( spot_blend, 0.001, 1.0 );
    memcpy( &lamp->position, position, sizeof( vec3 ) );
    lamp->position.w = 1.0f;
    /* The type ID for spot light. */
    lamp->type = 4;
```

```
        /* Create the direction vector for the spot based on the XYZ
    rotation angle that the function receives. */
        create_direction_vector( &lamp->spot_direction,
                                 &up_axis,
                                 rotx,
                                 roty,
                                 rotz );

        return lamp;
    }
```

**3.** On the line right after the end bracket of the function you created in the last step, add the following block to create a function that is able to convert the spot direction vector to homogeneous object coordinates:

```
    void LAMP_get_direction_in_object_space( LAMP *lamp,
                                             mat4 *m,
                                             vec3 *direction ) {
        mat4 invert;
        mat4_copy_mat4( &invert, m );
        mat4_invert( &invert );
        vec3_multiply_mat4( direction,
                            &lamp->spot_direction,
                            m );
        vec3_normalize( direction,
                        direction );
        vec3_invert( direction,
                     direction );
    }
```

**4.** Locate the following line in the `templateAppInit` function and comment it:

```
    lamp = LAMP_create_point_sphere( ( char * )"point2",
                                     &color,
                                     &position,
                                     10.0f );
```

and then on the next line, add the following code to create a new spot:

```
    lamp = LAMP_create_spot( ( char * )"spot",
                             &color,
                             &position,
                             /* The spot XYZ rotation angle. */
                             -25.0f,
                              0.0f,
                             -45.0f,
                             /* The field of view in degree. */
                             75.0f,
                             /* The spot blend. */
                             0.05 );
```

At this point, everything is almost ready in your application to be able to handle a spot. The last step is to send over the necessary uniform variables. But first move to the next section to learn how to modify your existing `lighting.gfx` shader to be able to use a spot light.

## Spot Light Shader Code

Open the `lighting.gfx` file and follow these steps to be able to support spots:

**1.** Add the following spot direction property to the `lamp` structure of the GL_VERTEX_SHADER section:

```
lowp vec3 spot_direction;
```

**2.** Declare the following `varying` variable on the line after the `texcoord0` declaration to be able to pass the spot direction in tangent space to the fragment shader:

```
varying lowp vec3 spotdir;
```

**3.** Inside the `main` function, add the following line right after the line where you affect the `lightdir`. For a spot, you will need to send both the `lightdir` and `spotdirection` to the fragment shader.

```
/* Convert current spot direction from homogeneous object space to
tangent space to make sure that all lighting data are in the same space
before proceeding with the appropriate lighting calculation. */
spotdir = LAMP_VS.spot_direction * tbn;
```

**4.** Move to the GL_FRAGMENT_SHADER section and add the following spot cutoff and spot blend properties to the `lamp` structure:

```
lowp float spot_cos_cutoff;
lowp float spot_blend;
```

**5.** At the end of the list of fragment shader varyings, on the line after the `texcoord0` declaration, append the following variable (which you declared in step 2):

```
varying lowp vec3 spotdir;
```

**6.** On the line after the end bracket of the `point_sphere_lamp` function, add the following code block to create a new function that is able to handle a spot:

```
void spot_lamp( in lamp _lamp,
                in highp vec3 _lightdir,
                in lowp vec3 _spotdir,
                inout lowp vec4 _final_color ) {
    lowp vec3 normal = texture2D( BUMP, texcoord0 ).rgb * 2.0 - 1.0;
    lowp vec3 nlightdir = normalize( _lightdir );
    lowp float ndotl = max( dot( normal, nlightdir ), 0.0 );
    if( ndotl > 0.0 ) {
        /* Calculate the dot product between the normalized light direction
and the spot direction. */
        lowp float ldots = max( dot( nlightdir, _spotdir ), 0.0 );
        /* If the result is greater than the spot cos cutoff, it means that
the fragment receives light and is inside the cone of light projected by
the spot. */
```

```
            if( ldots > _lamp.spot_cos_cutoff ) {
                lowp float ndoth =
                max( dot( normal,
                          normalize( nlightdir + position ) ), 0.0 );
                /* Progressively smooth the edges of the light circle of
    the spot based on the current dot product of the spot direction and
    the light direction. */
                lowp float spot =
                ldots * clamp(
                ( ldots - _lamp.spot_cos_cutoff ) / _lamp.spot_blend,
                0.0, 1.0 );
                /* Multiply the result by the attenuation. */
                _final_color += MATERIAL.diffuse *
                                _lamp.color *
                                ndotl * spot;
                _final_color += MATERIAL.specular *
                                _lamp.color *
                                pow( ndoth, MATERIAL.shininess ) *
                                spot;
            }
        }
    }
```

7. Inside the `main` function, comment the line that calls the `point_sphere_lamp` function, and on the next line, add the following call to let the execution pointer trigger the spot lighting calculation:

```
    spot_lamp( LAMP_FS, lightdir, spotdir, final_color );
```

8. In order to finalize the spot light implementation, get back to the `templateApp.cpp` and add the following block of code before the end bracket of the `program_draw` function:

```
    /* To handle spot lights. */
    else if( lamp->type == 4 ) {
        vec4 position;
        sprintf( tmp, "LAMP_VS.position" );
        LAMP_get_position_in_eye_space(
        lamp,
        &gfx.modelview_matrix[ gfx.modelview_matrix_index - 1 ],
        &position );
        glUniform3fv( PROGRAM_get_uniform_location( program, tmp ),
                1,
                ( float * )&position );
        /* Calculating the direction of a spot is slightly different than for
    a directional lamp, because the cone has to be projected in the same space
    as the object that might receive light. */
        vec3 direction;
        sprintf( tmp, "LAMP_VS.spot_direction" );
        LAMP_get_direction_in_object_space( lamp,
        &gfx.modelview_matrix[ gfx.modelview_matrix_index - 1 ],
        &direction );
        glUniform3fv( PROGRAM_get_uniform_location( program, tmp ),
                1,
```

```
                    ( float * )&direction );
          /* Send the spot cos cutoff to let the shader determine if a
     specific fragment is inside or outside the cone of light. */
          sprintf( tmp, "LAMP_FS.spot_cos_cutoff" );
          glUniform1f( PROGRAM_get_uniform_location( program, tmp ),
                    lamp->spot_cos_cutoff );
          /* Send the spot blend. */
          sprintf( tmp, "LAMP_FS.spot_blend" );
          glUniform1f( PROGRAM_get_uniform_location( program, tmp ),
                    lamp->spot_blend );
     }
```

**9.** Build and run your project. You now have a fully working spot light that can receive an arbitrary position, direction, and field of view, just like in Figure 10-7.

Before wrapping up this exercise, make sure that you test multiple values to be able to tweak and adjust the spot to fit your requirements.

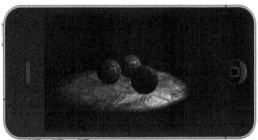

**FIGURE 10-7:** Scene illuminated using a spot light

## MULTIPLE LIGHTS

I still have a lot to say about lighting, but unfortunately, it is time for me to wrap up this chapter. In the last exercise of this chapter, you will modify your existing code to be able to handle multiple lamps, and render them simultaneously in real time.

Switching your current implementation to be able to handle multiple lights at this point is very easy. All you have to do is create an array of lamps. Then inside your C/C++ implementation, as well as in the shader program, you only need to loop for the number of lamps you want to place in your scene.

Duplicate chapter10-5 and rename it **chapter10-6**, then follow the instructions below to be able to dynamically allocate a specific amount of lamps rendered simultaneously (as demonstrated in Figure 10-8).

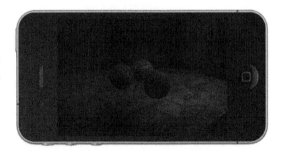

**FIGURE 10-8:** Scene illuminated using two point sphere lights

Follow these steps to learn how to modify your app to be able to render your scene using two point sphere lamps:

**1.** Inside the templateApp.cpp at the top of the file, replace the lamp pointer variable definition from this:

```
LAMP *lamp = NULL;
```

to this:

```
/* Define the maximum amount of lamps your implementation can handle
```

```
simultaneously. For this example, you're defining 2. */
#define MAX_LAMP 2
/* Declare an array of lamp pointers.*/
LAMP *lamp[ MAX_LAMP ];
```

**2.** Inside the `program_draw` function callback, comment the block where you are handling the lamp uniforms for the different lamp types, starting from the line after the `char tmp` definition until the line right before the end of the function.

**3.** For demonstration purposes, you are going to use two point sphere lamps. Insert the following block of code before the end bracket of the function to send only point sphere lamp uniforms:

```
i = 0;
/* Since your lamps are now in an array, simply loop and dynamically
create the uniform name for the lamp index in the shader program, and
gather the necessary data for a specific lamp index as long as the loop is
rolling. */
while( i != MAX_LAMP ) {
    sprintf( tmp, "LAMP_FS[%d].color", i );
    glUniform4fv(
    PROGRAM_get_uniform_location( program, tmp ),
    1,
    ( float * )&lamp[ i ]->color );

    vec4 position;
    sprintf( tmp, "LAMP_VS[%d].position", i );
    LAMP_get_position_in_eye_space(
    lamp[ i ],
    &gfx.modelview_matrix[ gfx.modelview_matrix_index - 1 ],
    &position );
    glUniform3fv(
    PROGRAM_get_uniform_location( program, tmp ),
    1,
    ( float * )&position );

    sprintf( tmp, "LAMP_FS[%d].distance", i );
    glUniform1f(
    PROGRAM_get_uniform_location( program, tmp ),
    lamp[ i ]->distance );
    ++i;
}
```

If you wanted to implement all lamp types, you could simply integrate all of the `if` statements that you commented in step 2 and index the lamps' data and uniforms as demonstrated in the preceding code.

**4.** Comment the following line (which is the last line before the `templateAppInit` function end bracket):

```
lamp = LAMP_create_spot
```

and on the next line, add the following block to create two point sphere lamps, one white and one red, that will be located on the top right and bottom left of the scene:

```
/* Create the first lamp, basically the same as you did before, except
you are initializing it at index 0 of the lamp pointer array. */
lamp[ 0 ] =
LAMP_create_point_sphere( ( char * )"point1",
                          &color,
                          &position,
                          10.0f );

/* Invert the XY position. */
position.x = -position.x;
position.y = -position.y;
/* Modify the color to be red. */
color.y =
color.z = 0.0f;
/* Create the second lamp. */
lamp[ 1 ] =
LAMP_create_point_sphere( ( char * )"point2",
                          &color,
                          &position,
                          10.0f );
```

**5.** In the `templateAppExit` function callback, remove the line that frees the lamp from local memory and replace it with the following lines to free each `lamp` of the array:

```
unsigned int i = 0;
while( i != MAX_LAMP ) {
    lamp[ i ] = LAMP_free( lamp[ i ] );
    ++i;
}
```

You have everything ready on the client side. Now all you have to do is modify the shader program to also support the same amount of lamps that you've initialized here, which you'll learn how to do in the next section.

## MAKING THE SHADER PROGRAM DYNAMIC

Open the `lighting.gfx` file and follow these steps to be able to multiply lights using the same structure that you have been building since the beginning of this chapter:

**1.** At the top of the `GL_VERTEX_SHADER` section, declare the following definition:

```
#define MAX_LAMP 2
```

**2.** Modify the `uniform lamp` and `varying lightdir` to be arrays of the same size as the maximum lamp value, like this:

```
uniform lamp LAMP_VS[ MAX_LAMP ];
...
...
varying highp vec3 lightdir[ MAX_LAMP ];
```

**3.** Inside the `main` function, comment the `lighdir` and `spotdir` affectation and add the following block to dynamically loop and create the `lightdir` for an array of point sphere lamps (before `position = -normalize( position * tbn );`):

```
/* Loop while you've got some lamps. */
   for( int i = 0; i < MAX_LAMP; ++i ) {
      lightdir[i] = ( LAMP_VS[i].position - position ) * tbn;
   }
```

Please note that if you want to use lamps of different types, you should send the `lamp->type` to the shader program and then create an `if` statement to determine which calculations should be effectuated before sending the data to the fragment phase.

**4.** At the top of the `GL_FRAGMENT_SHADER` section, add the following definition:

```
#define MAX_LAMP 2
```

**5.** Modify the same variables as in step 2, but this time for the `GL_FRAGMENT_SHADER` by replacing the declaration with the following:

```
uniform lamp LAMP_FS[ MAX_LAMP ];
```

**6.** Inside the `main` function of the fragment shader, comment the `spot_lamp` function call, and on the next line, add the following block to be able to use two point sphere lamps:

```
/* Loop while you've got some lamps. */
for( int i = 0; i < MAX_LAMP; ++i ) {
   point_sphere_lamp( LAMP_FS[i], lightdir[i], final_color );
}
```

**7.** Your application is now ready to roll. Compile and run it, and you should now see on your screen two point sphere lamps that affect the lighting condition of the scene.

To build a fully dynamic system that is able to handle any combination of lamp types automatically, you just have to make some adjustments inside the `program_draw` function. All you have to do is finalize the block of code that is handling the work of sending only the necessary uniforms for the current lamp type (pointed by the index) and pass the `type` for each lamp that you want the shader to handle. Then simply create an `if` to evaluate the right `varyings` to calculate inside the vertex shader and dispatch them to the appropriate functions in the fragment shader.

In addition, please note that I skipped the full conversion of the lamp uniform data send block and only focused on the point sphere uniforms (because that's what you used in this exercise). Since the whole converted block is over one hundred lines of code that have a lot of redundancy, I'll leave it to you to modify it.

## SUMMARY

With the knowledge that you have gathered in this chapter, you are now able to integrate full-fledged per-pixel lighting with normal mapping into your games and 3D apps.

The complex lighting shader that you created throughout this chapter will allow you to handle a single or multiple lights inside your scenes.

Please remember that per-pixel lighting is very GPU-hungry, and that a shader that contains loops and branching can be quite heavy to handle on portable devices. However, with the basics and the knowledge you've gathered in this chapter, you can tweak, adjust, modify, and profile your code to make it work optimally for your applications.

In your games and 3D apps, you can implement a system that is able to cull and clip lamps based on their distance, radius, or some other factors used in your games to limit as much as possible the work on GPU and offload it to CPU. That is the key for maintaining good performance on mobile devices while using per-pixel lighting. As usual, before moving on to the next chapters, stay a few more hours on this one, tweaking and testing different parameters and combinations.

Another key thing in game and graphics programming is to know your limitations. Before implementing anything into your game or 3D apps, always do some standalone tests of the technique that you are trying to integrate, to learn what you can and cannot do and profile as much as you can, so you won't have any surprises or performance drops.

When you are ready, move on to the next chapter, which is about advanced graphics effects.

# 11

# Advanced FX

**WHAT'S IN THIS CHAPTER?**

➤ Learning how to render to texture

➤ Learning about post-processing and implementing a bloom effect

➤ Learning how to use multiple render passes and combining the results to create a final rendering image

➤ Learning how to correctly project textures from a spot light

➤ Discovering how to use a Frame Buffer Object (FBO) with a depth attachment

➤ Implementing real-time shadows using a depth texture

➤ Learning the basics of a particle system

In this chapter, you will learn how to create a new range of advanced effects. You will first discover how to use the built-in OpenGL ES mechanism and be able to render your scene to a texture.

By implementing a multipass process, you will discover how to be able to reuse the offscreen textures as well as how to use them to create fullscreen post-processing effects, such as bloom.

Going forward in this chapter, I will show you how to project a texture to your scene from a projector point of view. Projecting textures is very useful and visually appealing, and will allow you to gain the necessary basics in order to implement real-time shadows.

Next, you will learn about a shadowing technique called projected shadow map. In this implementation process, you will learn how to create a Frame Buffer Object (FBO) and attach it to a depth texture.

At the end of this chapter, you will discover how to implement particles by converting regular vertex points into a textured particle that is always facing the camera. You will then learn how to control the size and distance attenuation and how to texture the points (GL_POINTS). With the knowledge you will gain in this chapter, you will be able to implement your very own particle system.

## RENDER TO TEXTURE

The concept of rendering to texture is pretty simple. You first render a frame using the same viewport size or using a lower resolution (generally one-half or one-third of it) to draw the scene. Then you save the render result into a texture, erase the color and depth buffer, and redraw the scene again. During the second pass drawing, or at the end of the second pass, you reuse that texture to create different effects by using the offscreen texture in the scene or using it fullscreen.

This technique can be used for multiple types of effects, such as post-processing effects like bloom, night vision, heat vision, and underwater, and so on. You can also use it for real-time reflection, shadows, depth of fields, and many others.

On modern mobile devices, there are basically two ways to render to texture. The first is to use the default render to texture functionality of OpenGL ES, which requires less video memory, but it is slower than the second method that I'm about to introduce.

The second method is to use the Frame Buffer Object (FBO) functionality provided by GLES2 (which was originally part of the GL_OES_framebuffer_object extension). The performance of using an FBO to render to texture is better; however, it requires more memory.

In order to get familiar with the techniques, in the following exercise you will learn how to use the first method.

## POST-PROCESSING EFFECTS

In order to create state-of-the-art, post-processing effects, you will need to use a multipass approach. Multipass consists of rendering the scene multiple times and storing the previous pass results into textures that you will then reuse to create the final image.

In this first exercise, you will implement a bloom effect. The idea behind this effect is to first render the scene from the viewer's eyes at a lower screen resolution, only drawing the specular highlights of the scene, like in Figure 11-1; and save the resulting color buffer into a texture.

**FIGURE 11-1:** Scene rendered using only specular colors

Then you will need to render the scene again at full resolution, but this time only using the diffuse color as shown in Figure 11-2.

Next, using the texture that you gather from the first pass, you will apply it on a fullscreen quad with additive blending using a blur filter to create a "blurred" version of the texture as shown in Figure 11-3.

**FIGURE 11-2:** Scene rendered using only the diffuse color

**FIGURE 11-3:** Fullscreen quad with blur filter

The final image that will be displayed onscreen is the result of Figure 11-2 and Figure 11-3 blended together, which will give you the effect shown in Figure 11-4.

Available for download on Wrox.com

To get started, duplicate the template_chapter11-1 project directory and rename it **chapter11-1**. Then open the project into your integrated development environment and get familiar with the structure that you will be using for this exercise.

**FIGURE 11-4:** Final rendering with bloom effect

The structure is basically a continuation of the last chapter's project, and contains a modified version of the point light shader code that you created earlier. This modified version calculates the diffuse and specular separately and combines the two colors to create the final result for a fragment.

In addition, the scene now contains a 1 by 1 unit quad called "fullscreen". You will be using this object and scale it in 2D to fit the current fullscreen dimension to be able to overlay the texture that you render offscreen to create the desired post-processing effect.

At the moment, the fullscreen object is attached to a GFX file called "blur.gfx", which is where you will be adding the necessary code to blur the offscreen texture.

Build and run the initial template for this exercise to see the differences between the lighting conditions that I set for this exercise and the ones that were used in the last chapter. Please note that, for your convenience, I repackaged the LAMP implementation and bundled it into a new struct named LIGHT, where all the same functionalities that you implemented in the previous chapter remain.

Now follow these steps to start implementing the render to texture functionalities to create a bloom effect:

**1.** At the top of the file (as usual right after the `#include` statement), create the following global variables:

```
            /* The color buffer texture ID. */
unsigned int colorbuffer_texture = 0,
            /* The width and height of the texture. When it comes to
texture in OpenGLES, a width and height using a power of 2 will always give
better performance compared to a non-power of two texture (assuming that
the non-power of 2 texture extension is supported by your hardware). */
            colorbuffer_width   = 128,
            colorbuffer_height  = 256;

/* The number of pixels to use in order to blur the texture vertically and
horizontally. */
float blur_radius = 2.0f;

/* Pointer to the fullscreen object. */
OBJMESH *fullscreen = NULL;

/* Flag to be able to track the current rendering pass, because you will
have to determine if the scene should be rendered with only diffuse or only
specular colors. */
unsigned char pass = 0;
```

**2.** Move to the `templateAppInit` callback and add the following block on the line just before the end bracket of the function:

```
/* Generate a new texture ID.*/
glGenTextures( 1, &colorbuffer_texture );
/* Bind the new texture ID. */
glBindTexture( GL_TEXTURE_2D, colorbuffer_texture );
/* Make sure that the texture coordinates will be clamped to the range
of 0 to 1. */
glTexParameteri( GL_TEXTURE_2D, GL_TEXTURE_WRAP_S, GL_CLAMP_TO_EDGE );
glTexParameteri( GL_TEXTURE_2D, GL_TEXTURE_WRAP_T, GL_CLAMP_TO_EDGE );
/* Specify that the texture pixels will be linearly interpolated when
magnified or minified. */
glTexParameteri( GL_TEXTURE_2D, GL_TEXTURE_MAG_FILTER, GL_LINEAR );
glTexParameteri( GL_TEXTURE_2D, GL_TEXTURE_MIN_FILTER, GL_LINEAR );
/* Create a new 2d image. */
glTexImage2D( GL_TEXTURE_2D,
              0,
              /* Only RGB, no alpha is necessary. */
              GL_RGB,
              /* Specify that the width and the height of the texture
are based on the values that you set above. This is necessary to properly
render the color buffer to the texture, because you are going need to
resize the glViewport to fit theses values. */
              colorbuffer_width,
              colorbuffer_height,
```

```
                           0,
                           GL_RGB,
                           /* Specify that you want the image to be RGB 16 bits. */
                           GL_UNSIGNED_SHORT_5_6_5,
                           /* No pixel data is needed, because you are going to
            dynamically fill the texture when requesting to render the current color
            buffer to it. */
                           NULL );
```

**3.** For convenience, get the "fullscreen" object pointer and set the object to be invisible (still inside templateAppInit, before the end bracket of the function).

```
fullscreen = OBJ_get_mesh( obj, "fullscreen", 0 );
fullscreen->visible = 0;
```

**4.** Add the following line at the beginning of the templateAppExit function to delete the texture ID when the application quits:

```
glDeleteTextures( 1, &colorbuffer_texture );
```

You are now ready to add the necessary code to create the different rendering passes. In the next section, you'll learn how to draw and copy the result of the color buffer to the texture you just initialized.

## First Rendering Pass

In every game or 3D app that you are going to create, you will sooner or later need to use multiple rendering passes (aka *multipass*). Multipasses can create a very huge array of nice effects and give you the opportunity to combine multiple offscreen images to create a final rendering that will be drawn onscreen.

For the current exercise, only two rendering passes are necessary, but it is normal to have even more rendering passes than that.

Follow these instructions to implement the specular color pass and save the resulting color buffer to the texture you created earlier:

**1.** Insert the following code between the brackets of the first_pass function:

```
/* Tag that the first pass is about to be drawn onscreen. */
pass = 1;
/* This is really important! Resize the glViewport to fit the texture width
and height, but do not recalculate the aspect ratio of the perspective
matrix. The image will be scaled to fit the screen resolution, so you have
to make sure that the perspective ratio in which the scene is drawn fits
the original fullscreen viewport size.*/
glViewport( 0, 0, colorbuffer_width, colorbuffer_height );
/* Call the draw_scene function and render the scene at a lower resolution
with the same width and height of the texture that you want to save the
color buffer result to. */
draw_scene();
/* Bind the color buffer texture ID to be able to save the image. */
glBindTexture( GL_TEXTURE_2D, colorbuffer_texture );
```

```
/* The function to call in order to transfer the current result of the
color buffer to an arbitrary texture ID previously bound to the current
GL context. */
glCopyTexSubImage2D( GL_TEXTURE_2D,
                     0, 0, 0, 0, 0,
                     colorbuffer_width,
                     colorbuffer_height );
```

**2.** In `templateAppDraw`, replace the `draw_scene();` line, and call `first_pass();` instead.

**3.** In the `program_draw` callback function, replace the code inside the MATERIAL.diffuse `else if` statement to set the diffuse color to 0 (black) only if you are drawing the first pass. In other words, replace this:

```
glUniform4fv(
program->uniform_array[ i ].location,
1,
( float * )&objmesh->current_material->diffuse );
```

with this:

```
if( pass == 1 ) {
   vec4 black = { 0.0f, 0.0f, 0.0f, 1.0f };
   glUniform4fv( program->uniform_array[ i ].location,
                 1,
                 ( float * )&black );
}
else {
   glUniform4fv( program->uniform_array[ i ].location,
                 1,
                 ( float * )&objmesh->current_material->diffuse );
}
```

**4.** Build and run the program in order to visualize exactly what you are sending to the texture (which should be the same as previously shown in Figure 11-1).

## Second Pass

You now have the specular color pass saved into your color buffer texture. What you need to do next is render the scene using only the diffuse color, which means that this time, the specular color will have to be black or at least the brightness of the image should be turned down to avoid overexposure.

Follow these instructions to build the necessary code for the second render pass:

**1.** Locate the `second_pass` function and add the following code between the function brackets:

```
/* Tag that you are about to draw the second pass. */
pass = 2;
/* Restore the viewport to its original "fullscreen" dimension. */
glViewport( 0, 0, viewport_matrix[ 2 ], viewport_matrix[ 3 ] );
/* Draw the scene again. */
draw_scene();
```

**2.** In the `program_draw` callback, locate the MATERIAL.specular `else if` statement (as you did in step 3 for the first rendering pass, but this time is for specular color). Replace this line:

```
glUniform4fv( program->uniform_array[ i ].location,
              1,
              ( float * )&objmesh->current_material->specular );
```

with the following `if` statement:

```
if( pass == 2 ) {
   vec4 black = { 0.0f, 0.0f, 0.0f, 1.0f };
   glUniform4fv( program->uniform_array[ i ].location,
                 1,
                 ( float * )&black );
}
else {
   glUniform4fv( program->uniform_array[ i ].location,
                 1,
                 ( float * )&objmesh->current_material->specular );
}
```

**3.** Inside the `templateAppDraw` function callback, before the end bracket of the function, call the second pass as follows:

```
second_pass();
```

**4.** Build and execute the program. As you can see, what you have now is the same as previously shown in Figure 11-2. The specular render pass has been stored into the texture and you are now drawing the scene with only the diffuse color ON.

## Fullscreen Pass and Blur Shader

Before moving on to the fullscreen pass, you first need to make sure that you have the blur shader ready to roll. Follow these steps:

**1.** Open the `blur.gfx` file and modify the fragment shader section (`GL_FRAGMENT_SHADER`) to look like this:

```
/* The texture that you rendered in the first pass. */
uniform sampler2D DIFFUSE;
/* The radius of the blur per pixel. (ex: 1.0/128.0, for 1px) */
uniform mediump vec2 BLUR_RADIUS;
/* The texture coordinates.*/
varying lowp vec2 texcoord0;

void main( void ) {
   /* Get the RGBA color for the current UV and multiply it by a
weight factor. */
   lowp vec4 final_color =
   texture2D( DIFFUSE, texcoord0 ) * 0.227;
   /* Offset the UV in the current blur radius direction and multiply the
resulting color of the texture fetch operation by a precalculated weight,
accumulating the final color for the current fragment. */
   final_color +=
   texture2D( DIFFUSE, texcoord0 +
   vec2( 1.384 * BLUR_RADIUS.x, 1.384 * BLUR_RADIUS.y ) ) * 0.316;

   final_color +=
```

```
texture2D( DIFFUSE, texcoord0 +
vec2( 3.230 * BLUR_RADIUS.x, 3.230 * BLUR_RADIUS.y ) ) * 0.070;

/* Assign the final color to the fragment. */
gl_FragColor = vec4( final_color.rgb, 1.0 );
}
```

**2.** Go back to the `templateApp.cpp`, and inside the `fullscreen_pass` function, add the following code to draw a fullscreen quad and pass the necessary uniforms to the shader program:

```
/* Activate the projection matrix, because you are about to switch it to
a 1:1 pixel ratio. */
GFX_set_matrix_mode( PROJECTION_MATRIX );
GFX_load_identity();
/* Calculate the half-screen size to have the origin of the projection
located at the center of the screen. */
float half_width  = ( float )viewport_matrix[ 2 ] * 0.5f,
      half_height = ( float )viewport_matrix[ 3 ] * 0.5f;
/* Set the projection. */
GFX_set_orthographic_2d( -half_width,
                          half_width,
                         -half_height,
                          half_height );
/* Re-activate the model view matrix. */
GFX_set_matrix_mode( MODELVIEW_MATRIX );
/* Reset it to its identity. */
GFX_load_identity();
/* Disable the depth test (there's no need for this test, because you
are drawing in 2D), enable blending, and disable cull face. */
glDisable( GL_DEPTH_TEST );
glDepthMask( GL_FALSE );
glDisable( GL_CULL_FACE );
glEnable( GL_BLEND );
/* Set the current blend equation and blend function to additive. */
glBlendEquation( GL_FUNC_ADD );
glBlendFunc( GL_SRC_ALPHA, GL_ONE );
/* Activate the texture channel 1 (because you will use this as the
diffuse channel. */
glActiveTexture( GL_TEXTURE1 );
/* Bind the colorbuffer texture that contains the result of the
first pass. */
glBindTexture( GL_TEXTURE_2D, colorbuffer_texture );
/* Make sure that the fullscreen object is visible. */
fullscreen->visible = 1;
/* Set the scale of the fullscreen object to be the same as the screen
dimensions. */
GFX_scale( ( float )viewport_matrix[ 2 ],
           ( float )viewport_matrix[ 3 ],
           1.0f );
/* Rotate the fullscreen quad object, because the texture coordinates
inside the OBJ file are inverted. (You could avoid this call by manually
tweaking the UVs of the object instead.) */
GFX_rotate( 180.0f, 1.0f, 0.0f, 0.0f );
/* Get the blur shader program. */
```

```
PROGRAM *program = OBJ_get_program( obj, "blur", 0 );
/* Set the program for drawing, because you are about to send over the
necessary
 uniforms to blur the texture shader program. */
PROGRAM_draw( program );
/* As mentioned earlier, to do a "proper" blur, you have to execute two
passes, horizontally and vertically. Set the blur radius to draw the first
blurring pass horizontally. */
vec2 radius = { blur_radius / ( float )colorbuffer_width,
                0.0f };
/* Send the uniform for the blur radius. */
glUniform2fv(
PROGRAM_get_uniform_location( program,
( char * )"BLUR_RADIUS" ),
1,
( float * )&radius );
/* Draw the fullscreen quad onscreen to blur and get it additively
blended with the current colors onscreen. */
OBJ_draw_mesh( obj,
               OBJ_get_mesh_index( obj, "fullscreen", 0 ) );
/* Same as above, but this time vertically. */
radius.x = 0.0f;
radius.y = blur_radius / ( float )colorbuffer_height;
glUniform2fv(
PROGRAM_get_uniform_location( program,
( char * )"BLUR_RADIUS" ),
1,
( float * )&radius );
OBJ_draw_mesh( obj,
               OBJ_get_mesh_index( obj, "fullscreen", 0 ) );
fullscreen->visible = 0;
/* Restore the GL states back to their original values.*/
glDisable( GL_BLEND );
glEnable( GL_CULL_FACE );
glEnable( GL_DEPTH_TEST );
glDepthMask( GL_TRUE );
```

3. Before the end bracket of the `templateAppDraw` function callback, call the `fullscreen_pass` function as follows:

```
fullscreen_pass();
```

4. You now have a fully working bloom post-processing effect up-and-running. Build and run your app. It should look exactly like what was shown previously in Figure 11-4.

This may look very simple, but remember that this process is very memory-intensive for the GPU. Always use post-processing effects and multiple render passes with care!

Before moving on, feel free to tweak the texture size and blur radius, and use the optimization techniques that you've learned so far, to optimize the workflow of this program.

In the next tutorial, you'll learn how to implement a projected texture.

# PROJECTED TEXTURE

Texture projection has always been used in game programming. It is relatively fast and easy to implement, and can create nice eye-candy effects.

In this exercise, you will first learn how to project a texture from a spot. The technique demonstrated here will also allow you to better understand the approach that will be used in the section of this chapter that covers real-time shadows.

To get started, duplicate `template_chapter11-2` and rename it **chapter11-2**. The template is similar to the one in the previous exercise; however, this time the lighting shader is an isolated version of the spot light you implemented in the previous chapter.

If you take a look at the associated Blender file, you will see that there is a "projector" quad located in the middle of the scene. The purpose of this quad is to make the `projector.png` texture load automatically. This is the texture that you are going to project from the spot light.

Now build and run the application, and familiarize yourself with the code structure that you will be using.

Follow these steps to learn how to implement a projected texture into your games and 3D apps:

**1.** At the top of the `templateApp.cpp`, declare the following global variables:

```
/* For convenience, declare a pointer to the projector texture. */
TEXTURE *texture = NULL;
/* The model view and projection matrix from the projector (the spot point
of view). */
mat4 projector_matrix;
```

**2.** In the `program_draw` callback, add the following two `else if` statements to the current `if` statement in order to send the projector texture channel ID and the projector matrix to the lighting shader:

```
else if( !strcmp( program->uniform_array[ i ].name,
         "PROJECTOR" ) ) {
   /* Bind the projector texture to the texture channel 0. */
   glUniform1i( program->uniform_array[ i ].location,
               0 );
   program->uniform_array[ i ].constant = 1;
}
else if( !strcmp( program->uniform_array[ i ].name,
         "PROJECTORMATRIX" ) ) {
   glUniformMatrix4fv(
   program->uniform_array[ i ].location,
   1,
   GL_FALSE,
   ( float * )&projector_matrix );
}
```

**3.** Before the end bracket of the templateAppInit function, add the following block to make the projector object invisible, and then to get the projector texture, and clamp the texture UVs within a range of 0 to 1:

```
OBJ_get_mesh( obj, ( char * )"projector", 0 )->visible = 0;
texture = OBJ_get_texture( obj, ( char * )"projector", 0 );
glBindTexture( GL_TEXTURE_2D, texture->tid );
glTexParameteri( GL_TEXTURE_2D,
                 GL_TEXTURE_WRAP_S,
                 GL_CLAMP_TO_EDGE );
glTexParameteri( GL_TEXTURE_2D,
                 GL_TEXTURE_WRAP_T,
                 GL_CLAMP_TO_EDGE );
```

**4.** Add the following code block inside the draw_scene_from_projector function:

```
/* Set up the projection matrix to use the same field of view as the
spot. The idea behind this block is to pretend to render the scene from the
eye of the spot, and then, later on, reuse the projection and model view
matrix to transform the vertex position inside the shader program to be in
that same coordinate system. The result of this operation will allow you to
automatically generate the UV coordinates from the projector (the spot) and
project the texture on the objects of the scene. */
GFX_set_matrix_mode( PROJECTION_MATRIX );
GFX_load_identity();
GFX_set_perspective(
light->spot_fov,
( float )viewport_matrix[ 2 ] / ( float )viewport_matrix[ 3 ],
1.0f,
20.0f,
-90.0f );

GFX_set_matrix_mode( MODELVIEW_MATRIX );
GFX_load_identity();
/* Execute a look_at to be able to gather the model view matrix. Note
that the position of the light and the camera as well as the projection
matrix are the same. This will allow you to pretend that the scene is
rendered from the light point of view without really drawing anything, just
gather the necessary matrices to be able to project the texture from the
spot. */
GFX_look_at( ( vec3 * )&light->position,
             &center,
             &up_axis );
/* Create a bias matrix that will allow you to transform the coordinates
from object space to screen space. */
projector_matrix.m[ 0 ].x = 0.5f;
projector_matrix.m[ 0 ].y = 0.0f;
projector_matrix.m[ 0 ].z = 0.0f;
projector_matrix.m[ 0 ].w = 0.0f;

projector_matrix.m[ 1 ].x = 0.0f;
projector_matrix.m[ 1 ].y = 0.5f;
```

```
projector_matrix.m[ 1 ].z = 0.0f;
projector_matrix.m[ 1 ].w = 0.0f;
projector_matrix.m[ 2 ].x = 0.0f;
projector_matrix.m[ 2 ].y = 0.0f;
projector_matrix.m[ 2 ].z = 0.5f;
projector_matrix.m[ 2 ].w = 0.0f;

projector_matrix.m[ 3 ].x = 0.5f;
projector_matrix.m[ 3 ].y = 0.5f;
projector_matrix.m[ 3 ].z = 0.5f;
projector_matrix.m[ 3 ].w = 1.0f;

/* Multiply the bias matrix with the current model view and projection
matrix and store the result as the projector_matrix. */
mat4_multiply_mat4(
&projector_matrix,
&projector_matrix,
GFX_get_modelview_projection_matrix() );
```

**5.** Inside the `draw_scene` function, right after the `mat4_invert` call, add the following block to bind the projector texture ID to the texture channel 0 and to keep an original copy of the projector matrix. (In order for this to work properly, you will have to re-apply the `projector_matrix`.)

```
/* Bind the projector texture ID to the texture channel 0. */
glActiveTexture( GL_TEXTURE0 );
glBindTexture( GL_TEXTURE_2D, texture->tid );
/* Create a local copy of the projector matrix, because it will have to
be updated independently for each object and sent over to the shader
program. */
mat4 projector_matrix_copy;
mat4_copy_mat4( &projector_matrix_copy, &projector_matrix );
```

**6.** On the line before the `OBJ_draw_mesh` call, add the following two lines to transform the original `projector_matrix` before sending it over to the shader:

```
mat4_copy_mat4( &projector_matrix,
               &projector_matrix_copy );
mat4_translate( &projector_matrix,
               &projector_matrix,
               &objmesh->location );
```

**7.** Inside the `templateAppDraw`, insert the following line of code right after the start bracket of the function to render the scene from the projector point of view. This call is executed before the `draw_scene` call in order to get the latest matrix from the spot.

```
draw_scene_from_projector();
```

In a few steps, you have implemented all the necessary code to be able to project the texture onto your scene. Now it's time to tweak the shader program to handle the uniform you have sent over.

# PROJECTOR SHADER

Open the `lighting.gfx` shader file and follow these steps to project the radioactive texture onto your text scene:

**1.** At the top of GL_VERTEX_SHADER section of the GFX file, insert the following variables:

```
/* The projector matrix for the current object. */
uniform highp mat4 PROJECTORMATRIX;
/* Varying to send over the projected coordinate to the fragment shader.
(Of course, the operation to apply the texture to the object will have to
be pixel-based.) */
varying highp vec4 projectorcoord;
```

**2.** Before the end bracket of the main function, insert the following line to transform the current vertex position as it would be if the scene was rendered from the spot:

```
projectorcoord = PROJECTORMATRIX * vec4( POSITION, 1.0 );
```

**3.** Move on to the GL_FRAGMENT_SHADER section and add the following two variables to the existing list declared at the top of the fragment shader:

```
/* The projector texture channel ID (which is 0). */
uniform sampler2D PROJECTOR;
/* To bridge the projector coordinates calculated in the vertex shader. */
varying highp vec4 projectorcoord;
```

**4.** On the line just before the `gl_FragColor` affectation, insert the following `if` statement:

```
/* Check if the w component is greater than 0, which will get rid of the
back projection of the texture. */
if( projectorcoord.w > 0.0 )
   /* Add the projector color to the current diffuse color and reuse the
ndotl and spot attenuation factor to properly shade the fragment. Note
that this time, you use the texture2DProj because your coordinates are
projected texture coordinates. */
   diffuse_color += texture2DProj(
   PROJECTOR,
   projectorcoord ) * ndotl * spot;
```

**5.** Build and run the program. You should see on your screen the radioactive texture projected from your spot light, as shown in Figure 11-5.

Many different effects can be easily produced using the projected texture technique. You can use this method to project a pre-calculated shadow texture (as you are about to learn in the next section), draw a cursor on a terrain (like in most RTS games), or even replace the spot

**FIGURE 11-5:** Projected texture

calculations completely and use a projected texture to simulate a spot effect (which in some cases can even result in better performance than the one you created in the last chapter).

Now that you understand projected texture as well as multiple rendering passes, move on to the next section to learn how to combine these two techniques to produce real-time shadows on your mobile device.

# PROJECTED REAL-TIME SHADOWS

If you are searching online to find out how to do real-time shadows on a mobile device, you are not going to find any demos that are usable in a real game scenario (or at least there weren't at the time this book was written).

Since the processing power of a mobile device is somewhat limited, the approach that I am about to show you provides the best results at the minimum processing cost (on both CPU and GPU).

The technique that you are about to code combines what you have learned so far in this chapter. The idea is to first render the scene offscreen, writing only the depth value into a depth texture. To be able to do that, you will have to create a frame buffer and attach a depth texture to it.

A frame buffer is an offscreen object that you can use directly to render to a texture. This will allow you to render your scene from the projector (in this case, the spot light), as you did in the previous exercise, and get the depth texture automatically written with the depth values.

Once this first rendering pass is effectuated, you simply have to render the scene from the camera point of view; and, at the fragment processing phase, compare the Z value of the fragment with the value of the depth texture. If the depth value of the fragment is lower, the fragment is shadowed.

To get ready to do the exercise, duplicate `template_chapter11-3` and rename it **chapter11-3**. This version of the template is the same as you used in the previous exercise. However, there are a few differences. The projected texture references in both the C/C++ implementation as well as in the lighting shader have been removed. In addition, this time the `"projector"` object is using a simple shader called `"writedepth"`, which does not do anything else except write the depth buffer.

Are you ready to implement real-time shadows? Just follow these steps to effectuate the necessary modifications to the application and get dynamic shadows up-and-running in no time:

1. Inside the `templateApp.cpp`, declare the following global variables that you will be using for the frame buffer and the depth texture:

```
/* Variable to remember the original frame buffer ID. On iOS, by default,
the screen uses a frame buffer, but not on Android. This will allow you to
either set back the original frame buffer ID, or to simply detach the frame
buffer (by passing the value 0). */
int main_buffer;
/* The depth texture ID. */
unsigned int depth_texture,
/* The frame buffer ID used for creating the shadow map in real time. */
                shadowmap_buffer,
/* The width and height of the depth texture that will be attached to the
```

frame buffer. The higher the width and height, the smoother the shadow will be, at the cost of performance and more video memory usage. */
```
                shadowmap_width  = 128,
                shadowmap_height = 256;
```

2. Move to the `templateAppInit`, and insert the following block to create the frame buffer and the depth texture before the end bracket of the function:

```
/* Get the current frame buffer ID that is bound to the current GL context.
If there is none, the value returned will be less than 0 (if you are using
Android); in this case, clamp the main_buffer variable to 0 to unbind the
framebuffer. If you are running the app on iOS, you will get the current
frame buffer ID and will reuse it to switch between the shadowmap_buffer ID
and the original ID created by the system. Very convenient! */
glGetIntegerv( GL_FRAMEBUFFER_BINDING, &main_buffer );
if( main_buffer < 0 ) main_buffer = 0;
/* Generate a new frame buffer ID. */
glGenFramebuffers( 1, &shadowmap_buffer );
/* Bind the new frame buffer ID. */
glBindFramebuffer( GL_FRAMEBUFFER, shadowmap_buffer );
/* Create a new texture ID. */
glGenTextures( 1, &depth_texture );
/* Bind the new texture ID. */
glBindTexture( GL_TEXTURE_2D, depth_texture );
/* Set the magnification and magnification filter to not use
interpolation. */
glTexParameteri( GL_TEXTURE_2D,
                 GL_TEXTURE_MIN_FILTER,
                 GL_NEAREST );
glTexParameteri( GL_TEXTURE_2D,
                 GL_TEXTURE_MAG_FILTER,
                 GL_NEAREST );
/* Set the texture wrap to be clamped to the edge of the texture. Just like
in the projector tutorial, this will force the UV values to stay in the
range of 0 to 1. */
glTexParameterf( GL_TEXTURE_2D,
                 GL_TEXTURE_WRAP_S,
                 GL_CLAMP_TO_EDGE );
glTexParameterf( GL_TEXTURE_2D,
                 GL_TEXTURE_WRAP_T,
                 GL_CLAMP_TO_EDGE );
/* Create a blank depth texture using the size of the shadow map specified
above. Note that your GL implementation needs to have the extension the
GL_OES_depth_texture available for this tutorial to work and be able to
create a texture using the GL_DEPTH_COMPONENT pixel format. */
glTexImage2D( GL_TEXTURE_2D,
              0,
              GL_DEPTH_COMPONENT,
              shadowmap_width,
              shadowmap_height,
              0,
              GL_DEPTH_COMPONENT,
              /* Request a 16-bit depth buffer. */
              GL_UNSIGNED_SHORT,
              NULL );
```

```
/* Unbind the texture. */
glBindTexture( GL_TEXTURE_2D, 0 );
/* Attach the depth texture to the frame buffer. This will allow you to use
this texture as a depth buffer. */
glFramebufferTexture2D( GL_FRAMEBUFFER,
                        /* The type of attachment. */
                        GL_DEPTH_ATTACHMENT,
                        /* Specify that the attachment is a 2D texture. */
                        GL_TEXTURE_2D,
                        /* Pass the texture ID in parameter. */
                        depth_texture,
                        0 );
```

3. Before the end bracket of the `draw_scene_from_projector` function, insert the following code block to be able to use the "writedepth" shader and render the scene to fill the depth buffer of the `shadowmap_buffer` Frame Buffer Object:

```
/* Bind the shadowmap buffer to redirect the drawing to the shadowmap
frame buffer. */
glBindFramebuffer( GL_FRAMEBUFFER, shadowmap_buffer );
/* Resize the viewport to fit the shadow map width and height. */
glViewport( 0, 0, shadowmap_width, shadowmap_height );
/* Clear the depth buffer, which will basically clear the content of
the depth_texture. */
glClear( GL_DEPTH_BUFFER_BIT );
/* Cull the front face. Because you are trying to render real-time
shadows, you are only interested in the back face of the object, which
basically is the surface that casts the shadow. By culling the front face,
you will be able to cast shadows for the scene and allow objects to cast
shadows on themselves. */
glCullFace( GL_FRONT );

unsigned int i = 0;
/* Get the writedepth shader program. */
PROGRAM *program = OBJ_get_program( obj, "writedepth", 0 );
/* Assign the shader program to all materials. */
while( i != obj->n_objmaterial ) {
   obj->objmaterial[ i ].program = program;
   ++i;
}
/* Draw the scene as you normally do. This will fill the
depth_texture values. */
   i = 0;
   while( i != obj->n_objmesh ) {
      objmesh = &obj->objmesh[ i ];
      GFX_push_matrix();
      GFX_translate( objmesh->location.x,
                     objmesh->location.y,
                     objmesh->location.z );
      OBJ_draw_mesh( obj, i );
      GFX_pop_matrix();
      ++i;
   }
   /* Restore that the back face should be culled. */
   glCullFace( GL_BACK );
```

4. Right after the start bracket of the `draw_scene` function, add the following line to bind the previous frame buffer (iOS) or unbind the current frame buffer (Android):

```
glBindFramebuffer( GL_FRAMEBUFFER, main_buffer );
```

5. Still inside the `draw_scene` function, on the line after the `unsigned int i` declaration, add the following code to affect the `"lighting"` shader to all objects before drawing the regular pass and bind the `depth_texture` to the texture channel 0:

```
/* Get the lighting shader program. */
PROGRAM *program = OBJ_get_program( obj, "lighting", 0 );
/* Affect the lighting program to all materials for the current OBJ
structure. */
while( i != obj->n_objmaterial ) {
   obj->objmaterial[ i ].program = program;
   ++i;
}
/* Bind and make the depth_texture active on the texture channel 0. */
glActiveTexture( GL_TEXTURE0 );
glBindTexture( GL_TEXTURE_2D, depth_texture );
/* Reset the counter to loop through the objects. */
i = 0;
```

6. In the `templateAppExit`, insert the following lines to delete the depth texture and the shadow map buffer:

```
glDeleteFramebuffers( 1, &shadowmap_buffer );
glDeleteTextures( 1, &depth_texture );
```

At this point, everything is ready for real-time shadows. In the next section, you'll make some minimal changes to the lighting shader in order to draw the shadow onto your scene.

## CASTING SHADOWS USING THE DEPTH TEXTURE

Inside the `lighting.gfx`, all you have to do is transform the current vertex position to be the same as viewed from the spot (as you did in the previous exercise), and compare the current fragment Z value with the Z value of the depth texture. If the fragment Z value is smaller than the depth value previously recorded, the fragment is shadowed, or else it should be drawn regularly. To implement this approach in code, simply replace this line:

```
gl_FragColor = ( diffuse_color + specular_color );
```

with this block of code:

```
/* Pre-calculate the depth for the current fragment and give it a little
offset for self-shadowing. The offset value can be tweaked to fit your
requirements (0.005 provides good results on my devices). */
lowp float shadow = ( projectorcoord.z / projectorcoord.w ) + 0.005;
/* If the projector W coordinate is greater than 0, it means that the
```

```
fragment is not part of the projector back projection. */
if( projectorcoord.w > 0.0 )
/* Check if the projected coordinate Z value is lower than the depth
calculated above. If it is, that means the fragment is in shadow; if it
isn't, the fragment is lighted. */
shadow = texture2DProj( PROJECTOR, projectorcoord ).z <
shadow ? 0.2 : 1.0;
/* Multiply the final color by the shadow intensity. */
gl_FragColor = ( diffuse_color + specular_color ) * shadow;
```

Now build and run the app, and you'll get real-time shadows as shown in Figure 11-6.

Notice how easy it was to combine the approaches of the two previous exercises to get a completely different end result. In addition, if you wanted to add soft shadows, all you have to do is integrate the blur code that you created in the first exercise of the chapter and use it to affect the shadow value.

**FIGURE 11-6:** Real-time shadow map using a depth texture

## A FEW MORE WORDS ABOUT THE FRAME BUFFER OBJECT

At the beginning of this chapter, you learned how to use the default GLES method to render to texture. Since you now have the capabilities to create an offscreen Frame Buffer Object (FBO), you will be delighted to know that you can also attach a color texture to directly render to texture.

The render to texture performance of an FBO is greatly superior to the default render to texture technique of OpenGL ES. Of course, this enhanced performance is at the cost of more memory, because it requires you to create an FBO, a depth attachment, and a color attachment. The code structure that is required to create and attach a color texture to an FBO is as follows (you can integrate the corresponding code into the structure to make it work):

```
/* Insert here the same frame buffer creation code, depth texture creation
code, and depth attachment code as you did in the previous exercise. */

/* Create a new "colorbuffer_texture" as you did in the first exercise of
this chapter. */

/* Attach the "colorbuffer_texture" ID as the color attachment 0 of the
current frame buffer. */
glFramebufferTexture2D( GL_FRAMEBUFFER,
                        GL_COLOR_ATTACHMENT0,
                        GL_TEXTURE_2D,
                        colorbuffer_texture,
                        0 );
```

Once the texture is attached as a color attachment, you simply have to bind the FBO ID before drawing and render your scene as you would normally do. Once the drawing is done, you can reuse the texture ID of the texture attached to the frame buffer color attachment for post-processing effects.

As an extra exercise, re-implement the first exercise of this chapter using an FBO, in order to compare the FPS between the two methods.

## PARTICLES

Fire, smoke, water, explosions — all of these effects require you to use particles. Basically each particle in these effects is nothing more than a textured point always facing the camera. The fastest and easiest way to render particles on a mobile device is to use GL_POINTS. You've already dealt with points earlier in this book, and it is now time to learn how to tweak them to be able to use them as particles to create a wider range of special effects.

Before starting, please note that since a particles system in modern game engines can be quite large and complex, the following tutorial focuses only on how to deal with points as if they were particles. You will learn how to adjust the size of the points based on the distance with the viewer, learn how to texture them, and gain the necessary knowledge to be able to implement your own particle system that fits your specific needs and requirements.

Start by duplicating the template_chapter11-4 project and rename it **chapter11-4**.

In this tutorial, you will be working with only one sphere. This sphere has been linked to the "particles.gfx" shader program and to the particle.png texture. At the moment, if you run the template, you will see that the sphere is using the vertex normal to colorize each vertex. But by the end of this exercise, you will learn how to convert each vertex position into a textured particle that will be rendered onscreen using additive blending and with proper alpha sorting, as shown in Figure 11-7.

**FIGURE 11-7:** Drawing particles

To implement particles into the app, follow these steps:

1.  Load templateApp.cpp, and add the following line before the end bracket of the templateAppInit to modify the drawing mode of the first (and only) triangle list of the sphere to use points instead of triangles or triangle strips:

    ```
    OBJ_get_mesh( obj, "sphere", 0 )->
    objtrianglelist[ 0 ].mode = GL_POINTS;
    ```

2.  On the line before the OBJ_draw_mesh call inside the templateAppDraw function, add the following block:

    ```
    /* If the current object name is the sphere. */
    ```

```
if( strstr( objmesh->name, "sphere" ) ) {
    /* Enable blending. */
    glEnable( GL_BLEND );
    /* Turn off the depth mask. This is very important when drawing
particles. This will allow the particle to pass the depth test but will not
write the depth buffer. Otherwise, you would have to manually sort every
point of the geometry and render them from back to front to insure proper
additive alpha sorting. */
    glDepthMask( GL_FALSE );
    /* Set additive blending. */
    glBlendEquation( GL_FUNC_ADD );
    glBlendFunc( GL_SRC_ALPHA, GL_ONE );
    /* Rotate all the points around the object origin. */
    objmesh->rotation.x += 0.5f;
    objmesh->rotation.y += 0.5f;
    objmesh->rotation.z += 0.5f;
    GFX_rotate( objmesh->rotation.z, 0.0f, 0.0f, 1.0f );
    GFX_rotate( objmesh->rotation.y, 0.0f, 1.0f, 0.0f );
    GFX_rotate( objmesh->rotation.x, 1.0f, 0.0f, 0.0f );
    /* Draw the mesh. From here, the particles.gfx shader will be called and
it will handle the point sizes, attenuations, and the points' texture
coordinates. */
    OBJ_draw_mesh( obj, i );
    /* Disable blending and re-enable the depth mask writing. */
    glDisable( GL_BLEND );
    glDepthMask( GL_TRUE );
}
/* If the current object is not the sphere, draw it normally. */
else
```

3. Open the `particles.gfx` file, and inside the `GL_VERTEX_SHADER` section, add the following instructions on the line just before the `gl_Position` affectation:

```
/* Get the length (distance) of the vertex in eye position. This will allow
you to calculate the size attenuation of the point relative to the viewer. */
highp float d = length( epos );
/* Set the point size to 24 pixels (but it could be any value between 1 and
the maximum point size your implementation supports), and use the
attenuation vector declared at the top of the main function to affect the
size based on the linear and quadratic attenuation values. This is very
similar to what you did previously for the lighting attenuation code. */
gl_PointSize = 24.0 / sqrt(    attenuation.x +
                             ( attenuation.y * d ) +
                             ( attenuation.z * d * d ) );
```

4. Move on to the `GL_FRAGMENT_SHADER` section and replace the following fragment color affectation:

```
gl_FragColor = vec4( normal, 1.0 );
```

with this:

```
/* Use the GLSL built-in gl_PointCoord variable as the texture coordinates.
This will allow you to texture the point as you would normally do for a
triangle. Note that the values of gl_PointCoord will always be clamped in
```

```
              the range of 0 to 1; no texture tiling is possible. */
              gl_FragColor = vec4( normal, 1.0 ) *
                              texture2D( DIFFUSE, gl_PointCoord );
```

**5.** Build and run the program.

Congratulations! In a few easy steps, you now have a sphere entirely drawn using textured particles. By taking this approach to the next level, you can easily create your own full-fledged particle system.

## SUMMARY

This chapter was definitely a lot of fun! You learned how to implement multiple render passes, which will allow you to create more realistic real-time renderings by combining offscreen textures with your rendering results.

You have also learned how to project a texture in real time from an arbitrary spot light source in your scene.

Using the depth texture extension, and with the power of an FBO, you can now cast shadows onto your scene. And using a color attachment, you can create faster fullscreen post-processing effects.

With what you've learned in this chapter, you are also ready to implement your own particle system and render textured hardware-accelerated points onscreen to create multiple types of special effects.

Before leaving this chapter behind you, make sure that you test different values, and try hacking around the exercises of this chapter. Use the optimization techniques that you learned earlier in this book to try to get the most FPS while using the different effects demonstrated in this chapter.

In the next chapter, you are going to learn how to use bone animations.

# 12

# Skeletal Animation

## WHAT'S IN THIS CHAPTER?

➤ Learning about the skeletal animation system

➤ Learning about the MD5 file format

➤ Loading an MD5 mesh

➤ Animating an MD5 mesh

➤ Learning how to use different interpolation methods to get smoother animations

➤ Blending two actions together

➤ Additively blending two actions together

In this chapter, you will learn about skeletal animation. I will first introduce and compare the traditional ways of handling character animation and describe the modern way to handle them.

Moving forward in this chapter, you will learn about the MD5 file format, which is a format especially built for skeletal animation. You will then learn how to use the book's API to load and animate an MD5 mesh.

Once the necessary code is in place to play back animations, you'll learn how to use different interpolation methods to dynamically generate frames between action frames. As a result, your animation transitions will become smoother and a lot more realistic.

Finally, you will learn how to interpolate multiple actions together using either regular blending (multiply) or additive blending to create an infinite number of action combinations.

# TRADITIONAL VS. MODERN ANIMATION SYSTEMS

Traditionally, animation in games was basically done the same way as in cartoons. Animation sequences were built using multiple versions of the same mesh corresponding to each frame of an action. Then at run time, a different version of the mesh is presented to the user as the current animation frame increment. This technique is called *keyframe animation.*

This approach has many limitations and is simply not practical for modern games, because action combinations have to be manually prerecorded.

Imagine for a second that you are using a keyframe animation system and that your player can run, shoot, and jump. This would require you to manually create all the possible combinations of actions, resulting in the following list:

➤ Run

➤ Shoot

➤ Jump

➤ Run + Shoot

➤ Run + Jump

➤ Run + Jump + Shoot

At run time, all these actions have to be linked manually by the programmer, and from an artist's point of view, it is a real nightmare to create them manually frame-by-frame.

In modern games, these problems and limitations have been successfully fixed using a technique called bone animation or *skeletal animation* (the term I'll be using throughout this chapter).

The idea behind this method is very simple. All you need is a base skeleton or armature that is built from bones and joints, as shown in Figure 12-1.

Then each vertex of the mesh has to be associated to a bone and will then be transformed at run time based on the location and rotation of this bone at a specific frame. In addition, skeletons can be reused by more than one character as long as they are sharing the same bones.

Since the vertex positions drawn onscreen are affected by the final pose of the skeleton, you can then easily combine multiple actions and create an infinite number of variations by blending or adding skeleton poses.

**FIGURE 12-1:** Bob's skeleton

So, returning to the example mentioned at the beginning of this section, if your character can run, jump, and shoot, all you need is these three actions prerecorded. Then at run time, you simply have to mix them together to create the final skeleton pose based on the game logic or player input.

These days, every modern game engine uses a skeletal animation system in one way or another. Due to its extreme flexibility, more-complex frameworks can be created to support rag doll physics, inverse kinematics, or dynamic locomotion, or even allow the player to control the skeleton bones in real time.

## THE MD5 FILE FORMAT

In order to start exploring the skeletal animation possibilities, you will be using the MD5 file format for the exercises and tutorials in this chapter. MD5 is a text-based format (human readable, and very easy to understand) that was originally developed by iD Software for the game Doom 3 and then extended in Quake 4.

When using any skeletal animation system, the mesh file and the action files are saved separately, and the MD5 format is no exception. The MD5 mesh file is generally saved using the `.md5mesh` extension, and the action files are saved using the `.md5anim` extension.

This book's SDK provides a simple yet very effective implementation that will allow you to load and animate MD5-based characters.

Before going forward, if you need more information concerning the MD5 format specifications, visit the website `http://tfc.duke.free.fr/coding/md5-specs-en.html`.

Since the book's MD5 implementation is rather lengthy (over a thousand lines of code), feel free to consult the source files `md5.cpp` and `md5.h` (located under the `SDK/common/` directory of the book's SDK) for more information about the functionalities implemented.

Finally, in order to get you started and enable you to export MD5-animated characters from within Blender, I included a Python script in the `SDK/md5_exporter/` directory that will allow you to export MD5 mesh and action files that are fully compatible with this book's MD5 API.

## LOADING AN MD5 MESH

It's time to start implementing some real practical code! In the first exercise for this chapter, you will start by loading an MD5 mesh file and familiarize yourself with this book's MD5 API.

Duplicate the `template_chapter12-1` project directory and rename it **chapter12-1**. The template includes the same viewer functionalities (swipe up, down, left, and right to rotate the character) that you integrated in Chapter 3.

In addition, for this exercise, I've already re-implemented the directional lamp shader code that you created in Chapter 10. You will reuse this code to illuminate your MD5 mesh (available inside the `lighting.gfx` shader program file).

This exercise will strictly focus on loading and drawing an md5mesh using its default bind pose contained in the mesh file. You will also learn how to manually load a Wavefront material file (`.mtl`) and associate the necessary material data to the mesh, because the default material format used by MD5 (`.mtr`) is unfortunately not supported by the exporter provided with this book's SDK.

Follow these instructions to load and render an MD5 mesh onscreen:

**1.** At the top of the `templateApp.cpp`, add the following definitions:

```
/* The material file. */
#define MTL_FILE ( char * )"bob.mtl"
/* The MD5 mesh file. */
#define MD5_MESH ( char * )"bob.md5mesh"
```

**2.** Declare the following global variables (as usual after the `#include`) to be able to load the `.md5mesh` and `.mtl` files from disk:

```
/* A fresh OBJ pointer, which you will strictly use to load the
materials associated to the MD5 mesh. */
OBJ *obj = NULL;
/* An empty MD5 structure pointer. For more information about this
structure, feel free to consult the file md5.cpp and its associated .h
located inside the common directory of the SDK. */
MD5 *md5 = NULL;
```

**3.** Just before the end bracket of the `templateAppInit` function, add the following block to initialize the OBJ structure and manually load the `.mtl` file linked to your project and build the libraries:

```
/* Manually initialize a blank OBJ structure. You do not need to use the
OBJ_load function this time, because there's no geometry to load, only a
material file. */
obj = ( OBJ * ) calloc( 1, sizeof( OBJ ) );
/* Manually load the material file using the filename you defined
at the beginning of the current source file. */
OBJ_load_mtl( obj, MTL_FILE, 1 );
/* Build the textures. */
unsigned int i = 0;
while( i != obj->n_texture ) {
    OBJ_build_texture(
    obj,
    i,
    obj->texture_path,
    TEXTURE_MIPMAP | TEXTURE_CLAMP | TEXTURE_16_BITS,
    TEXTURE_FILTER_3X,
    0.0f );
    ++i;
```

```
    }
    /* Build the shader programs (in this case, there's only one). */
    i = 0;
    while( i != obj->n_program ) {
        OBJ_build_program( obj,
                           i,
                           program_bind_attrib_location,
                           NULL,
                           1,
                           obj->program_path );
        ++i;
    }
    /* Build the materials and associate the material_draw callback function
to each of them to be able to set the uniform variables of the
shader program. */
    i = 0;
    while( i != obj->n_objmaterial ) {
        OBJ_build_material( obj, i, NULL );
        /* Set a material callback so every time the material is about to be
used for drawing, the material_draw function will be triggered by the
execution pointer. */
        OBJ_set_draw_callback_material( obj, i, material_draw );
        ++i;
    }
```

4. On the next line right after the code you added in step 3, append the following code block to load the md5mesh file from disk, and query the OBJ material library in order to associate the materials to each part of the mesh (please note that the materials have been renamed according to the mesh parts' names):

```
    /* Load the MD5 mesh file from the disk. */
    md5 = MD5_load_mesh( MD5_MESH, 1 );
    /* Convert the triangles to triangle strips. */
    MD5_optimize( md5, 128 );
    /* Build the VBO and VAO and construct the normals and tangents for each
face of the meshes. */
    MD5_build( md5 );
    /* Loop while there are some mesh parts. */
    i = 0;
    while( i != md5->n_mesh ) {
        /* The current mesh pointer. */
        MD5MESH *md5mesh = &md5->md5mesh[ i ];
        /* Query the OBJ material database to get the objmaterial pointer for
the current mesh part. Note that for the MD5 format, each part name is
considered as a shader that corresponds to the same material entry name in
the OBJ material file. */
        MD5_set_mesh_material( md5mesh,
                               OBJ_get_material(
                               obj,
                               md5mesh->shader,
                               0 ) );
        /* Next mesh please... */
```

```
        ++i;
    }
    /* Free the mesh data that was used to build the mesh, because this data
is no longer required for drawing. */
    MD5_free_mesh_data( md5 );
    /* Disable the cull face to make sure that even backfaces will be drawn
onscreen. */
    glDisable( GL_CULL_FACE );
```

5. Move to the `templateAppDraw` function, and on the line just before the end bracket of the function, add the following code to actually draw the MD5 onscreen using the default bind pose saved in the MD5 mesh file (since no action sequences have been assigned to the mesh yet):

```
    GFX_push_matrix();
/* If auto rotate is ON, simply turn the geometry on the Z axis,
demo reel style. */
    if( auto_rotate ) rot_angle.z += 1.0f;
    /* Rotate the X and Z axis based on the rotation specified by the user. */
    GFX_rotate( rot_angle.x, 1.0f, 0.0f, 0.0f );
    GFX_rotate( rot_angle.z, 0.0f, 0.0f, 1.0f );
    /* Draw the MD5 model onscreen.*/
    MD5_draw( md5 );
    GFX_pop_matrix();
```

6. In the `templateAppExit` function, add the following lines to free from the local memory the structures that you initialized at the beginning of the app:

```
    obj = OBJ_free( obj );
    md5 = MD5_free( md5 );
```

7. Now build and run the application. With the code that you have created, you are now able to load an MD5 mesh and draw it using its default T position, just like in Figure 12-2.

You now have the necessary framework in place to be able to start adding animation. Move on to the next section to learn how easy it is to assign an animation sequence (aka action) to the current MD5 mesh displayed on your mobile screen.

**FIGURE 12-2:** Hi, my name is Bob!

## ANIMATING THE MESH

Your MD5 model is loaded and ready to be animated. The beauty of the skeletal animation system is that actions are completely separated from the mesh and are stored as a separate file. In this tutorial, you will learn how to load an action file from disk and play it back frame-by-frame in real time.

Start by duplicating the chapter12-1 project directory and rename it **chapter12-2**. Then link the bob_idle.md5anim action file to your project (the file can be found in the SDK/data/chapter12-2 directory).

Follow these steps to learn how to add an action strip to the MD5 structure, and as a result, animate the model:

**1.** Declare the following variable at the top of the templateApp.cpp:

```
/* To store the idle MD5ACTION pointer. */
MD5ACTION *idle = NULL;
```

**2.** On the line before the MD5_free_mesh_data function call, add the following block to load the animation from disk and start the playback:

```
/* Load the action from the disk. */
MD5_load_action( md5,
                 /* The internal name for this action. */
                 ( char * )"idle",
                 /* The action file name. */
                 ( char * )"bob_idle.md5anim",
                 /* Use a relative path to load the action file. */
                 1 );
/* Retrieve the pointer of the idle action. */
idle = MD5_get_action( md5, ( char * )"idle", 0 );
/* Set the frame rate that you want to use to play back the animation. */
MD5_set_action_fps( idle, 24.0f );
/* Start playing the animation using looping. */
MD5_action_play( idle,
                 /* The method to use to interpolate between frames.
For this first example, simply use the MD5_METHOD_FRAME method to represent
that each frame of the sequence will be played sequentially one after the
other (no interpolation between each animation frame). */
                 MD5_METHOD_FRAME,
                 /* Specify whether or not the animation should loop
when the end frame is reached (either 1 or 0). */
                 1 );
```

**3.** Inside the templateAppDraw, on the line just before the MD5_draw call, add the following statement to increase the animation time step:

```
/* Increase the time step of the animation. Note that the
MD5_draw_action function will return 1 (in this case, when the
current frame number changes) if a new skeleton pose has been
generated, which indicates that you need to update the current pose
of the MD5 skeleton. Since you are using the MD5_METHOD_FRAME
method, a new version of the skeleton's pose will be generated only
when the current animation frame increases. For each new "skeleton
pose," all the skin of the mesh will have to be updated and the VBOs
have to be refreshed. */
    if( MD5_draw_action( md5, 1.0f / 60.0f ) )
    { MD5_set_pose( md5, idle->pose ); }
```

**4.** Compile and execute the application. You should now have the idle animation up-and-running (the guard standing still and looking around while lifting his lamp), just like in Figure 12-3.

For each frame, a new version of the skeleton is created, and all the vertices (the skin of the mesh) are transformed, depending on the associated bone position and rotation.

As you can see, even at 24 FPS, it's still a bit choppy. In the next section, you'll learn how to generate frames between frames and make the animation smoother.

## LERP

For a skeleton animation system, frames are basically just markers that modify the bones' positions and rotations at a specific frame or time in the animation sequence.

Since these "frames" are basically just markers, you can easily generate an infinite number of middle frames between the current and the next.

**FIGURE 12-3:** Is there anybody there?

While generating middle frames, bone positions will always have to be linearly interpolated, but since the bone rotations are using quaternions, you can either interpolate them linearly or spherically, making the transitions even smoother. (If you are not familiar with quaternions, please visit http://en.wikipedia.org/wiki/Quaternion.)

To change the current frame interpolation method to create middle frames using LERP, comment the following line inside the `templateAppInit` function:

```
MD5_action_play( idle,
                 MD5_METHOD_FRAME,
                 1 );
```

Then, on the next line, add the following call:

```
MD5_action_play( idle,
                 MD5_METHOD_LERP,
                 1 );
```

Now build and run the application and observe how smoothly the frames are interpolating between each other by generating middle frames using linear interpolation.

Of course, the `MD5_METHOD_FRAME` is the fastest method (CPU-wise), because it requires only one skeleton update for each frame. However, the animation looks a lot better with the `MD5_METHOD_LERP` method than the (choppy) `MD5_METHOD_FRAME`, which basically has no interpolation whatsoever.

From a CPU point of view (as well as GPU, because the VBO has to be updated), it is more expensive to generate these middle frames. In your own games and 3D apps, you will have to make a choice to either use middle frame generation or not.

Now move on to the next section to learn how to modify your existing app to use spherical interpolation (SLERP).

## SLERP

Quaternions are great to handle bone rotation and give you a maximum amount of flexibility. (I personally can't think of a better method.)

In the previous section, you changed the frame interpolation method to linear. But you can also change it to spherical (commonly called SLERP) for an even more realistic transition between bone rotations, at the cost of a bit more CPU processing compared to the linear interpolation. (Unfortunately, everything that looks better in computer graphics requires more calculations.)

To use spherical interpolation on the bone rotations between each middle or subframe (as it is also called), simply change the MD5_METHOD_LERP to MD5_METHOD_SLERP (inside the templateAppInit function), and then build and run your application to see the changes.

Looking good, isn't it? Well it's not over yet — there's obviously a lot more to talk about when it comes to skeletal animation. In the next section, you'll learn how to blend (or mix if you prefer) multiple animation sequences together.

## BLENDING ANIMATION

In the previous exercise, you witnessed how easy it is to interpolate between two skeleton frames. But what about two different animation sequences?

The interpolation process also works between skeleton poses, so it is not a problem to blend multiple skeletons posed together using the same concept.

Start by duplicating the chapter12-2 project directory and rename it **chapter12-3**. Load the project into your IDE and link the bob_walk.md5anim file (which is located in the SDK/data/chapter12-3 directory) to your project.

Then follow these instructions to learn how to progressively blend (mix) two action sequences together based on an arbitrary blend factor:

1. At the top of the templateApp.cpp, declare the following global variables:

```
/* The walk action pointer. */
MD5ACTION *walk = NULL;
/* The joints array that will be used to hold the final pose of the
skeleton after the idle and walk actions are blended together. */
MD5JOINT *final_pose = NULL;
```

2. In the templateAppInit function, on the line right after the MD5_load_action call, add the following line to load the walk animation:

```
MD5_load_action( md5,
                 ( char * )"walk",
                 ( char * )"bob_walk.md5anim",
                 1 );
```

**3.** On the line before the `MD5_free_mesh_data` function call, add the following block to get the `walk` action pointer and start the animation playback (as you did for the `idle` action):

```
/* Get the walk animation pointer. */
walk = MD5_get_action( md5, ( char * )"walk", 0 );
/* Set the rate of the animation playback. */
MD5_set_action_fps( walk, 24.0f );
/* Play the walk action using spherical interpolation between frames and
loop when the end frame is reached. */
MD5_action_play( walk,
                 MD5_METHOD_SLERP,
                 1 );
```

**4.** On the next line right after the code block you added in step 3, insert the following code to create an array of joints capable of holding the full skeleton defined in the MD5 mesh file:

```
/* Initialize a temporary skeleton to be able to store the final
pose after blending the idle and walk animation. */
final_pose = ( MD5JOINT * )
             calloc( md5->n_joint, sizeof( MD5JOINT ) );
```

**5.** Now move on to the `templateAppDraw` function and replace the following lines:

```
if( MD5_draw_action( md5, 1.0f / 60.0f ) )
{ MD5_set_pose( md5, idle->pose ); }
```

with this block of code to smoothly effectuate the transition between the `idle` and the `walk` animation poses:

```
/* Control the direction of the blending, from idle to walk and from
walk to idle (for demonstration purposes only, of course). */
static unsigned char blend_direction = 0;
/* The blend factor to use to mix the two animation sequence together.
This factor is basically a value from 0 to 1 that determines how much the
two actions will be blended together (from the first to the second). */
static float blend_factor = 0.0f;
/* If the blend_direction is 0, increase the blend factor to
progressively push lazy Bob to start walking. */
if( !blend_direction ) blend_factor += 0.001f;
/* If the blend_direction is a value other than 0, progressively
decrease the blend factor (to let Bob have a rest) and interpolate the
walk animation back to the idle action. */
else blend_factor -= 0.001f;
/* If the blend_factor is less than 0 or greater than 1, invert
the blend_direction. */
if( blend_factor < 0.0f || blend_factor > 1.0f )
{ blend_direction = !blend_direction; }
/* Increase the time step for all the actions with statuses that are
set to PLAY. */
MD5_draw_action( md5, 1.0f / 60.0f );
```

```
        /* This is the interesting part. This function receives two skeleton
    poses and blends them together based on a blend factor. The resulting
    skeleton will then be stored in the final_pose array of joints. */
        MD5_blend_pose( md5,
                        /* The final skeleton. */
                        final_pose,
                        /* The first action to use for blending. */
                        idle->pose,
                        /* The second action to use for blending. */
                        walk->pose,
                        /* The method to use to blend the two skeletons together
    based on the blend factor passed to the function. Note that joint's
    position will always be linearly interpolated, and the rotation
    interpolation will use the method specified by this parameter. */
                        MD5_METHOD_SLERP,
                        /* Make sure that the blend_factor always stays between
    the range of 0 to 1. */
                        CLAMP( blend_factor, 0.0f, 1.0f ) );
        /* Use the final_pose skeleton to calculate and update the vertex
    positions of the skeleton's skin and the VBO with the latest interpolated
    skeleton. */
        MD5_set_pose( md5, final_pose );
```

**6.** In the `templateAppExit` function callback, add the following line to free the `final_pose` joints that you initialized earlier:

```
    free( final_pose );
```

**7.** Run the program and let the animation roll for a while. Observe how the actions get blended and progressively fade as the `blend_factor` between animations increases or decreases, as shown in Figure 12-4.

The technique demonstrated in this tutorial is ideal for transitioning from one action to another, such as from walking to running or vice versa.

Of course, this method has its limitations, as you cannot really add animation together because the mix is done based on a factor. In order to create a combination of two (or more) actions, move on to the next section to learn about additive blending.

**FIGURE 12-4:** Idle and walk actions blended at 50 percent

## ADDITIVE BLENDING

As mentioned in the previous section, blending (mixing) poses is used strictly for transitions. If you want to combine actions, you will have to use additive blending. Additive blending is very easy to understand, as demonstrated in Figure 12-5.

**FIGURE 12-5:** Blending animations additively

Using the additive blending technique, you can combine multiple actions that take care of specific parts of the skeleton.

In a more complex and elaborate skeletal animation system, you would probably have access to toggle ON/OFF each bone of the body. But to keep things simple, the additive animation system included in this book's SDK controls the addition of actions automatically. This implementation simply analyzes which bones are animated and which ones are not by comparing the current and the next frame rotation and position value of each bone. As a result, the implementation will only "add" the active bone(s) to the actions received in parameters (as you'll see when you try out the code in this section).

In order to test additive animation blending, start by duplicating the chapter12-3 project directory and rename it **chapter12-4**.

Then to be able to create a blended "Idle + Walk" animation sequence, all you have to do is to replace the following line inside the templateAppDraw callback:

```
MD5_blend_pose( md5,
        final_pose,
        idle->pose,
        walk->pose,
        MD5_METHOD_SLERP,
        CLAMP( blend_factor, 0.0f, 1.0f ) );
```

with the following:

```
MD5_add_pose( md5,
        final_pose,
        /* The md5action pointer of the first action. */
        idle,
        /* The md5action pointer of the second action. */
        walk,
        /* The interpolation method to use to interpolate the first
and second action pose together. */
```

```
MD5_METHOD_SLERP,
    /* The weight of the walk action (the second action pass in
parameter to the function), since you are using addition, the idle
animation will always have the priority. This factor will control how much
percentage of the walk animation will be added to the idle animation. */
    CLAMP( blend_factor, 0.0f, 1.0f ) );
```

Please note that the function `MD5_add_pose` takes in parameter the two `MD5ACTION` pointers instead of the action pose. This function will internally use the `MD5ACTION->pose` (which you can also set manually in code if you want) to construct the `final_pose` of the skeleton based on which bones are animated.

Build and run the program. You have now created a new action sequence by additively blending the `idle` and the `walk` sequence, and your screen should look similar to Figure 12-6.

Using this technique, you can now combine as many actions as you want and create an infinite number of variations. You can also mix the `MD5_add_pose` with `MD5_blend_pose` calls and vice versa to pre-blend or pre-combine animation poses before calling the `MD5_set_pose` function and drawing the final skeleton onscreen.

**FIGURE 12-6:** Additive blending (Idle + Walk) actions

## SUMMARY

This chapter was short and sweet, even though skeleton animation is a very extensive subject. (There are just *so many* possibilities!) There are many different frameworks available, and they all do things somewhat differently; however, they are all built using the same concepts that you have learned in this chapter (actions, pose, skin, joint control, blending, and adding).

With the knowledge that you have gathered in this chapter, you are now able to load and animate arbitrary meshes and control their actions in real time.

In addition, you can now integrate realistic character animation into your own games and 3D apps. You also now know how to create dynamic skeleton poses on-the-fly based on your game logic and/or player input(s).

As usual, make sure that you fully grasp all the notions demonstrated here. Test, test, test, and tweak the tutorials that you have created in order to master and re-implement skeletal animation in your own apps!

# INDEX

Printed and bound by CPI Group (UK) Ltd, Croydon, CR0 4YY

27/10/2024

14580379-0001